SUFFERING AND THE
GOODNESS OF GOD

Other Crossway Books in the Theology in Community Series

The Deity of Christ (2011)

Fallen: A Theology of Sin (2013)

The Glory of God (2010)

Heaven (2014)

The Kingdom of God (2012)

The Love of God (2016)

"When people are hurting they need biblical answers, not platitudes. Here the editors and authors have thoroughly combed the Scriptures to give us the answers we need in tough times. This book should help both those who are suffering and those called upon to comfort and encourage others in their suffering."

Jerry Bridges, author, *Trusting God Even When Life Hurts*

"The skeptic chides: 'If God is good, he is not God; if God is God, he is not good.' With Scripture to answer the pain of real-life questions, and with real-life pain to question Scripture, these theologians address the hardest questions with honesty, tenderness, and deep truth."

Bryan Chapell, Pastor, Grace Presbyterian Church, Peoria, Illinois

"Those who read this book will thank the gifted team of authors for their careful, biblical, theological, philosophical, and ethical engagement with the problem of suffering and evil. This timely book addresses these crucial and challenging issues with clarity, conviction, and pastoral sensitivity. Readers will be strengthened, edified, and encouraged. I highly recommend this most important book."

David S. Dockery, President, Union University

"Morgan and Peterson have assembled a fine community of biblical scholars and theologians, all committed to Christ and the church, to address the problem of suffering. There are no easy answers to this problem, but there are plenty of wrong answers, misunderstandings, and confusion. This book—this community—will point you in the right direction."

Stephen J. Nichols, President, Reformation Bible College; Chief Academic Officer, Ligonier Ministries

"This volume should be warmly embraced by readers anxious to receive realistic good news from the Bible on this perennially-important subject. The writers are biblical, pastoral, reflective, and honest. I am grateful for their helpful and theologically-rich analysis."

Paul R. House, Associate Dean and Professor of Divinity, Beeson Divinity School

"Chapter by chapter, the authors root and ground their reflections in Scripture, modeling how to move from biblical exposition to a biblical theology. The reflections are not only theoretical and necessary but also practically engaging. There is much wisdom in this work, and it is my prayer that it will become must-reading for every serious Christian who wants to learn afresh how to handle God's Word rightly for today's church and to proclaim the gospel powerfully to today's world."

Stephen J. Wellum, Professor of Christian Theology, The Southern Baptist Theological Seminary

SUFFERING AND THE GOODNESS OF GOD

Christopher W. Morgan and Robert A. Peterson,
editors

WHEATON, ILLINOIS

Chapter 7 is an abridgment of "The Problem of Evil," chapter 9 in *The Doctrine of God* (P&R Publishing), copyright © 2002 by John M. Frame, 160–82.
Chapter 10 is an abridgment of "The Religious Problem of Evil," chapter 14 in *The Many Faces of Evil* (Crossway Books), copyright © 2004 by John S. Feinberg, 447–75.

Cover image: Church of the Madonna dell'Orto, Venice, Italy / Cameraphoto Arte Venezia / Bridgeman Images
Cover design: Jordan Singer

First printing 2008
Reprinted with new cover, 2018
Printed in the United States of America

Trade paperback ISBN: 978-1-4335-5727-9
ePub ISBN: 978-1-4335-1940-6
PDF ISBN: 978-1-4335-0478-5
Mobipocket ISBN: 978-1-4335-0479-2

Library of Congress Cataloging-in-Publication Data
Suffering and the goodness of God / Christopher W. Morgan and Robert A. Peterson, editors.
   p. cm.—(Theology in community)
  Includes bibliographical references and index.
  ISBN 978-1-58134-859-0 (hc)
  1. Suffering—Biblical teaching. 2. Theodicy—Biblical teaching. 3. Bible—Criticism, interpretation, etc. I. Morgan, Christopher W., 1971– II. Peterson, Robert A., 1948–
BS680.S854S84 2008
231'.8—dc22
                        2008011652

Crossway is a publishing ministry of Good News Publishers.

To our parents, Bill and Karen Morgan
and Arthur (deceased) and Marjorie Peterson

CONTENTS

SERIES PREFACE

THEOLOGY IN COMMUNITY

As the series name *Theology in Community* indicates, *theology* in community aims to promote clear thinking on and godly responses to historic and contemporary theological issues. The series examines issues central to the Christian faith, including traditional topics such as sin, the atonement, the church, and heaven, but also some which are more focused or contemporary, such as suffering and the goodness of God, the glory of God, the deity of Christ, and the kingdom of God. The series strives not only to follow a sound theological method but also to display it.

Chapters addressing the Old and New Testaments on the book's subject form the heart of each volume. Subsequent chapters synthesize the biblical teaching and link it to historical, philosophical, systematic, and pastoral concerns. Far from being mere collections of essays, the volumes are carefully crafted so that the voices of the various experts combine to proclaim a unified message.

Again, as the name suggests, theology *in community* also seeks to demonstrate that theology should be done in teams. The teachings of the Bible were forged in real-life situations by leaders in God's covenant communities. The biblical teachings addressed concerns of real people who needed the truth to guide their lives. Theology was formulated by the church and for the church. This series seeks to recapture that biblical reality. The volumes are written by scholars, from a variety of denominational backgrounds and life experiences with academic credentials and significant expertise across the spectrum of theological disciplines, who collaborate with each other. They write from a high view of Scripture with robust evangelical conviction and in a gracious manner. They are not detached academics but are personally involved in ministry, serving as teachers, pastors, and missionaries. The contributors to these volumes stand in continuity with the historic church, care about the global church, share life together with other believers in local churches, and aim to write for the good of the church to strengthen its leaders, particularly pastors, teachers, missionaries, lay leaders, students, and professors.

For the glory of God and the good of the church,
Christopher W. Morgan and Robert A. Peterson

ACKNOWLEDGMENTS

Allan Fisher, of Crossway, for believing in us and this series and encouraging us in the preparation of this work.

Rick Matt and Dana Ergenbright for editing parts of the manuscript. Special thanks are due Beth Ann Brown for editing the entire manuscript.

Jeremy Ruch and Phillip Mayberry, Robert's teaching assistants, for reading the manuscript. To David Calhoun, Robert's colleague, for offering helpful comments on every chapter.

Chris's colleagues Don Dunavant and Jeff Mooney and students Matt Leonard and David Massey for reading sections of the manuscript.

CONTRIBUTORS

David B. Calhoun (Ph.D., Princeton Theological Seminary), Professor of Church History, Covenant Theological Seminary

William Edgar (Dr. Théol., Université de Genève), Professor of Apologetics, Westminster Theological Seminary, Philadelphia

John S. Feinberg (Ph.D., University of Chicago), Professor of Biblical and Systematic Theology, Trinity Evangelical Divinity School

John M. Frame (M.Phil., Yale University), Professor of Systematic Theology and Philosophy, Reformed Theological Seminary, Orlando

Walter C. Kaiser Jr. (Ph.D., Brandeis University), Colman M. Mockler Distinguished Professor of Old Testament and President Emeritus, Gordon-Conwell Theological Seminary

Dan G. McCartney (Ph.D., Westminster Theological Seminary), Professor of New Testament, Westminster Theological Seminary, Philadelphia

Christopher W. Morgan (Ph.D., Mid-America Baptist Theological Seminary), Professor of Theology, California Baptist University

Robert A. Peterson (Ph.D., Drew University), Professor of Systematic Theology, Covenant Theological Seminary

Robert W. Yarbrough (Ph.D., University of Aberdeen), Associate Professor of New Testament, Trinity Evangelical Divinity School

INTRODUCTION

As we write these words, five hundred thousand Southern California residents, including two of Chris's colleagues, have evacuated their homes due to raging fires. Destruction and loss will hit some severely, others minimally. Thankfully, most involved will suffer little; just the inconvenience of staying at a hotel or friend's house and headaches from minor smoke inhalation. Others, however, will lose their homes and keepsakes. Some will suffer the excruciating pain of being burned by fire, while a few will undergo a much deeper pain of losing loved ones.

In a few months, another tragedy will take center stage, and all but a few will move on, and in time the event will become a distant memory. Yet some calamities are so massive that they remain permanently etched in our minds. These events often compel us to raise questions about suffering and good and evil.

Some of these heartbreaking events occur on a national scale. Recall September 11, 2001. The September 12 edition of *The New York Times* was filled with related stories, including: "New York firefighters, impelled by instinct and training, rushed to the World Trade Center yesterday to evacuate victims. Then the buildings fell down. The firefighters never came out. More than 300 firefighters were unaccounted for when the day ended."[1]

1. Jane Fritsch, "A Day of Terror: The Response; Rescue Workers Rush In, and Many Do Not Return," *New York Times*, September 12, 2001.

Commemorating the sixth anniversary, the *Times* ran an article simply called "September 11, 2001":

> It was the day when the unreal became the unimaginable. September 11, 2001, the crystalline morning when planes dropped from the skies and toppled the World Trade Center and punctured a hole in the Pentagon, was a demarcation point that shattered the security of the country and introduced a nebulous and virulent enemy previously unfamiliar to most citizens. Nearly 3,000 people died that morning, the vast majority of them in the gnarled rubble of the Lower Manhattan towers, others at the Pentagon and in a rural Pennsylvania field. A numbed country with red-rimmed eyes came to understand the ugly menace of terrorism. . . .
>
> It was a day that marked the start of another time that, six years later, has had an aftermath but not an end.[2]

Other tragic events play out on the global stage. A few years later we saw another gruesome event. Germany's *Deutsche Welle* announced, "Asia Marks Tsunami Anniversary, Still Struggles to Rebuild."

> Aid from the West . . . is helping Asian countries come back from the deadly tsunami of 2004. But the effects of the giant waves are still being felt. Remembrances are being held across Asia today on the two-year anniversary of the Indian Ocean tsunami whose devastating waves killed 230,000 people across the region and left millions homeless. Many parts of the region are still struggling to recover from the catastrophe, even as new floods and landslides in Indonesia are again forcing tens of thousands to flee their homes. . . .
>
> On December 26, 2004, a 9.0-magnitude earthquake off the shore of the Indonesian province Aceh triggered giant waves that fanned out across the Indian Ocean. The tsunami took nearly 230,000 lives and left around two million people homeless in 13 nations, including Indonesia, India, Sri Lanka, Thailand, Malaysia and Bangladesh.
>
> The tsunami extended as far as the African continent, causing destruction in Somalia, Kenya and Tanzania, as well as on Madagascar. Many of the survivors lost their children; most lost their homes.[3]

Such events evoke questions in all of us. Australia's *Sydney Morning Herald* observed this tendency in an article published a few days after the destructive tsunami, "Waves of Destruction Wash Away Belief in God's Benevolence":

2. N. R. Kleinfield, "September 11, 2001," *New York Times*, September 7, 2007.
3. "Asia Marks Tsunami Anniversary, Still Struggles to Rebuild," *Deutsche Welle*, December 12, 2006.

"Why did you do this to us, God? What did we do to upset you?" asked a woman in India this week, a heart-wrenching question asked in common these past few days by Muslims, Buddhists, Hindus and Christians. Nothing could have prepared us for what happened when the tsunami unleashed its terror. So we seek answers where answers are hard to come by, in either secular or sacred realms.[4]

Who can contemplate such devastation and loss for long? Our hearts become numb and our thinking seems futile.

While global and national tragedies trouble us, those that hit closer to home keep us awake at night. There was a period in Chris's life when it seemed to be dangerous to be his friend. The two-year-old son of one of his best friends, a pastor, was diagnosed with a brain tumor and given little time to live. Another missionary friend and his family were worshiping the Lord in Pakistan when terrorists bombed their church, injuring them and others with shrapnel. The twenty-five-year-old fiancé of a close friend was diagnosed with Hodgkin's disease and needed chemotherapy. The daughter, a church secretary and children's Sunday school teacher, of one of Chris's deacons was murdered by her jealous ex-husband and left two young girls motherless. Time and time again tragedy struck his closest of friends. During that same two-year period Chris grieved over the suicides of two people to whom he had sought to minister. One was a young man who was diagnosed with paranoid schizophrenia. Chris became his friend, shared the gospel with him, and tried to help him, but to no avail. He imitated his father and shot himself on his twenty-sixth birthday. The suicide note, rambling and incoherent, was addressed to Chris. The other young man struggled with depression and drug addiction. Chris witnessed to him and drove him to the psychiatrist on a number of occasions. Sadly, late one night Chris received a phone call from the young man's screaming grandmother. Chris drove to her home and found the twenty-eight-year-old hanging from the ceiling. Chris lowered him down, checked his pulse, and tried to revive him but was unsuccessful.

In the past two years Robert has known many sufferers too. The bright, successful daughter of members of his church small group suddenly became afflicted with headaches so severe that she had to drop out of college. Only extensive jaw surgery brought hope of relief, and only time will tell how successful it has been. Robert's son, Curtis, grieved with other friends the loss of a former high school classmate who, when he stopped

4. Edward Spence, "Waves of Destruction Wash Away Belief in God's Benevolence," *Sydney Morning Herald*, December 30, 2004.

to help a stranded motorist, was killed by a car that swerved off the road. A dedicated church leader, friend, and rocket scientist (no kidding) was struck down by pancreatic cancer and died within four months, leaving behind a widow and two children. Robert's father succumbed to Alzheimer's and passed away after suffering the debilitating effects of the disease for fourteen years. After longing for a child, a couple who attend the seminary where Robert teaches were elated at the birth of a beautiful daughter only to be crushed by the realization that she suffers from an aggressive form of leukemia that required chemotherapy one month after her birth. Robert's wife has become close friends with a woman whose former husband, a godly and powerful preacher, committed suicide after being unable to cope with clinical depression that resulted from the amputation of a leg due to a freak accident.

Along with much pain, suffering frequently brings many questions and overall confusion. After all, why do bad things happen to good people? Why would God allow his people to suffer injustice? Why is there such apparent inequity in suffering? Why do some people seem to get off lightly while others endure one crushing blow after another? How are we to understand God in light of these terrible realities? How are we to respond when suffering comes to our door? How can we help others who are experiencing pain?

Such questions are not new. In fact, many biblical figures faced them while suffering—including Job at the hands of his friends; Joseph, who knew the rejection of being sold into slavery by his own brothers; Jeremiah who knew oppression and physical abuse from the very Israelites to whom God sent him to preach; James, the son of Zebedee, whom Herod Agrippa I beheaded; Paul, who endured beatings, stoning, shipwreck, physical deprivation, and untold anxiety; and Peter, whom early church tradition says was crucified upside down.

We too at one time or another will all experience suffering, either personally or vicariously through those we love. The form suffering takes and its degree may vary, but we will all be acquainted with it. This means that we all bring specific questions out of our own experience to this book and therefore will seek different kinds of answers. Philosophers and theologians wonder how suffering can be consistent with God's sovereignty and goodness, and the reality of evil. Pastors want to know what the Bible says about suffering so they can teach accurately and help others respond appropriately. Missionaries query how and why God sometimes advances his gospel through persecution. Friends or family members of sufferers want to know how to comfort them. And believers who are experiencing suffering want to know why God allows it, how they can survive it, and how they are to respond to it.

Each person described can find some help in this book. We hope it will assist not because we claim to have perfect answers to these extraordinarily difficult questions. No, on this side of heaven, suffering will remain mysterious. Pat answers do not suffice, and indeed they often only add to the hurt. Nevertheless, while the Bible does not tell us everything we would like to know about suffering, it does teach much about it. After all, we know in part (1 Cor. 13:9). The Bible offers us much insight into who God is, who we are, where evil and suffering ultimately come from, how Christ suffered for us, how we are united to him even in his sufferings, how we are to respond to suffering, and how suffering fits within the larger biblical story. Such truths are not magic wands that erase our pain, wipe away our fears, and answer all of our questions. But when joined with a loving church, strength from the indwelling Holy Spirit, and dependence on the Lord, biblical teachings help significantly.

The contributors to this volume bring a variety of expertise and experiences to this weighty subject. They are highly accomplished academically in various disciplines: Old Testament, New Testament, theology, church history, and philosophy. Three have written books on suffering. The contributors write as professors, pastors, church leaders, and missionaries. And though all of them have experienced a measure of suffering themselves, been close to those who suffer, and ministered to sufferers, two in particular write out of difficult and lengthy personal battles with suffering. For almost twenty years, David Calhoun has been battling cancer, and for the same length of time, John Feinberg has been taking care of his wife who has Huntington's chorea, a terrible disease that gradually claims the minds and bodies of its victims.

Robert Yarbrough begins *Suffering and the Goodness of God* by placing the issue in contemporary perspective through eleven insightful observations. Walter Kaiser then interacts extensively with the Old Testament material, and Dan McCartney does the same with the New Testament teachings. Christopher Morgan and Robert Peterson seek to illuminate suffering by locating it within the larger biblical story. Upon that exegetical and biblical theological foundation, John Frame explores the philosophical and theological issues related to the "problem of evil." William Edgar then urges the church both to understand and to address the evil of oppression in our world today. The final two chapters concentrate on personal suffering. David Calhoun recounts how God uses Christian poetry to encourage him in the face of cancer, while John Feinberg offers personal reflections on accompanying his wife in her journey of terrible suffering.

In sum, *Suffering and the Goodness of God* examines contemporary questions, interprets key biblical texts, recounts the overall biblical story, addresses central issues in theology and philosophy, speaks to church and individual concerns, engages personal, pastoral, and academic questions, and offers hope through testimonies of God's sustaining grace.

We pray that you will experience the comfort and hope found in the Lord that the apostle Paul testifies to in 2 Corinthians 1:3–4:

> Blessed be the God and Father of our Lord Jesus Christ, the Father of mercies and God of all comfort, who comforts us in all our affliction, so that we may be able to comfort those who are in any affliction, with the comfort with which we ourselves are comforted by God.

Soli Deo Gloria,

Christopher W. Morgan and Robert A. Peterson

1

CHRIST AND THE CROCODILES

Suffering and the Goodness of God in Contemporary Perspective

ROBERT W. YARBROUGH

Even newspaper brevity could not hide the harrowing nature of what happened in Costa Rica in early May 2007.[1] A thirteen-year-old boy was wading in a placid lagoon. Suddenly he screamed. A crocodile's jaws had closed on his leg. Like a rag doll he was whisked beneath the water. He surfaced just once. Witnesses say he called to his older brother, "Adios, Pablito." He blurted out to horrified onlookers never to swim there again. Then there were only ripples.

One report observed that crocodiles do not normally chase and assault their prey. They just lie motionless until something blunders within their kill zone. Another report stated that crocodile attacks are fairly common in Central America and Mexico. An Internet search will readily turn up reports of fatal incidents in Africa, Australia, and elsewhere.

---

1. Reuters, "Crocodile Makes Off with Boy," *TVNZ*, 5 May 2007, http://tvnz.co.nz/view/page/1098603 (July 11, 2007).

Hardly less unnerving, particularly if you happen to be a parent, is a June 2007 report from North America.[2] A family of four was asleep in their tent in a Utah campground: dad, mom, and two brothers, ages eleven and six. In the dark of night the eleven-year-old was heard to scream, "Something's dragging me!" The frantic parents suspected a violent abduction. Only hours later did they realize that a black bear had slit an opening in the tent with a claw or tooth, sunk its fangs into the nearest occupant, and fled with its flailing booty still in the sleeping bag. The boy's lifeless body was eventually found a quarter-mile away.

The victim's grandfather, according to news reports, agonized: "We're trying to make sense of this. . . . It's something that just doesn't make sense. . . . Some things you're prepared for, but we weren't prepared for news that our grandson and child was killed by a bear. That's one of the hardest things we're struggling with—the nonsensical nature of this tragedy."[3]

In this age of Internet connectivity we are aware of life's incomprehensible cruelties like never before. Sometimes we hear such shocking news within minutes of its occurrence. We even glimpse it live if a videocam or camera phone is at the scene. Most of us have images of the December 2004 tsunami, caught on film under blue skies amid white beaches and palm trees during Christmas holidays, seared in our memories. About 230,000 souls departed this earth within scant hours. Terrible! Yet more people died of AIDS in a single nation (South Africa) in the next year (2005) than in the tsunami.[4] The world is full of the wails of the suffering and perishing to an extent humans can hardly quantify, let alone comprehend. Like the stunned grandfather above, at times all we can do is stop, ponder the ailing and dead, and wrestle with the question, why?

This points to the contemporary significance of the issue of suffering: we cannot escape the fact that it nips at humanity's flanks in all locales and at all hours. Too frequently the nip is a vicious bite that finds the jugular. And natural disaster, whether a tsunami or a wild animal, is just a small part of the picture. All too much suffering has a direct connection to human intention or negligence: beatings and murders, skirmishes and wars, robberies and riots, tortures and rapes, displacements and bombings, plagues and famines and genocides resulting from human malice. Or take just a single disease: on the day you read this, about 2,500 people will die

2. Catherine Elsworth, "Bear Kills Boy After Pulling Him from Family Tent," *Telegraph.co.uk.*, June 20, 2007, http://www.telegraph.co.uk/global/main.jhtml?xml=/global/2007/06/20/wbear120.xml (July 11, 2007).
3. Ibid.
4. Richard L. van Houten, "HIV/AIDS in 2006," *REC Focus* 6, no. 3–4 (December 2006), 7.

of malaria, "most of them under age five, the vast majority living in Africa. That's more than twice the annual toll of a generation ago."[5] Each year one million people die of malaria, and the number is rising. As world population increases, so does suffering.

At the same time, the Christian church around the world and through the ages has the charge of believing and proclaiming the excellencies of a good and loving God, who they claim created this world and whom they profess to love and joyfully commend to others. The juxtaposition of these conflicting claims—the empirical claim of daily calamity on a global scale, and the confessional claim of God's present and eternal benevolence—touches off the turbulence that this volume explores. By way of introduction, this chapter will unfold eleven theses on suffering's significance in a world created and ultimately redeemed by the God of historic Christian confession. The cumulative argument will be that suffering must be in the foreground, not the background, of robust Christian awareness today. Yet far from jeopardizing the credibility of claims of God's goodness, it serves to highlight those claims and draw us toward the God who makes them.

Thesis 1: Suffering Is Neither Good nor Completely Explicable
Current world threats and conditions have given rise to acute consciousness of the human plight. It is therefore understandable that books addressing suffering abound. A quick Amazon.com check will list dozens, with new ones appearing steadily. More than a few of these give the impression that, seen from the right perspective, suffering is actually not all that bad and in fact may just be an illusion. Alongside this move may come the claim to explain (away) suffering to a significant degree—to give a coherent account of its origin, causes, or purposes such that its scandal is essentially dispersed by proper exercise of reason, faith, or some combination of these. I recall a pastor being asked in a Bible study class why God allows sickness and death to come to the people we love and need. His quick and unflinching reply: to bring glory to himself. Maybe there was a history to this exchange between pastor and church member that I was missing, but the tone and implied substance of the reply struck me as pastorally unwise and theologically underdeveloped. (For more on suffering and God's glory see Thesis 6, below.)

Something is afoot in the world that is on a collision course with God's wrath, which may be as inscrutable, finally, as the suffering God permits. The Bible uses many words to point to this *something*: sin, evil, wrong-

5. Michael Finkel, "Bedlam in the Blood: Malaria," *National Geographic*, July 2007, 41.

doing, lawlessness, transgression, suffering, death. Scripture also refers to a superhuman being intimately connected with all that exalts itself against God and delights in defying his truth and trashing his creation: the Devil, the Evil One, Satan, the ruler of this age, the Father of Lies, and the father of murder. The existence of sin and the Devil, and God's ongoing determination to root them out and finally destroy them, are reminders that a primary existential calling card of this world's fallenness—human suffering—is not in itself good. Of course God can use it for good purposes and unerringly does so.[6] But suffering in itself is not a good thing—as we realize when suffering invades, infects, and affects our lives personally.

If suffering is not something blithely to be called "good," neither should we allege that it is fully understandable.[7] The enormity of human agony associated with either individual or collective experiences of suffering rightly leaves the godliest of persons scratching their heads, if not howling in misery and perhaps repenting in sackcloth and ashes (see the book of Job). Such agony has driven many to suicide in despair. Why *did* God permit or cause the tsunami, or in another era the Holocaust? Why the woe of Hurricane Katrina? Why the maimed veterans of the Iraq and Afghan wars and of dozens of previous military actions? Why the human carnage on the ground in the lands in which those wars were and are being fought? Why Joni Eareckson Tada's paralysis,[8] or fifteen million AIDS orphans in Africa? Even Jesus asked a question about the mystery of sin and suffering: "My God, my God, why have you forsaken me?" (Matt. 27:46).[9] How much more should we decline to claim for ourselves a reasoned, settled mastery of suffering, its causes and purposes, and its effects?

Thesis 2: Suffering in Itself Is No Validation of Religious Truth

The Baal prophets oozed blood from self-inflicted wounds (1 Kings 18). Jesus spoke of agonized self-denial that advertised itself (Matt. 6:16) and Paul of self-immolation by burning (1 Cor. 13:3). The quasi-religious Stoics of antiquity upheld suicide as a noble trump card for making a rational statement in the face of cosmic adversity. Many religious assertions are

6. Lee Eddleman, a personal mentor for four decades, observes that if suffering "leads us to a deeper sense of God's lovingkindness, i.e., leads us to joy (cf. 'who for the joy set before Him endured the cross'), then it becomes at least a blessing from Him" (personal correspondence).

7. Cf. Peter Hicks, *The Message of Evil and Suffering* (Downers Grove: InterVarsity, 2006), 141.

8. For one of her own many published comments see "Hope . . . the Best of Things," in *Suffering and the Sovereignty of God*, ed. John Piper and Justin Taylor (Wheaton, IL: Crossway Books, 2006), 191–204.

9. All Scripture quotations in this chapter are taken from *The Holy Bible: English Standard Version* (ESV).

backed by reports of individual or collective suffering for the sake of the cause. Mormons recall the opposition they and their early leaders faced, for example, in Illinois and Missouri. Certain Muslim groups can point to present or historic sufferings to bolster their claims about proper politico-religious order in Islam. Real or perceived unjust suffering at Israeli or US-British hands may be used to justify suicide bombings at least partially in the name of religious interests.

This volume will study and at times commend suffering as a possible condition or entailment of a living faith in Jesus Christ. But it should be understood that suffering in itself, although commanded and modeled by Jesus, is by no means always a token of faithful Christian discipleship. There are many reasons for this. Our suffering may be brought on by our own folly rather than noble decisions or actions. Ministers who molest children cannot plead the sanctity of their vocation to avoid a prison sentence. Or our suffering may be the result of false religious claims, not true ones. A theology professor who loses his job for teaching that is way off base may be getting his just deserts. Or our suffering may be the result of immaturity or bad judgment or self-righteousness. A youthful church staff member who is dismissed for upbraiding the congregation during Sunday morning worship could be serving as a courageous prophet—but she could also be giving in to petty anger, a rebellious spirit, and an unwillingness to trust the Lord of the church regarding matters for which she has no business condemning others.

The point here is that keen discernment is required for accurate assessment of suffering. It is not as easy as saying, "I suffer for these convictions; therefore, these convictions are sound." That could be the case. But those words could also be delusional. In an era like ours, where both suffering and demands to be heard based upon it are ubiquitous, careful reflection guided by Scripture's teaching, God's personal guidance, and the collective wisdom of God's people are essential. Hence this book.

Thesis 3: Accounting for Suffering Is Forced upon Us by Our Times

This book originates in the United States, a land of relative security and affluence. There have been decades within living memory where North Americans, most of us healthy, well-fed, and gainfully employed, could live relatively untouched by acute personal consciousness of many kinds and dimensions of suffering. Starvation, imprisonment for Christian faith, and being "tortured for Christ" (the title of Richard Wurmbrand's famous book) have sounded distant, exotic, and vaguely unnecessary. Naivete and obliviousness to suffering, especially by Christians for their faith in Jesus, probably should never have been so prevalent in the North American church, composed of ostensible followers of Jesus, who took up a cross and taught his disciples to do likewise. But suffering has been widely overlooked or suppressed, as in too many quarters it continues to be.

The days are now over for this mentality to be countenanced. A summer 2007 edition of a national newsweekly, for example, carried a four-page ad for The Voice of the Martyrs smack in the middle.[10] There were two tear-out cards. Anyone with a mailing address can request a free monthly newsletter. Much the same information and offer appeared in the July 2007 *Reader's Digest*. Anyone with Internet access can visit www.persecution. com and find out more than enough to break even a stony heart. (Just google "Christian persecution" for numerous other sites.) Anyone with a conscience and a sense of urgency to honor Christ can find multiple ways to become aware of, and respond to, the dire, ongoing, and increasing human misery and need.

The point is that what the din and self-preoccupation of the American way of life (often equating to pursuit of material security and self-indulgence, measured by gospel standards) may formerly have obscured—the terrible suffering of persecution—has now gone mainstream. There is no excuse for pastors or churchgoers failing to wrestle with *our* and *my* obligation to put a shoulder to the wheel of the task of selfless and long-term Christian response—and perhaps even personal exposure—to suffering for Christ's sake.

Nor can we reduce the task here to responsiveness to only *Christian* suffering. Jesus wept over Jerusalem, not just for followers who he knew would suffer for his name. The problem of suffering includes but extends beyond the circles where fellow Christians are especially affected. It may be that our collective will to embrace this issue with moral seriousness will prove to be either our salvation or our undoing. It may be, for example, that the responsiveness of upcoming generations—believers between, say, childhood and young adulthood—to the gospel message propounded by their parents and leaders hinges largely on the urgency with which we respond to the suffering that cries out to us from every direction and emerges from the shadows of our own lives. Will we encourage the young to a response that will move beyond the probably pitiable foundation we may manage to lay? Or will we, like contemporaries of Jesus, be guilty of raising a generation who are twice as much children of hell as we are (Matt. 23:15)? To flinch or take umbrage at this question probably indicates lack of knowledge of the

10. *U.S. News and World Report*, June 25, 2007, 39–42.

enormity of the task at hand. It could also indicate self-righteousness in the face of crisis that should long since have driven us to profound repentance and transformed life direction.

Thesis 4: Suffering May Be a Stumbling Block to Gospel Reception

One impediment to suffering getting due attention in some quarters is lack of awareness of its corrosive effect, in principle, on people's receptivity to the saving gospel message. In early Christian centuries the suffering caused by earthquakes, plagues, and other calamities was actually blamed on Christians, who were sometimes hounded and punished for their presumed destructive mischief. Suffering served to impede reception of the Christian message.[11] In more recent times, the Lisbon earthquake (1755) shook the faith of Europe as it claimed the lives of perhaps one-third of Lisbon's 275,000 inhabitants. It took place on November 1, All Saints' Day, a religious holiday when many would have attended mass. Philosophers of immense influence like Voltaire, Rousseau, and Kant concluded that the notion of a benevolent God directly superintending all human affairs was no longer tenable. This conviction persists today among many, from the unlettered to the intellectual elite.

The catastrophic loss of life in the trenches of World War I and the historically unprecedented brutality of new war technology (machine guns, high explosives, chlorine gas) are widely credited with shattering the cultural optimism of Europe and prompting a turn away from Christian or even theistic belief in Western intellectual culture, including the United States. World War II brought its own set of moral monstrosities, as wars always do—but with the unique features of the Holocaust and then the atomic bomb detonations in Japan. Looking back on the twentieth century as a whole, it is indeed justified to speak of "a century of horrors."[12]

North America has been untouched by the devastation of its cities, countryside, and population that many other nations of the world have experienced in recent generations. This may account, in part, for why a much larger percent of the population here still attends church than in other nations. We may well be thankful that we have been spared so much grief. At the same time, we should not let our good fortune make us callous to the effect of suffering on most of the world's population. We are a land still rich in the presence of churches and denominations that are committed,

11. Though not always: see Rodney Stark, *The Rise of Christianity* (Princeton: Princeton University Press, 1996).
12. See Alain Besançon's book by that title, subtitled *Communism, Nazism, and the Uniqueness of the Shoah* (Wilmington, DE: ISI Books, 2007).

in principle, to sending the light of the Christian message to all peoples, locally and beyond. But we will be hamstrung in our mission to the extent that an overly rosy view of life and God, derived from our relative freedom from destitution and suffering on the scale common elsewhere, infects and distorts our theological reasoning and outreach. Historically this has sometimes taken the form of a hypocrisy eager to preach the salvation of souls but too stingy to address listeners' material needs as well.

To summarize, the problem of suffering may seem distant to us, whose "suffering" may arise chiefly every decade or two when we or a loved one receives an unfavorable medical report. We need to open our eyes to a larger historical and geographical context. We cannot pray for, speak to, and serve with integrity alongside Christians of our era worldwide if we underestimate the relevance of suffering to all we seek to do in Jesus' name. We will either lack motivation for radical discipleship, not being gripped by and possibly sharing in the pain of others elsewhere, or we will tend to propagate and export a distorted rendering of the gospel, one that comports with our prosperous setting but does not ring true among the majority of the world's peoples, who on a daily basis live close to bare survival's jagged edge.

Thesis 5: Suffering Creates Teachable Moments for Gospel Reception

Jesus did not evade the issue of suffering and neither should we. One day as he was teaching (Luke 13:1–5), he was informed of Pilate's murder of some Galileans who were in the very act of worshiping God. We do not know all Jesus said. But we know he leveraged the shock of the hour into an object lesson, urging listeners to make a life change. He even took it a step further by pointing to a building collapse that claimed the lives of eighteen people. The lesson he drew from this tragedy was the same: Repent, lest you too perish!

There is much more to say about suffering than "Consider your ways and turn to God!" But Jesus reminds us of that standing imperative. If we dare deepen our comprehension of suffering vis-à-vis God's goodness—cognizant that "he who increases knowledge increases sorrow" (Eccles. 1:18)—we do well to seek ways to emulate Jesus' acknowledgment of suffering as an occasion for human affirmation of God.

We have already argued that this does not make suffering in itself a good thing (Thesis 1 above). But it does encourage us to enlarge our outlook to incorporate suffering into our view of what it means to come to Christ and then to honor and serve him. We do not trust in him so that we can evade suffering, nor do we present Christ as an assured means of escape from hard times. Rather we trust so that in good times *and* bad our lives will reflect fidelity to him and the courage that Jesus modeled and imparts. The same suffering that hardens some or drives them to faithless despair can be an occasion for the bold move of hope in Christ in spite of suffering's disincentives to affirm and believe in God.

We do well to remain intent on enlarging our spiritual understanding so that we become tougher and wiser when it comes to absorbing and responding to suffering. As we do so we will become more effective messengers of the gospel to others whose sufferings may likewise be the occasion of making the right choice when faced with the question: should I let adversity drive me away from the Bible's testimony to God's good purposes and eternal promise, or should I believe that the message of Jesus and the cross are still adequate grounds for personal faith in him? It is often suffering that makes this anguished but fruitful outcry unavoidable and that also paves the way for the best, though usually not the easiest, response.

Thesis 6: Suffering Will Bring Glory to God in the Lives of Believers Subjected to It

Joseph affirmed this when he uttered the famous words to his conscience-stricken brothers, "As for you, you meant evil against me, but God meant it for good, to bring it about that many people should be kept alive, as they are today" (Gen. 50:20). Jesus stated that behind a case of congenital blindness stood divine intention: the blindness came about not because of the victim's or his parents' sin, as many supposed, "but that the works of God might be displayed in him" (John 9:3). Jesus' opponents demanded of the man, "Give glory to God" (John 9:24). Through many years of suffering blindness, this man was in a position to do precisely that when Jesus touched his life, and he responded with brave and costly devotion.

People of authentic Christian faith are still glorifying God through sometimes unspeakable travail. A recent issue of *Trinity Magazine* (Spring 2007) soberly recounts a pair of such situations. Since I teach in the institution that produces this publication, Trinity International University, these tragedies strike me with personal force. In the first case, Gwen Voss, a twenty-seven-year-old librarian of great beauty, intelligence, and importance to Trinity's Rolfing Memorial Library and the international ministry it supports, was admitted to the hospital for a fairly common procedure, the reopening of a collapsed lung. Her long-awaited wedding date lay just one week ahead. She was, doctors thought, one day from discharge. But during an amiable conversation with her mother at her bedside, an undetected embolism

moved from her leg to her heart. Unconsciousness and death were immediate despite forty-five minutes of resuscitation efforts, including fervent
prayers by her parents and fiancé. Finally, her father, Tim, chair of the
Human Performance and Wellness Department in Trinity College, told
the doctor, "Let her go."

The brief account of this September 2005 event and its aftermath does
not even bear a writer's name.[13] Two things stand out. One is the depth
of the parents' grief. From her mother, Kathy: "That first year, there are
times when you feel you can hardly breathe." From her father, Tim: "Now,
a year later, I find myself really beginning the grieving process as a dad of
not having Gwen in my life."

The second striking feature is the depth of conviction that, despite the
sudden death blow, God was not unfaithful. From Kathy: "As a mom, I
wanted to say, 'God, you had no right to give her and take her away from
me.' But reading Philippians [2], I realized that Christ did not cling to his
own rights, and God did not cling to his own Son." From Tim, who has often
sought solitude outdoors: "God really does come beside you—a strength,
a peace, a covering." He continues: "At your core, you know that you are
not alone . . . even when the people in your life, your job, are not enough.
You really need God. He is acquainted with grief, with the depth of grief.
He finds ways to make himself evident."

Christian believers, particularly any who have faced a similar staggering
loss and yet have tasted divine comfort, may well agree that the testimony
of Tim and Kathy Voss, both to their agony and God's sufficiency, gives
due deference and honor to God.

No less poignant is the case recounted by my colleague John S. Feinberg.[14]
Before he and his wife, Pat, married in 1972, they took special care to as-
sure that the long-term illness of Pat's mother could not be passed along to
their children, should they have any. Doctors confirmed that neither Pat nor
any offspring were in danger; the malady had no hereditary dimensions or
implications. Yet some fifteen years later, in 1987, Pat was diagnosed with
her mother's disease. As I write twenty years later, her condition slowly
worsens. The prognosis is death. Any or all three of their children may
succumb to the same affliction. John writes:

> Although I had spent much time in my life up to this point thinking about
> the theological problem of evil (I wrote my doctoral dissertation on it [at
> the University of Chicago]), I couldn't make sense of what was happening.

13. *Trinity*, Spring 2007, 18–20.
14. "Facing My Questions," *Trinity*, Spring 2007, 21–23. See chap. 10 of this volume.

How could this happen to us when we had given our lives in service to the Lord? I knew that believers aren't guaranteed exemption from problems, but I never expected something like this. I was angry that God had allowed this to happen.

John Feinberg writes of finding particular challenge and insight in verses from Ecclesiastes 7 and Matthew 20. Although he states that "in November 1987, Pat's diagnosis gave me a view of the future that just about destroyed me," he goes on to speak repeatedly of his wonderful wife and children, his love for them that the hardships have only enhanced, and of his gratitude:

> While there are still many things about our circumstances that I don't know or fully understand, I do know some things with certainty. I know that throughout eternity I'll be thanking God for the wife and family he gave me and for the ministry he has allowed us to have in spite of (and even because of) the many hardships. I am so thankful that God is patient with us and always there with his comfort and care.

As in the case of Tim and Kathy Voss, John and Pat Feinberg had a head-on collision with suffering. Their convictions and, in their view, the reality of a benevolent God who is personally present, have resulted in a testimony that surely glorifies God. It would be facile and flippant to say "terrible thing x" happened so that "wonderful thing y" would result, x being death and disease and y being God's glorification. The Vosses and the Feinbergs do not trumpet final answers that dissolve the pain and questions that they will, no doubt, carry to their graves. Yet it is clear that adversity, and their suffering, have not had the last word. Among believers, suffering is an important factor in God's answering the prayer Jesus taught us: "Our Father who art in heaven, hallowed be thy name." His name is hallowed through his children's suffering.

Thesis 7: Suffering Is the Price of Much Fruitful Ministry

Christians are called to be servants—of God, of one another, of their spouses and other family members, of friends, of the world at large. Jesus "went about doing good" (Acts 10:38) and came not to be served but to serve and give his life (Mark 10:45). His selfless pattern was an intentional example for his followers: "For I have given you an example, that you also should do just as I have done to you" (John 13:15).

Jesus' call to serve is also, probably too frequently for our liking, a call to suffer. "Suffering seems to be one of those things God has for us that has to be dealt with personally in order to come to grips with it in others, Christian or not."[15] John Feinberg has written several powerful books on God, on evil, and on suffering.[16] But this enviable ministry in print has come at the price of circumstances none of us would wish on anyone or volunteer for ourselves. Many great sermons on suffering have grown out of lives torn apart by pain, whether the preacher's own or those to whom he ministered. Some years ago Warren Wiersbe produced a useful sampling of such sermons by Arthur John Gossip (1873–1954), whose wife had just died; by John Calvin (1509–1564), whose health and surroundings constituted a severe trial for much of his adult life; by Frederick W. Robertson (1816–1853), who wrestled with depression and died young; and many others.[17]

Today books abound on the integral link between Christian service and testimony on the one hand, and suffering on the other. Dietrich Bonhoeffer's (1906–1945) rich legacy, still very much alive through his printed works, harks back to years under Nazi oppression and eventually imprisonment and execution. Peter Hammond has written extensively about his harrowing experiences in Sudan.[18] Isaiah Majok Dau, a Sudan native, grew up amidst the terrors of Islamist oppression of the southern part of his native country. While the persecution of millions was not always overtly religious, at least tens of thousands died as the result of their confession of faith in Christ. Dau has produced one of the most important modern studies of suffering in Christian perspective, written from within the epochal war in Sudan and interacting with ruminations at least related to the subject of suffering by many Western theologians for whom the whole issue is largely theoretical.[19] The aftermath of the history Dau analyzes continues today in events unfolding in Darfur with its government-sanctioned janjaweed, terrified local populaces, and windswept mass graves.

Dan Baumann was falsely accused of espionage in Iran and endured prison and the threat of execution as a result of his Christian vocation and activities.[20] Bonnie and Gary Witherall followed the Lord's call to service to Lebanon, where Bonnie was killed in cold blood in the midst of selfless

15. Personal correspondence from Lee Eddleman, who adds, "For some the reality of the cross may suffice."
16. *No One Like Him: The Doctrine of God* (Wheaton, IL: Crossway Books, 2001); *The Many Faces of Evil* (Wheaton, IL: Crossway Books, 2004); *Where Is God? A Personal Story of Finding God in Grief and Suffering* (Nashville: Broadman and Holman, 2004).
17. *Classic Sermons on Suffering* (Grand Rapids, MI: Kregel, 1984).
18. See, e.g., *Faith under Fire in Sudan* (Newlands, South Africa: Frontline Fellowship, 1998).
19. *Suffering and God: A Theological Reflection on the War in Sudan* (Nairobi: Paulines Publications Africa, 2002). Worth noting also is the fictional but true-to-fact rendering of the Sudan civil war by Philip Caputo, *Acts of Faith* (New York: Vintage, 2005).
20. *Imprisoned in Iran: Love's Victory over Fear* (Seattle: YWAM, 2000).

service through medical care and Christian outreach in the city of Sidon.[21] New details continue to emerge regarding Stalin's Russia, where Orthodox Christians were put to death to the tune of six hundred bishops, forty thousand priests, and one hundred twenty thousand monks and nuns. Many more rank-and-file believers were killed, of course. "They suffered and died for their faith, for the fact that they did not renounce their God. In dying they sang His praises, and He did not abandon them."[22]

This is but a smattering of reference to a large and increasing literature that we ignore to our peril. The blood of our (often fatally) faithful sisters and brothers cries out to us from the ground. Their service was fruitful, and their enduring testimony is immensely rich. But there was a daunting entailment: Jesus' call to take up a cross became something more than a metaphor.

Thesis 8: Suffering Is Often the Penalty for Gospel Reception

A tension has arisen in some quarters in recent decades between viewing the gospel as a means of blessing, of gain, of prosperity on the one hand and viewing it as a call to personal loss and self-abnegation on the other. "Health-and-wealth" renderings of the Christian faith have arisen that focus largely on the benefit promised those who respond to the gospel message in the right way.[23] This has not been limited to North America, from which it has been aggressively exported. My own travels in Eastern Europe and Africa confirm how widely this notion of Christian teaching and life has spread in many corners of the globe. It can also be documented in rapidly growing segments of Christian populations in Asia and South America. Prosperity teaching is spread widely through satellite television and vies with older, historic, more balanced, and more austere understandings of what it means to believe in and follow Christ.

It is not to be doubted that God can and frequently does shower boon of all sorts, material included, on his beloved children. Yet offsetting the siren song of wealth and plenty are sobering reminders that God may choose to make the reception of his saving word a decidedly mixed blessing.

Consider this actual email plea to "Brother Mohammed," a convert from Islam to Christianity who ministers on a North American university cam-

---

21. Gary Witherall with Elizabeth Cody Newenhuyse, *Total Abandon: The Powerful True Story of Life Lived in Radical Devotion to God* (Carol Stream, IL: Tyndale, 2005).

22. Otets Arsenii, *Father Arseny (1893–1973): Priest, Prisoner, Spiritual Father*, trans. Vera Bouteneff (Crestwood, NY: St. Vladimir's Seminary Press, 1998), 1.

23. For a recent slice of the discussion see David Van Biema and Jeff Chu, "Does God Want You to Be Rich?" *Time*, September 18, 2006, 48–56.

pus, from "Salwa." (All names have been changed for security purposes.) Salwa and her husband, both devout Muslims, are studying in the States, and Salwa saw the Jesus film. According to their faith and custom, Salwa should not be communicating with a man who is not her husband, and she should certainly not be entertaining thoughts of believing in Christ à la Christian teaching. Now she finds herself in a gripping quandary. She writes clandestinely for counsel:

> Brother Mohammed,
> How are you today. Hope every thing is OK.
>
> First, I hesitated so much before sending this e-mail. I did not want to do something behind my husband's back, but I'm just looking for the truth and trying to find some answers to many many questions I have. And I know for sure that we use this method (e-mail) for only that reason.
>
> You might know the reason for this e-mail. I think you've heard the condition that I'm in since I saw the movie. I was wondering if someone from the same background that I came from can help me finding my way. Now, I'm really confused! Mohammed, how did you find your way? How did you start? and when? How did you become a believer? and how do you behave after that? What is the difference between now and then?
>
> What about what we all learned under the umbrella of Islam? I have endless questions. Mohammed, please, help me find my way! I can not help thinking of Jesus since I saw the movie but, what I've been taught for the 30 years prevents me from submitting. Were we wrong? were we right? where is the truth? Life is not long enough, so we need to search for the truth as soon as we can.
>
> My husband does not know about this e-mail, so, please, you respond to this e-mail only, not to the other ones. He has an access to my campus e-mail. Thanks, I appreciate your interest in helping me.
>
> Salwa

Who can fail to be moved by this situation? If Salwa continues to follow through on this, the personal and social cost to her will likely be staggering. This is assuming that she does not become one of several thousand "honor killings" that take place each year in certain quarters of the Arab world.

Following Christ may in fact have a result quite different from the blandishments of prosperity-teaching proponents. It is not only the woman "Salwa" who grapples with this; it is also "Mohammed," her contact—he has family members in the Middle East ready to do him harm for leaving Islam. He lives in delicate contact with them, praying for them and socializing when it seems safe, but trying to avoid situations in which they could find it easy to strike him down for embracing Christian convictions.

There are tens of millions of Christians resident in the Middle East[24] whose testimony faces just this sort of stony reception. There are hundreds of millions of Muslims whom Christians worldwide are called to love, pray for, and evangelize. It is hard to see how this task can even be taken seriously, let alone aggressively pursued, under the auspices of a message that conditions "Christians" to seek their own material benefit. Certainly such a message has nothing credible to offer "Mohammed," "Salwa," or innumerable others in analogous settings. The contemporary setting calls for clear-eyed recognition of the real cost of discipleship for vast reaches of today's world population.

Perhaps the last words of this section should call attention to the terse lines of a memorial posted in honor of American medical missionary Martha Myers, gunned down with several others in Yemen in December 2002. The penalty for her commitment to her calling was ultimate. The account speaks for itself:[25]

> Slain Missionary, Dr. Martha Myers, "Gave Her All to People Who Were Suffering"
>
> BIRMINGHAM, Ala.—Dr. Martha C. Myers, the Southern Baptist missionary shot to death by an extremist in Yemen Dec. 30, was remembered as a person "mature beyond her years, especially in her Christian commitment," by a former teacher.
>
> Dr. Mike Howell, her biology professor at Samford University, described Myers as a well-rounded person but one who was "absolutely serious" about becoming a medical missionary.
>
> "She was a brilliant, hard-working person, good in things other than biology," he said. "She sang in the A Cappella Choir and edited the literary magazine, but there was never any doubt among the faculty that she was headed to the medical mission field."
>
> Dr. Myers graduated from Samford in 1967 and the University of Alabama Medical School in 1971. An obstetrician, she served at Jibla Baptist Hospital in Yemen for more than 25 years.
>
> "There aren't many people willing to dedicate their life to people, but she gave her all to people who were suffering," Howell said. "That's the greatest calling of a Christian."

---

24. See Tarek Mitri, "Who Are the Christians of the Arab World?" *International Review of Mission* 89 (2000): 12–27.
25. January 3, 2003, http://www.samford.edu/News/news2003/010303_1.html (July 3, 2007), used by permission. Samford University dedicated a life-size bronze statue of Dr. Myers in May 2007. The statue is located in the university library in an area that houses the Marla Haas Corts Missionary Biography Collection.

Her father, Dr. Ira Myers of Montgomery, Ala., recalled his daughter speaking of the great need for medical care in Yemen. "She just depended on the Lord to take care of her," he said. "This is what she felt she ought to be doing and she did it."

Myers was killed along with two other hospital staff members, administrator William Koehn and purchasing manager Kathleen Gariety. Koehn's daughter, Janelda Pearce of Mansfield, Texas, is also a graduate of Samford's nursing school.

A classmate of Myers at Samford, Bonnie Barnes Voit of Cullman, Ala., recalled that Myers had a commitment to medical missions that was "as clear as crystal" when they met as freshmen in 1963. "This clear call she felt to serve others empowered her even as a freshman majoring in premed."

Catherine Allen of Birmingham, another classmate, said Myers was "very focused and very productive." It was this focused personality and "a distinct calling of God" that enabled Myers to serve for so long in Yemen, said Allen.

"The Yemen hospital was the most enduring, visible and viable International Mission Board witness in the Middle East," said Allen, a former administrator of the Woman's Missionary Union.

Myers and Koehn were buried on the grounds of the hospital they had served for a quarter of a century.

That is an official summation of a recent martyrdom in Christ's service. Thanks to a personal friend who visited Yemen shortly after Dr. Myers's death, I can fill in some background, edited from my friend's personal journal.[26] There were three murders that day: Kathy Gariety, Martha Myers, and Bill Koehn. But the target was Martha. She was an obstetrician/surgeon at the hospital. She died penniless, having sold her furniture and other possessions to give to the poor. She traveled all over the region inoculating children and caring for the sick. She had earlier befriended her killer's wife and had shared Christ with her. Consequently he determined to kill her and planned the murder for many months. During this time he became associated with Al Qaeda. On the day of the killings he called the hospital and had Martha paged. This way he would know that she would be at the telephone in the hospital office. He smuggled a pistol in with him, went straight to the office and shot and killed her. He then shot Bill Koehn, who was seated at the desk beside Martha, and Kathy Gariety, who also happened to be in the office. He went to the next room and shot the pharmacist, who would later recover.

26. This person remains anonymous for security reasons.

There is an interesting sequel. The first time Baptist personnel from the hospital went into Jibla after the shooting, people hid in their doorways. Given the law of retribution that is so much a part of their culture, they were afraid that the hospital staff would be out for blood, seeking vengeance. When it became obvious that no attack was forthcoming, the people flocked to the staff members, fell on their necks, and wept with them. Bill's widow, Martha Koehn, continues to serve at the hospital where her husband and Martha Myers are buried, up on the hill above the staff housing. The burial site is shown in the photograph below (used by permission):

Thesis 9: Suffering Nobly Borne Testifies to God's Goodness

This book is not only about suffering but also about God's goodness. It is suffering that poses the major problem. Who is going to resent God's goodness? Yet we live at a time when divine beneficence, at least in any form associated with religion and particularly with Christianity, is hotly disputed.[27] Telling responses to these attacks are appearing,[28] and more,

---

27. See, e.g., Christopher Hitchens, *God Is Not Great: How Religion Poisons Everything* (New York: Twelve, 2007); Sam Harris, *Letter to a Christian Nation* (New York: Knopf, 2006); Richard Dawkins, *The God Delusion* (Boston: Houghton Mifflin, 2006).
28. See, e.g., Keith Ward, *Is Religion Dangerous?* (Grand Rapids, MI: Eerdmans, 2007); Alister and Joanna Collicutt McGrath, *The Dawkins Delusion? Atheist Fundamentalism and the Denial of the Divine* (Downers Grove, IL: InterVarsity, 2007); Michael Patrick Leahy, *Letters to an Atheist* (Spring Hill, TN: Harpeth River Press, 2007).

perhaps more reflective ones, may be expected. But while many people in the world probably sympathize with these attacks, far fewer will read or even be aware of their rebuttals. How does goodness in the world, when it becomes evident and visible, come to be associated with God?

The Bible suggests that people infer at least certain divine attributes from creation (Rom. 1:20). Jesus pointed to birds, flowers, and grass as signs that God cares for humans, too (Matt. 6:26–30). Scripture is studded with claims that God superintends the world and that his provision is rich and good. An example can be seen in Psalm 104:10–15:

> You make springs gush forth in the valleys;
>   they flow between the hills;
> they give drink to every beast of the field;
>   the wild donkeys quench their thirst.
> Beside them the birds of the heavens dwell;
>   they sing among the branches.
> From your lofty abode you water the mountains;
>   the earth is satisfied with the fruit of your work.
> You cause the grass to grow for the livestock
>   and plants for man to cultivate,
> that he may bring forth food from the earth
>   and wine to gladden the heart of man,
> oil to make his face shine
>   and bread to strengthen man's heart.

Yet even if it is true that many find God to be good as the result of the natural blessings they receive from his hand, others do not. The Bible acknowledges this, too (Rom. 1:21). The goodness of God in the world at large cannot be quantified and "proven" to the earth's inhabitants. If God is good, and if acknowledgment of him in his goodness is integral to coming to terms with him as the God who saves, impressing this goodness on people becomes vital. How can this be accomplished? The question becomes all the more urgent in the postmodern setting with its suspicion of truth claims and metanarratives.

One response to this problem is to show that, even in the face of contemporary philosophical animus against historic Christian belief,[29] credible strategies still abound for effective testimony even in the academy where

---

29. See John W. Cooper, *Panentheism: The Other God of the Philosophers* (Grand Rapids, MI: Baker Academic, 2006).

post-, non-, and anti-Christian views are so entrenched and virulent.[30] But most Christians are not called to this venue of discussion and debate. What Christians at large *can* do is in some ways greater in scope and extent. They can bear their circumstances, including the painful ones, in ways that testify to God's goodness even if that testimony is rendered through tears. This may be as effective an apologetic for the goodness of the God they serve as anything else they could do or say.

When Jesus wept at Lazarus's grave, it moved even "the Jews" (in the fourth Gospel often a term describing Jesus' detractors) to pity: "See how he loved him!" (John 11:36). Jesus' grief, borne within his whole life's affirmation of the Father's goodness, moved his enemies' hearts to sympathy even though their minds were set on opposing his message. The same dynamic may be observed today. Often funerals of Christians become occasions for moving witness to the gospel message by those still living. I recall reports of a Christian physician killed in a car accident on a snowy road as he traveled for ministry purposes. During the closing hymn of the jam-packed memorial service his five sons stood, joined hands, and raised their arms aloft, proclaiming without words their belief in Christ's triumph over death despite their father's most lamented passing.

The argument here is in a sense no newer than Tertullian's ancient observation that the blood of Christian martyrs is often the seed of the church.[31] God uses pain and even death—not in the abstract but of his own loyal people—to testify to the word of life. What is called for today is a growing core of Christians not who have martyr complexes but whose daily lives are lived in such winsome, habitual, and cheerful self-sacrifice that they can weather even adverse circumstances with God-glorifying wisdom and grace. Job managed it in his day. Psalm 90, the only psalm attributed to Moses, shows that his belief in God's goodness was absolute despite acute earthly duress. Early Christians such as Paul and Peter wrote from within settings where difficulties abounded, but they did not hesitate to exhort others to "share in suffering as a good soldier of Christ Jesus" (as Paul writes to Timothy in 2 Tim. 2:3; cf. 1 Pet. 4:1). That is a major contention of Hebrews 11.

We live in a time when many have laid down their lives in faithfulness to their Lord who, they are convinced, is good and perfect in all his ways. The fact is that Christian suffering nobly borne may serve to impress upon a skeptical or indifferent world that the God of Christians is as good as

---

30. Pointing in fruitful directions is, e.g., Kevin J. Vanhoozer, *The Drama of Doctrine: A Canonical-Linguistic Approach to Christian Theology* (Louisville: Westminster, 2005).
31. *Apology*, 50.

or better than he is professed to be by those who endure hardship for his sake with aplomb and even praise. This witness, for some, may be more persuasive than formal argument alone could ever be.

Even if none are convinced, the virtue of the confession remains. People who have gone down in flames in one era have been known to kindle fires of fresh belief in subsequent times by their moving affirmation of God's goodness in the face of high cost to themselves. Cain's murdered brother, Abel, "through his faith, though he died, . . . still speaks" (Heb. 11:4).

Thesis 10: Suffering Unites Us with Other Sinners We Seek to Serve
Suffering is the quintessential leveler. "Never send to know for whom the bell tolls; it tolls for thee" (John Donne). We all face death eventually. In the meantime we are subject to the tremors of a world made uncertain by sickness, setback, sin, and the unwelcome unexpected in general.

A possible response to this is to stress the power of God to deliver us from what we dread. God's goodness, and his willingness and power to exercise it, are a grand theme of Scripture. Christians proclaim the God "who is able to do far more abundantly than all that we ask or think" (Eph. 3:20). Yet in the long run circumstances overtake the bravest and most sincere affirmations of God's victory over adversity. That ultimate victory is not in doubt. However, human capacity for leveraging it to our temporal, financial, medical, social, political, or other personal advantage will always prove limited in the current age.

Rather than chasing the wind of perpetual success and triumph, the Christian call is to recognize frankly how profoundly united we are with all other people on the face of the earth. It is our suffering, finally, that confirms and cements this solidarity. We watch our parents age and weaken and pass away, and eventually see the same decline in our own lives. We struggle with our children's problems and realize repeatedly that in the end they must work out their issues for themselves. Like others, we Christians receive disastrous medical test results. We lose our jobs. Our spouses may betray us. Our retirement funds take a hit when financial markets tank, and our good-faith efforts to further the Lord's interests may seem fruitless despite our best efforts. Or perhaps poor health and sporadic employment make retirement funds an unattainable dream.

The earth yields not only bounty but also thorns and thistles. Recently, word arrived of the death, after much suffering, of Harold O. J. Brown, founder of Care Net. This organization consists of 1,090 pregnancy centers across North America helping over one hundred thousand pregnant women annually find alternatives to abortion. This man's efforts, we could say, helped save a million lives or more. Yet he was not untouched by the general entropy of life in this fallen world. No one is.

This fact is one reason why suffering must be in the foreground of Christian thought and action today: it is a ready bridge between those who have the word of life and those who do not. This is apparently part of God's evangelistic strategy. Even Jesus was "a man of sorrows, and acquainted with grief" (Isa. 53:3). Was this part of what drove the centurion to profess Jesus' innocence, and why "all the crowds that had assembled" to gape at Jesus' death returned to their homes "beating their breasts" in apparent empathy? Christians' lives and message gain credibility in part because they are not spared the vicissitudes that batter everyone else in need of God's redemptive promise.

Thesis 11: Suffering Establishes True Fellowship among Christians
Paul longed to know not only the power of Christ's resurrection in his life but also the fellowship of his sufferings (Phil. 3:10). Reinhard Hütter in his volume *Suffering Divine Things* examines, among other matters, "the pathos characterizing the core of Christian experience."[32] Christians have in common not first of all that they "do" something to make themselves Christian but that they are acted on from outside their own puny force of intellect, feeling, or will. There is an "other" which "determines or defines a person prior to all action, in all action, and against all action, an 'other' which a person can only *receive*."[33] This "other" is, first of all, God himself in his saving self-disclosure. But it is also the adversities of life from within which God makes himself known. Luther in particular unfolded "the pathetic heart of Christian existence." He did this using "the terminology into which this Greek *pathos* and all its semantic variants have been translated into Latin, namely, as *passio*."[34]

Hütter explores this insight in its significance for a Christian doctrine of the church. It is equally important for hinting at the contemporary significance of suffering (related to the Greek word *pathos* and the Latin *passio*). It is certainly true that it is primarily God himself who in his redemptive activity has "caused us to be born again to a living hope through the resurrection of Jesus Christ from the dead" (1 Pet. 1:3). But this new birth does not take place in a vacuum. Rather it unfolds amidst earthly life, which is manifestly to some extent a vale of tears. Christians are divided in many ways

32. Reinhard Hütter, *Suffering Divine Things*, trans. Doug Stott (Grand Rapids, MI: Eerdmans, 2000), 31.
33. Ibid., 30 (Hütter's emphasis).
34. Ibid., 31.

by doctrinal, social, geographical, economic, racial, and other distinctives if not barriers. They have in common, however, not only their knowledge of God in Christ but also their subjection to forces and circumstances that constitute suffering.[35] They also share a common mandate *to* suffer, as many subsequent chapters in this book will demonstrate. Just as this creates important solidarity with other humans at large (Thesis 10 above), it is an insight—and ultimately an experience—rich with potential for encouraging mutual Christian sympathy, shared undertakings, and the affirmation of one another that is primary amidst a fellowship whose principal affective badge is their love for one another (cf. John 13:34–35).

Conclusion

Naturally the theses above do not begin to exhaust what could be said regarding the contemporary significance of suffering in a world replete also with tokens of God's goodness. We have said nothing, for example, of the fact that what befalls us in life is a perennial spur to a truer and better faith. We are forced to move beyond the important *relational* principle that believers have a gift of personal fellowship with God to the *doctrinal* principle that this personal fellowship is rooted in theological truth and does not replace it.[36] "Although charisma probably does indeed constitute the inner dynamic of the church, it is not its foundation."[37] Suffering is a bracing slap in the face that drives God's people again and again to clarify and purify the fundamental terms of acknowledgment and worship of their God. It drives us to turn our hearts to God in truer prayer. The rediscovery and application of a brutally realist God-centeredness is an urgent need in an era of much crass human-centeredness—typified recently in the ego-centered absurdity of Episcopal priest Ann Holmes Redding's simultaneous profession of both Christian and Muslim faith.[38]

Nor have we explored implications of the fact that whatever suffering Christians and everybody else must endure in this world, it pales next to

35. The connection between true knowledge of God and suffering aptly regarded may be disconcertingly direct. As Lee Eddleman observes (personal correspondence): "Deuteronomy teaches us that we are in constant danger of majoring on the wrong things; words and actions in themselves do not satisfy God. There is more. How does He get us there? Perhaps suffering?"
36. Cf. Hütter, *Suffering Divine Things* (p. 14), with reference to Heinrich Schlier's realization of the poverty of German Protestant Christianity (rich in claims to personal piety but deficient in resolve to discover and live out biblical *truth*) at the time of the Third Reich. Hütter speaks aptly here of the "charismatic principle" and the "dogmatic principle."
37. Ibid. Hütter is quoting Schlier.
38. Cf. Eric Young, "Episcopal Priest Suspended over Muslim-Christian Identity," *Christian Post Reporter*, July 7, 2007, http://www.christianpost.com/article/20070707/28350_Episcopal_Priest_Suspended_Over_Muslim-Christian_Identity.htm (July 9, 2007).

scriptural predictions of what awaits the divinely accursed both in this age[39] and in the age to come.[40] This has contemporary significance in that contemplation of both current and eschatological woe is an important incentive to cultivate a seemly sense of urgency in personal pursuit of God, in ecclesial labors including evangelism, and in mission generally.

But the last word of this introductory chapter belongs not to one more thesis or argument but to a story. We began speaking of a boy's death by crocodile in Costa Rica. No one could save him. A second story, very similar, has a different ending. In the Nseleni River near subtropical Empangeni, South Africa, two third-graders released from school with pinkeye decided to slip away for a secret swim. As they were leaving the water, a hidden crocodile's jaws closed on Msomi's leg. He shouted frantically for help. Companions wisely and understandably fled.

Except for Themba. He grabbed his friend Msomi in a tug-of-war with the determined reptile. Matters hung in the balance for a long turbulent moment. Suddenly Msomi broke free. He scampered out of the water, bleeding from his left leg and arm and from a cut across his chest. But he was saved.

And Themba the noble rescuer, a third-grade kid with the heart of a grizzled warrior? Msomi, visibly shaken, lamented from his hospital bed: "I ran out of the water, but as Themba tried to get out, the crocodile caught him and he disappeared under the water. That was the last time I saw my friend alive. I'll never forget what happened that day—he died while trying to save me."[41]

The crocodiles of crises and calamities beset us all. Eventually we wander into the kill zone where the unwanted lurks, biding its time. Suffering is ubiquitous and finally terminal in this age. But there is a God, and he is good, and those who seek him are saved. We are all Msomi, but there is a Themba. The chapters that follow explore our dilemma and our deliverance, beginning with two that survey the Old Testament and suffering from the pen of Walter Kaiser.[42]

39. Cf. Stephen Keillor, *God's Judgments: Interpreting History and the Christian Faith* (Downers Grove: IVP Academic, 2007).
40. See Christopher W. Morgan and Robert A. Peterson, eds., *Hell Under Fire* (Grand Rapids, MI: Zondervan, 2004).
41. Sibusiso Ngalwa, "Boy Dies Saving Friend from Crocodile," April 4, 2004, http://www.iol.co.za/?click_id= 14&art_id=vn20040404110517366C649996&set_id=1 (July 10, 2007).
42. My thanks to Luke Yarbrough for consultation and corrections to an earlier draft of this chapter. I am also indebted to Lee Eddleman for helpful observations.

2

SUFFERING AND THE GOODNESS OF GOD IN THE OLD TESTAMENT

WALTER C. KAISER JR.

The news media bring into our homes stories and pictures of suffering from all over the world. Our own lives, too, are visited by pain and heartache. From those around us, and even from our own hearts, questions sometimes arise as to God's goodness. The Old Testament does not give a systematic or philosophical explanation for suffering or the problem of pain. Yet it does use as many as twelve Hebrew words to discuss topics such as suffering, distress, and anguish.[1] In fact, the presence of evil is introduced from the start in the garden of Eden, followed by the fall of humanity, which brings with it the problem of suffering and pain.

Despite the prominence of the concept of suffering in the Old Testament, the "goodness" (Hebrew: *tob*) of God is set forth as well. What we find is that it is precisely in suffering that God's goodness and existence become most apparent, for it is there, in the dark places, that God meets his people and

---

1. The New Testament also has some twenty-one Greek terms, but the key Greek term is *pascho*, "to suffer, to endure." See B. Gaertner, "Suffer," in *The New International Dictionary of New Testament Theology*, vol. 3, ed. Colin Brown, trans. from the German (Grand Rapids, MI: Zondervan, 1978), 719–26.

comforts them. A prominent example of this teaching is found in Exodus 33:19 where, after the golden calf disaster, God speaks to Moses on Mount Sinai and promises, "I will cause all my goodness to pass in front of you, and I will proclaim my name, the LORD, in your presence."[2] The goodness of God is nothing less than all of the qualities of the living God, the character of God himself powerfully present for Moses in a moment of crisis.

Paralleling this display of God's goodness was the prophet Elijah's experience on Mount Sinai. Elijah was in despair at the way the king and queen of Israel had so quickly dismissed God's mighty display of power on Mount Carmel. So God commanded the prophet, "Go out and stand on the mountain in the presence of the LORD, for the LORD is about to pass by" (1 Kings 19:11). Both this narrative and the Exodus 33 narrative use the verb "pass by" and both occur on Mount Sinai, suggesting that these two contexts should be linked together in the mind of the reader. God chose to encourage the despondent Elijah with a new view of his majesty and magnificence, a fresh manifestation of the One who is the essence of all goodness itself.

The same promise of God's goodness is made to all of his children in Psalm 23:6: "Surely goodness and mercy shall follow me all the days of my life" (KJV). Again in Psalm 31:19 the psalmist David sings of this goodness: "How great is your goodness, which you have stored up for those who fear you, which you bestow in the sight of men on those who take refuge in you."

Therefore, if we are to gain a balanced view of the problem of pain and suffering, it must be considered in the context of the goodness of God. Given the fact that the topic of suffering and pain in the Old Testament is so large,[3] let us first look at some of the largest teaching passages and then, in the next chapter, list the reasons and purposes for suffering in the Bible.

---

2. Unless otherwise noted, Scripture quotations in this chapter are taken from *The Holy Bible: New International Version* (NIV).

3. The amount of literature on suffering in the Old Testament is not voluminous. Among the better known books are: J. L. Crenshaw, *A Whirlpool of Torment: Overtures to Biblical Theology* (Philadelphia: Fortress, 1984); T. E. Fretheim, *The Suffering of God: An Old Testament Perspective* (Minneapolis: Fortress, 1984); E. S. Gerstenberger and W. Schrage, *Suffering*, trans. John E. Steely (Nashville: Abingdon, 1977); W. C. Kaiser, *A Biblical Approach to Personal Suffering: Lamentations* (Chicago: Moody, 1982); A. S. Peake, *The Problem of Suffering in the Old Testament* (London, Epworth Press, 1904); J. A. Sanders, "Suffering as Discipline in the Old Testament and Post-Biblical Judaism," *Colgate Rochester Divinity School Bulletin* 28 (1955); D. J. Simundson, *Faith Under Fire: Biblical Interpretations of Suffering* (Minneapolis: Augsburg, 1980); E. Sutcliffe, *Providence and Suffering in the Old and New Testaments* (London: Nelson, 1953). For separate articles, see: L. R. Bailey, "The Bible on Suffering" [a review article], *Interpretation* 35 (1981): 301–3; A. Leaney, "The Eschatological Significance of Human Suffering in the Old Testament and the Dead Sea Scrolls," *Scottish Journal of Theology* 16 (1963): 290–96; J. Luyten, "Perspectives on Human Suffering in the Old Testament," in *God and Human Suffering*, ed. J. Lambrecht and R. F. Collins (London: Peeters Press, 1990): 1–30.

The Book of Job

Few cases in the Old Testament pose the problem of what seems to be the unmerited (or at least innocent) suffering of a righteous man more strikingly than the book of Job. How does Job's experience harmonize with the depiction of God's fairness and goodness? Is not Yahweh completely dependable and able to deliver Job from the horrible situation in which he finds himself? It seems that nothing less than divine justice and benevolent providence are at stake.

In the prologue to the book, readers are given a glimpse at what is going on behind the scenes, in the heavenly realms, as God calls Satan's attention to Job, a paragon of virtue. Satan insists that Job's piety is merely dependent on the Lord's great blessings, and it would not hold if he were to suffer. Satan gains permission and approval from God to afflict Job and to ascertain the genuineness of his piety, but the Lord sets limits to the testing.

Job, of course, is unaware of all of this. However, he passes the first test magnificently. Having learned of the loss of all his sheep, camels, and children, Job responds: "The LORD gave and the LORD has taken away; may the name of the LORD be praised" (Job 1:21b). In the second test Satan is allowed to touch his health, but Job still replies: "Shall we accept good from God, and not trouble?" (Job 2:10b). God has already declared Job's righteousness to Satan, but Job does not know this yet. Therefore, the principal issue is not who will win the wager made by God; rather, it is first a vindication of God himself and then of Job.

The dialogue that follows in Job 4–31 with Job's three friends is often tiresomely repetitive. There is very little, if any, movement in thought or new theology from one speech to the other in the three cycles. The most that can be seen is the friends' increasing exasperation with Job as he steadfastly refuses to accept that their arguments are personally applicable to him. Instead, Job wishes to argue his case in front of God, but alas, he cannot find God, nor force him to grant such a hearing and trial.

Typical of the arguments of the three friends are:

> Eliphaz:
> "Consider now: Who, being innocent, has ever perished?
>   Where were the upright ever destroyed?
> As I have observed, those who plow evil
>   and those who sow trouble reap it.
> At the breath of God they are destroyed;
>   at the blast of his anger they perish." (Job 4:7–9)

Bildad:
"Does God pervert justice?
    Does the Almighty pervert what is right?
When your children sinned against him,
    he gave them over to the penalty of their sin.
But if you will look to God
    and plead with the Almighty,
if you are pure and upright,
        even now he will rouse himself on your behalf
        and restore you to your rightful place." (Job 8:3–6)

Zophar:
"Yet if you devote your heart to him
    and stretch out your hands to him,
if you put away the sin that is in your hand
    and allow no evil to dwell in your tent,
then you will lift up your face without shame;
    you will stand firm and without fear.
You will surely forget your trouble,
    recalling it only as waters gone by.
Life will be brighter than noonday,
    and darkness will become like morning.
You will be secure, because there is hope;
    you will look about you and take your rest in safety.
You will lie down, with no one to make you afraid,
    and many will court your favor.
But the eyes of the wicked will fail,
    and escape will elude them;
        their hope will become a dying gasp." (Job 11:13–20)

The argument of the friends is that Job must have sinned and therefore deserves all of his misery. Since God is totally just and is the one who both rewards and judges, the fact that Job is suffering means that he must have sinned against God. Their case is reductionistic, namely, that righteousness always brings prosperity, whereas sin and wickedness routinely bring misfortune. Previously, Job enjoyed divine favor, as evidenced by his enormous wealth. But the fact that he is now sick and stripped of his possessions, having suddenly lost everything he had, is proof that he must have sinned grievously.

Job relentlessly and unambiguously presses his claim of righteousness:

"[I have] not denied the words of the Holy One." (Job 6:10c)

"My hands have been free of violence and my prayer is pure." (Job 16:17)

"My feet have closely followed his [i.e., God's] steps;
I have kept to his way without turning aside.
I have not departed from the commands of his lips;
I have treasured the words of his mouth
more than my daily bread." (Job 23:11–12)

"My lips will not speak wickedness,
and my tongue will utter no deceit.
I will never admit you are in the right;
till I die, I will not deny my integrity.
I will maintain my righteousness and never let go of it;
my conscience will not reproach me as long as I live." (Job 27:4–6)

Job continues to press his appeal to God. In Job 9:33, he calls for an "umpire," "arbitrator," or "mediator" to step in between his friends and himself and "lay his hand upon us both." Many, with good reason, see here a prophetic testimony to the need for a Messianic person who is both divine and human, and who can bring a reconciliation between God and Job, and ultimately between God and humanity. Again in Job 16:19 the sufferer calls for a "witness" who "is in heaven" and who can be his "advocate" as he "pleads [a cognate of "arbitrator" in Job 9:33] with God as a man pleads for his friend" (Job 16:21).

In his most famous outcry to God, in Job 19:25–27, Job expects to be thoroughly vindicated. Some debate whether Job means that he will finally be vindicated in this life or the next; but either way, he remains confident that God knows about his case. Even if his vindication does not come in his lifetime, this text shows his expectation of the resurrection of his body: "Yet in my flesh I will see God" (Job 19:26b). On that day, Job will have the moment before God he so desired during his testing. In chapter 31 Job details the mercy and generosity he himself has shown to all, especially to the poor and destitute. He insists that his actions and motives have been free from greed, sexual impurity, idolatry, and all charges of impropriety.

When the Lord finally speaks, he makes no charge against Job except that he has spoken out of ignorance about the divine role in all of this. In the prologue, God had declared Job "blameless and upright" (Job 1:1), which does not mean he was absolutely faultless; Job himself acknowledges his sin (Job 7:20–21; 13:26). Yet Job was without any duplicity, hypocrisy, or pretense. He loved God completely and steered away from evil. So the question remains: if his suffering was not for sins committed, then why was he suffering? Most significantly, in the epilogue God indicts each of Job's three friends for wrongly applying to Job the doctrine of retributive suffering: "You have not spoken of me what is right, as my servant Job has" (Job 42:8).

Despite the comfort that Job's three friends intend to give, all of their arguments are wrongly aimed at Job. They try their best to show Job that he must "put away the sin that is in [his] hand . . . then [he] will lift [his] face without shame" (Job 11:14–15). Even if Job has no other fault, his three friends conclude that he is surely doubting God and in rebellion against the divine wisdom (Job 15). Their persistent advice is, "Submit to God and be at peace with him" (Job 22:21).

A fourth, younger friend of Job, Elihu, argues, in the five chapters of Job 32–37, that Job's suffering is a result of God's attempt to teach and educate him. Elihu asks, "Who is a teacher like [God]?" (Job 36:22; cf. Job 35:11). Therefore, Job must learn what it is God has for him in this suffering and pain. It is significant that God does not condemn Elihu as he does the other three friends of Job!

In the end, none of the views of Job's three friends is accepted as divine wisdom regarding Job's case. Instead, if any sense is to be made of all the pain that Job is going through, the person of the Lord must be faced. When God answers Job out of the storm (Job 38), Job (and all his friends) is finally reduced to silence. God invites anyone to step forward who thinks he could have advised God when the world was being created, or who wants to argue with God to correct him (Job 40:1–2). Job certainly does not wish to take up this challenge, for he ends by saying, "I am unworthy—how can I reply to you? I put my hand over my mouth. I spoke once . . . twice, but I will say no more" (Job 40:4–5).

Ultimately neither Job nor his friends is able to explain why Job suffered so greatly, but the character of God is vindicated, the simplistic theories of the friends are refuted, Job's righteousness is confirmed, and Satan's wicked scheme is foiled.

Ecclesiastes

The motto of Ecclesiastes is not, as the NIV translation reads, "Meaningless! Meaningless! . . . Utterly meaningless! Everything is meaningless" (Eccles.

1:2). Neither is it "All is to no purpose!"[4] The Hebrew word *hebel* is best translated as "transience," or "transitoriness," for it has at its root the sense of a "fog," "mist," or "change."[5] In Ecclesiastes it is used to capture the suffering that arises from the enormous amount of change in our lives, the lack of permanence and stability that appears to be everywhere.

Whereas the book of Job highlights the suffering that comes to an individual, Ecclesiastes looks more holistically at life, culture, and the general direction of history. It poses a question that expresses another aspect of the turmoil of the human soul: "What does man gain from all his labor at which he toils under the sun?" (Eccles. 1:3). The problem in life, according to the writer of Ecclesiastes, also called the "Preacher" or the "Teacher," is that everything seems to be changing all the time. Life is just too brief and too temporary. Is it worth all the trouble, all the working, living, and striving?

Although today some conclude that this book gives a fatalistic answer to all of life and an upside-down view of traditional values, the book, on the contrary, deliberately supplies a positive answer at the end of each of the four major teaching blocks of texts, viz., (1) Ecclesiastes 2:24–26, (2) 5:18–20, (3) 8:15, and (4) 12:9–14.[6] The answer simply stated is: even things so basic to life as eating, drinking, and finding satisfaction in our work are not part of our "birthright," nor do they come to us automatically. Rather, they come from the hand of God, as a gift for those who believe and fear him. The person who rejects this, who greedily gathers everything up and stores it away, will only find that God takes all of what was stored and delivers it into the hand of one who pleases him (Eccles. 2:24–26). The goods of life, with all their pleasures and duties, must be viewed as gifts from God. In fact, God deliberately separates the gift of possessions from our ability to enjoy them (Eccles. 6:2) so that we might be driven back to

---

4. E. S. Gerstenberger, *Suffering*, 90.

5. See Daniel C. Fredericks, *Coping with Transience: Ecclesiastes on the Brevity of Life* (Sheffield, England: JSOT Press, 1993). A similar view is that of Glenn Fobert, *Everything Is Mist: Ecclesiastes on Life in a Puzzling and Troubled Temporary World* (Belleville, Ontario: Guardian, 2003). Tremper Longman III, *The Book of Ecclesiastes* (Grand Rapids, MI: Eerdmans, 1998) disagrees on p. 64 and says there are only a handful of passages where *hebel* is best translated as "temporary" (Ps. 39:11 [Hebrew, 39:12], Job 7:16; Ps. 144:4; and Prov. 31:30). Of the 330 commentaries Longman surveys, almost every one takes *hebel* negatively; yet if it is so negative, then why is it in the Bible? It was the early church father Jerome who rendered *hebel* into Latin as "*vanitas*"; thus the Septuagint rendered it *mataiotes*, meaning "emptiness, futility, purposelessness" and the like. But the early Greek translators such as Aquila, Theodotian, and Symmachus rendered it *atmos/atmis*, meaning "breath, vapor, mist." James 4:14 seems to reflect *atmis*, for it uses this word and says, "How do you know what will happen tomorrow? For your life is like the fog [*atmis*]—it is here a little while, then it is gone."

6. This is the argument I make in my book *Ecclesiastes: Total Life* (Chicago: Moody, 1979).

him, to the Giver of all. Possessing the stuff of life is no guarantee of happiness, for one must also receive the ability to enjoy the gifts.

It is clearly a violation of the author's intent to argue that Ecclesiastes teaches that all of life is a big zero, without purpose or point. The writer states it this way: "Now all has been heard; here is the conclusion of the matter: Fear God and keep his commandments, for this is the whole [or, entirety] . . . of man [note that the word *duty*, typically included here as "the whole duty," does not appear in Hebrew]. For God will bring every deed into judgment, including every hidden thing, whether it is good or evil" (Eccles. 12:13–14). If we insist the Teacher thought everything was meaningless, we then have to argue that these two verses are not part of the original text but were added later to get the book into the biblical canon. But there are no Hebrew manuscripts that lack these verses. Consequently, if our understanding of the body of Ecclesiastes contradicts the concluding verses, we need to revise our understanding to bring it in line with the divinely expressed purpose.

Additionally, Ecclesiastes 12:9–10 says that the Teacher "searched out and set in order many proverbs. The Teacher searched to find just the right words, and what he wrote was upright and true." That hardly sounds like pessimism, fatalism, and meaninglessness. We have seen that while the words of Job's friends are accurately reported, they are not endorsed as the words or perspective of divine revelation. But if we say that only some of the author Solomon's[7] words are approved by God in this book, and some are not, we are left perplexed as to which words have divine endorsement and which do not. The older view that this book was written by a "natural" or "unspiritual" man leaves us with twelve chapters in the Bible of what *not* to do and only two final verses of approved teaching—surely an unbalanced proportionality of revelatory material, to say the least.

Twelve times in this book God is depicted as the Giver, either of joy or life itself. The gifts of God fall into four categories, according to Whybray: (1) the gift of life itself (5:18; 8:15; 9:9; 12:7), (2) the gift of eternity in the hearts of all mortals (3:11), (3) good gifts to those who please him, and (4) unpleasant gifts to those who do not believe or fear him.[8] Moreover, as Ecclesiastes wrestles with the problem, "What does one gain from all one's work and living?" (see Eccles. 1:3), the word *joy* or *enjoyment* appears seven times,[9] disproving the idea that the book urges despair, resignation, pessimism, or fatalism.

---

7. Because of its own internal claims, I take Solomon to be the author of Ecclesiastes (Eccl. 1:1, 11). See a fuller development of this argument in my book *Ecclesiastes: Total Life*, 24–38.

8. R. N. Whybray, *Ecclesiastes* (Sheffield, England: Sheffield Academic Press, 1989), 80.

9. See Ecclesiastes 2:20–26; 3:10–15; 3:16–22; 5:10–20; 8:14–15; 9:7–10; 11:7–12:7.

In the midst of all the changes in life, there are anchor points in fearing God and observing his commandments. God has deliberately made everything beautiful and has built people so that they have a capacity and a hunger to know how everything fits together. Yet without knowing God, it is impossible to know "A" from "Z," the beginning from the end (Eccles. 3:11). "Change" is a fact of life (and often a source of suffering), but that does not have to be our final answer to reality or life. Knowing God is the greatest goal imaginable, for in knowing him there is joy and the ability to find pleasure and satisfaction in every sphere of life.

Lamentations

Under the inspiration and direction of the Holy Spirit, the prophet Jeremiah[10] has given us a description of some of the most intense human suffering and communal pain ever experienced. The book of Lamentations provides no cheap cures or panaceas for the problems Judah faced as its capital city, Jerusalem, was besieged and ultimately destroyed and its landscape was devastated. The pathos of this situation rings out in the words of Lamentations 2:20–22:

> Look, O Lord, and consider:
>   Whom have you ever treated like this?
> Should women eat their offspring,
>   the children they have cared for?
> Should priest and prophet be killed
>   in the sanctuary of the Lord?
> Young and old lie together
>   in the dust of the streets;
> my young men and maidens
>   have fallen by the sword.
> You have slain them in the day of your anger;
>   you have slaughtered them without pity.
> As you summon to a feast day,
>   so you summoned against me terrors on every side.
> In the day of the Lord's anger
>   no one escaped or survived;
> those I cared for and reared,
>   my enemy has destroyed.

10. On the question of the author and the time of composition, see my book *A Biblical Approach to Personal Suffering* (Chicago: Moody, 1982), 24–30.

It is impossible to deal with pain, especially of this intensity, by pretending that it does not exist. It cannot be talked out of existence nor is there a magical cure to make it go away. Lamentations explores the complexity of the suffering that comes as a result of God's judgment, as well as the challenge of comforting those who suffer, as Eugene H. Peterson explains beautifully:

> Suffering, in itself, does not lead a person into a deeper relationship with God. It is just as liable to do the opposite, dehumanizing and embittering [someone]. The person who experiences suffering can mistakenly interpret the experience as the rejection of God, concluding that because God hates sin, he hates the sinner. . . .
>
> The task of pastoral work is to comfort without in any way avoiding the human realities of guilt or denying the divine realities of judgment. There is no better place for learning how to do that than in Lamentations. In the midst of suffering Lamentations keeps attention on the God who loves his people so that the judgment does not become impersonal nor the guilt neurotic, nor misfortune merely general. It pays attention to the exact ways in which suffering takes place; it takes with absolute seriousness the feelings that follow in the wake of judgment; and then it shapes these sufferings and feelings into forms of response to God. Pain thus becomes accessible to compassion.[11]

At the heart of the message of Lamentations is that where pain, grief, and hurt are, there is God himself. Indeed, this is the focal point or "big idea" of the whole book:

> Because of the LORD's great love we are not consumed,
>   for his compassions never fail.
> They are new every morning;
>   great is your faithfulness.
> I say to myself, "The LORD is my portion;
>   therefore I will wait for him." (Lam. 3:22–24)

An encounter with God, then, is central to what the book has to say about suffering. There are no "cheery bromides" or easy answers to solve the problems. In fact, the book concludes with the rhetorical question, "Have [you] utterly rejected us and are [you] angry with us beyond measure"? (Lam. 5:22). However, it must be remembered that this question comes

11. Eugene H. Peterson, *Five Smooth Stones for Pastoral Work* (Atlanta, GA: John Knox, 1980), 96.

in the midst of a prayer, thereby assuming that there is still a personal relationship with God.

Lamentations deals straight on with the concept of God's anger, using almost the full range of the Old Testament's rich and varied vocabulary for wrath.[12] This concept may make us moderns uncomfortable. But God's anger is the sign that he still cares for us and is committed to shattering our apathy:[13] "The moment anger is eliminated from God, suffering is depersonalized. . . . Anger is an insistence on the personal—it is the antithesis of impersonal fate or abstract law."[14] God's anger is not despotic, unreasonable, or whimsical, but comes in response to violations of the covenant he has made with his people. Therefore, it is the sign that he has abandoned neither his promise-plan nor his people.

The communal aspect of suffering is emphasized in Lamentations. Instead of viewing suffering as a series of private acts of grief, here we find the whole community participating. Our pain must not be borne in private or in silence, but with the whole community that has endured what we have felt as well. In fact, these strong communal ties are one of the greatest helps amidst the sense of isolation that suffering brings. Lamentations does not give easy answers, for there are none, but it deals honestly with the pain and binds the suffering community together as they encounter God in the midst of their grief.

The Story of Joseph: Genesis 37, 39–48

The narrative of Joseph, the eldest son of Rachel and a child of Jacob's later years, really begins when he is seventeen years old. Since he is his father's favorite, as shown by the special coat Jacob gives him, his brothers become envious. He is also prone to tattling on them and telling them of the dreams he has been having in which they bow down to him, all of which merely exacerbate their hatred. Their jealousy leads them to sell him to a passing caravan of Midianites/Ishmaelites, and then to tell their father that Joseph was attacked and killed by a wild beast. He is taken off to Egypt to spend the next thirteen years apart from his family, many of those years in prison, with no way of getting word to his father that he is still alive.

Remarkably, we are never given any hint that Joseph adopted a bitter spirit against his brothers or even against God for allowing him to be placed so unfairly in such a precarious position. Did Joseph recall the boyhood

---

12. Wesley J. Fuerst, *The Cambridge Commentary: The Books of Ruth, Esther, Ecclesiastes, The Song of Songs, Lamentations: The Five Scrolls* (Cambridge: Cambridge University Press, 1975), 45.
13. Peterson, *Five Smooth Stones*, 108.
14. Ibid., 106.

dreams that had so annoyed his brothers and believe that what had been revealed to him in these same dreams was still God's plan for his life? The text does not comment one way or the other. Many times during his thirteen years of captivity he was promoted to positions of increasing authority, and perhaps this was enough to encourage Joseph to believe that the dreams would still come to pass. Surely it shows that the deception of others cannot derail the plan of God. All the years of isolation, loneliness, and separation from home and friends surely caused Joseph great suffering and hurt. But his confidence in the sovereignty of God sustained him and enabled him to speak kindly to his brothers when he saw them again, at last:

> Do not be distressed and do not be angry with yourselves for selling me here, because it was to save lives that God sent me ahead of you. . . . Don't be afraid. Am I in the place of God? You intended to harm me, but God intended it for good to accomplish what is now being done, the saving of many lives. (Gen. 45:5; 50:19–20)

None of that speech reversed thirteen years of hardship and pain, but it does demonstrate the stability that comes when individual suffering is seen as part of God's wider purpose. Once again, we are not given the rationale for suffering, or a philosophical explanation, but we are given a fixed point of reference for how to endure during trials.

Proverbs

It is possible, of course, to bring suffering on ourselves by disregarding the wisdom God has given to us by his common grace for everyday living. Persons who are idle and too lazy to work expose themselves to suffering hunger (Prov. 10:4; 19:15). Those who keep company with fools likewise risk coming to harm (Prov. 13:20). Stingy persons, who hold back on giving to others, find themselves in the throes of poverty (Prov. 11:24). There is another type of person who is called "simple," who, despite the risk of danger, refuses to take refuge and therefore suffers from his own foolishness (Prov. 22:3; 27:12). Then there is the rich oppressor who brings suffering to the poor by his refusal to deal justly and fairly with them (Prov. 13:23).

In such cases, it is difficult to blame divine providence for the resultant suffering. In effect, the pain comes because we insist on going against the grain of the universe. When we fail to use the benefits and resources given to us by virtue of common grace, and we rebel against the order God has placed in the world, we must bear the brunt of our own foolishness. We cannot look for some mysterious reason in divine providence that excuses our own stupidity.

Proverbs does not say that righteous living will always produce prosperity or a life free of trouble. Yes, prosperity can be a good thing if we do not make wealth our idol or the center of our lives. But being poor and righteous is better than being rich and wicked (Prov. 22:1; 28:6, 11). Proverbs teaches that God will ultimately punish the wicked, and their prosperity will be lost (Prov. 2:21–22; 5:22; 10:16, 25, 27; 11:5, 8). Judgment will come upon them both at the end of their lives and at the last day. Proverbs therefore highlights the type of suffering that we bring upon ourselves and others when we insist on kicking against the way God has ordered the world.

Psalms of Lament

Many find seven basic elements in a lament: (1) an invocation, (2) a plea to God for help, (3) one or more specific complaints, (4) a confession of sin or, alternatively, a declaration of one's innocence, (5) a prayer of imprecation or curse on one's enemies, (6) an expression of confidence that God will respond, and (7) a hymn or a blessing. The central point in the lament is the complaint that indicates where the sufferer is hurting and why he or she wants relief.

A prime example of this focal point in a lament can be seen in Psalm 73:13, where the psalmist complains, "Surely in vain have I kept my heart pure; in vain have I washed my hands in innocence." Again in Psalm 120:2, the cry goes up, "Save me, O Lord, from lying lips and from deceitful tongues." Such complaints are only representative, for laments run the whole gamut of emotions.

The book of Lamentations is the main example of the lament form. However, except for Lamentations 3, that book is mainly a communal lament similar to the communal laments of Psalms 44, 60, 74, 79, 80, 83, and parts of 89, as well as Jeremiah 14, Habakkuk 1, and Isaiah 63. Other psalms have a partial communal lament, such as Psalms 68, 85, 90, and 106. In all of these, the focal point of the lament is an issue that is present in the community. However, even though the division between communal and individual laments seems fairly straightforward,[15] often the speaking "I" of the psalms acts as a representative for the whole group. Alternatively,

---

15. Biblical laments have been categorized into these two categories since the early days of form criticism, mainly under two men: Hermann Gunkel, *The Psalms: A Form-Critical Introduction*, trans. Thomas M. Horner (Philadelphia: Fortress, 1967) and Joachim Begrich, "Das priestliche Heilsorakel," *Zeitschrift für die alttestamentliche Wissenschaft* 52n (1934): 81–92.

the speaker may be the king, who is offering the lament as a representative of the whole group.

The list of individual psalms of lament is even more extensive. Included in this list are Psalms 3–7, 10–14, 17, 22, 25–28, 31, 35, 36, 38–43, 51–59, 61–64, 69, 71, 73, 77, 86, 88, 102, 109, 120, and 130. One could also easily add parts of Jeremiah 15, 17, 18, and 20, Lamentations 3, and a number of the texts in Job.

These laments help us gain a more balanced view of life by reminding us that life is not continual happiness. Our Lord did not want his Word to give us a romanticized portrayal of life, one that does not account for its painful realities. Instead, God intended his revelation to fully equip us for our earthly journey; therefore he provided us the language of prayer and faith. Genuine expression of emotion does not always need to be spontaneous. Sometimes the structure of alphabetic acrostics, such as Lamentations 1-4 and a number of the psalms, helps direct the mourner's outpouring of grief, like riverbanks to channel his expression of anguish before God. Enormous depth characterizes these laments, as they flow from long hours of meditating on what is happening to the sufferer. In all these cases, the suffering and despair drive the mourner toward God rather than away from him. Pain, grief, and hurt are not downplayed but are named and discussed.

Psalm 77[16] is a lament composed by Asaph, who wrote twelve psalms. This psalm recounts a time of intense inner suffering, when Asaph's anguish knew few limits. Although his voice ascended to heaven tirelessly, his "soul refused to be comforted" (Ps. 77:2). His "spirit grew faint" (v. 3) as it appeared that God was not going to answer.

The questions came fast and furiously as the sufferer lay on his bed remembering all that troubled him. Six rhetorical questions are posed in verses 7–9: (1) "Will the Lord reject forever?" (2) "Will he never show his favor again?" (3) "Has his unfailing love vanished forever?" (4) "Has his promise failed for all time?" (5) "Has God forgotten to be merciful?" and (6) "Has he in anger withheld his compassion?" Like many others who go through dark nights of the soul, so the psalmist in Psalm 77 pours out his grief to God. It is not that he doubts God exists, for why then would he pour out his heart to him? But he doubts that God cares for him as an individual and for his nation. Sometimes people clumsily try to help us in our distress by saying, "Don't even think or talk about it; it does no good!"

---

16. For a fuller development of this psalm, see my *Preaching and Teaching from the Old Testament: A Guide for the Church* (Grand Rapids, MI: Baker Academic, 2003), 129–38, where I have included by permission the sermon preached by Rev. Dr. Dorrington Little, at the First Congregational Church of Hamilton, MA, on January 21, 2001.

But God wants us to name every hurt in his presence. Asaph knows this and pours out all his concerns.

Verses 10–15 form the next strophe with verse 10 serving as the focal point or "big idea" of the psalm: "Then I thought, 'To this I will appeal: the years of the right hand of the Most High.'" The psalmist thought, but only for a moment, that it was God who had changed! But this verse can also be read as an appeal to the stability of God. If so, then we move from the despair of verses 1–9 to a resounding reaffirmation of faith, with verse 10 serving as the hinge verse between the two sections. Now Asaph remembers all that God has done previously, listing some of these deeds in verses 16–19. He recalls the Red Sea crossing as evidence of the fact that God is indeed there in the midst of our afflictions.

What started out with despair that was leading to doubt (a word, incidentally, that never appears in the Hebrew Bible), has now moved to worship and adoration of the One and only true God who helps us in our distress, despair, hurt, and suffering. No, we are not forgotten by God, for his love and mercy are real and his promises are true. God does care; in fact, history has shown that this is the very hallmark of God.

The Suffering of God

If we are to properly understand suffering, we must also consider the fact that God himself is not unaffected by pain, but is afflicted just as we are.[17] The concept of the nearness of God in the Old Testament should suggest to us that he experiences many of the same emotions as we do. Surely God "was grieved that he had made man on the earth" (Gen. 6:6), as he prepared for the flood. The living God experiences deep agony, seen clearly in Hosea 11:8–9:

> How can I give you up, Ephraim?
>   How can I hand you over, Israel?
> How can I treat you like Admah?
>   How can I make you like Zeboiim?
> My heart is changed within me;
>   all my compassion is aroused.
> I will not carry out my fierce anger,
>   nor will I turn and devastate Ephraim.
> For I am God, and not man—
>   the Holy One among you.

17. A Japanese theologian, Kazoh Kitamori, wrote a book entitled *The Theology of the Pain of God: The First Original Theology from Japan* (Richmond, VA: John Knox Press, 1965).

Few statements are as forthright and as graphic as this. Every passion in the Lord is aroused as he contemplates both his abiding love for Israel as well as the need for his justice. God will not treat Israel as he treated the five cities of the plain, including Sodom and Gomorrah.

At other times Yahweh feels like an abandoned husband:

> This is what the LORD says:
> "What fault did your fathers find in me,
>   that they strayed so far from me?
> They followed worthless idols
>   and became worthless themselves.
> They did not ask, 'Where is the LORD,
>   who brought us up out of Egypt
> and led us through the barren wilderness . . . ?'" (Jer. 2:5–6)

The same is seen in Isaiah 1:2–3 or Micah 6:1–5. In ways that we cannot fully comprehend, Almighty God suffers along with his people. None of those who are united to him by covenant, then, suffers alone. He not only knows and cares, but he suffers with them. And, as the Almighty, he offers his repentant people his presence, power, and help. How, then, can we doubt the goodness of God? His goodness must be factored into all discussions of our suffering and pain.

Conclusion

God is for us and not against us. He does not want his people to suffer.[18] It is not God's continual and deepest wish that all of our desires should remain forever unfulfilled; that is erroneous teaching. But so is a health, wealth, and prosperity message, especially if it says God wants everyone to be happy and rich.

We cannot deny that the issue of suffering in the lives of God's people contains a good deal of mystery. We wonder why Job's righteousness should have provoked Satan in the first place. However, it is clear that our commitment to follow God and trust in his goodness and faithfulness, even in the throes of suffering, surely cuts the ground out from under Satan. All of the Old Testament speaks with a unified voice about the way that righteousness, pain, suffering, and distress interact with one another. The Torah will not contradict the Psalms, and the two of them will not oppose the wisdom literature or the prophets.

---

18. This conclusion has been aided by Doug Rudy, "Prosperity, Suffering, and Righteousness in the Wisdom Literature of the Old Testament," http://www.xenos.org/ministries/crossroads /OnlineJournal/issue2/suffrigh.htm (October 4, 2006), 1–17.

God's people will continue to suffer, and there will be no easy answers to that suffering, yet we have the assurance that God will be with us and will hear our cries to him. His goodness will meet us there, enabling us to endure and to emerge triumphant.[19]

We will further explore God's goodness in the next chapter, as we investigate various kinds of suffering in the Old Testament.

---

19. For a clear series of questions and answers to these issues, see David E. Pratte, "God Helps with Your Troubles: Bible Solutions for Problems, Suffering, and Hardship," 1998, http://www.biblestudylessons.com/cgi-bin/gospel_way/help_for_troubles.php (June 27, 2007).

3

EIGHT KINDS OF SUFFERING IN THE OLD TESTAMENT

WALTER C. KAISER JR.

The Old Testament gives us the most comprehensive survey of the problem of suffering from the standpoint of theistic religion which can be found anywhere."[1] Even though we are not given a unitary or systematic principle that explains all suffering, it does not mean that the topic is avoided in the Bible; much of its content focuses on that very problem. How did humanity become subject to suffering? Inasmuch as men and women were created "good" (Gen. 1:31), how was it that sin corrupted the good work of God and brought such misery to their lives and work? The whole plan of redemption announced in Scripture, culminating in the work of Christ on the cross, is dedicated to answering that question.

Ways of Organizing the Kinds of Suffering in the Old Testament
There is no single preferred method of organizing the huge amount of data that the Old Testament presents on this question. Neither is there an all-embracing, unitary solution to the problem of pain, evil, and suffering

1. H. Wheeler Robinson, *Suffering: Human and Divine* (New York: MacMillan, 1939), 31.

that can be teased from the text. Therefore, it is best to leave the question where the biblical text leaves it.

Gordon R. Lewis organizes his encyclopedia article on this topic by identifying six main types of suffering in the Bible.[2] Each type adds another facet to the question of why there is so much suffering in the world, but no one type, nor even all of them together, supplies the final answer, as if there were a complete or comprehensive answer to this huge question.

Lewis lists the following six types: (1) judgmental suffering, (2) empathetic suffering, (3) vicarious suffering, (4) testimonial suffering, (5) preventative suffering, and (6) educational suffering.

The first, judgmental suffering, comes as the result of sins against God's revelation as announced by his prophets. Our sin is the main cause of this type of suffering, and its consequences ought to be obvious to us without searching for someone to blame or assigning ourselves a "victim" status.

In the case of empathetic suffering, it is mostly God who experiences suffering. If we are to do justice to God's immanence (as well as his transcendence), we must understand that the sin God observed in the days of Noah caused him grief (Gen. 6:6). As mortals are afflicted, Isaiah 63:9 notes, so is God afflicted as well.

Lewis focuses almost exclusively on the death of Christ in the New Testament to demonstrate vicarious suffering, although Isaiah 52:13–53:12 surely anticipated the Messiah's suffering on behalf of the sins of the world.

Lewis's example of testimonial suffering in the Old Testament is Job. Satan desired to show God that Job would deny his faith if he were given the proper amount of trouble and pain. Despite Job's ignorance of Satan's schemes, he did not fold under the pressure but testified to his trust in God.

Preventative suffering is explained more apologetically and philosophically by Lewis. Pain, he argues, can be a warning signal from God of approaching physical dangers. Without the feeling of pain, we could daily run into cuts, burns, and bruises that would leave us a heap of scar tissues, if we survived.

Finally, Lewis points to educational suffering. He uses New Testament examples to show that this suffering is a work of God not primarily to make us comfortable but to produce character in us.

2. Gordon R. Lewis, "Suffering and Anguish," in *The Zondervan Pictorial Encyclopedia of the Bible*, 5 vols., ed. Merrill C. Tenney and Steven Barbabas (Grand Rapids, MI: Zondervan, 1975), 5:530–33. The list is from p. 530.

E. S. Gerstenberger finds five experiences of suffering in the Old Testament: (1) loss, (2) illness, (3) violence, (4) fear, and (5) failure.[3] Because he sees these as only scattered witnesses to what is going on within the broader narrative, he also correctly refuses to claim that these five provide us with a complete picture of the Old Testament.

In the first type, loss, Gerstenberger discusses three types of loss: (a) the loss of property, (b) the loss of other persons, and (c) the loss of honor. Each brings pain and causes suffering.

Job's illness provided a severe test, as did the Shunammite woman's loss of her son, perhaps to a sunstroke (until restored to life again; 2 Kings 4:20). Often the problem in the Old Testament was leprosy (Num. 12:12–16; 2 Kings 7:3). Occasionally there was an outbreak of the bubonic plague (1 Sam. 5:6–6:9) that raised the suffering level to new heights. Even pagan Philistines recognized the connection between this pestilence and the fact that they had taken from Israel the holy object, the ark of the covenant of God (1 Samuel 5 and 6).

Violence also accounts for experiences of suffering, such as the innumerable court intrigues that regularly characterized Oriental families (1 Kings 2:13–25; 2 Kings 8:7–15; 11:1–3). Violence could also arise from organizations that became demagogic or clearly selfish. The prophet Samuel warned that such might be the result of the desired monarchy, but Israel refused to listen to him (1 Samuel 8).

In addition, Gerstenberger lists fear as a source of suffering. But here he mostly has in mind the fear caused by the superhuman powers of demons, "hairy ones" (Lev. 17:7; Isa. 34:14), and the so-called night monster, "Lilith." However, Gerstenberger overemphasizes this category, giving it a place that is disproportionate to the text and to biblical religion.[4]

Finally, failure is Gerstenberger's fifth type of suffering in the Old Testament. He has in mind being "put to shame" (Isa. 37:27; Ps. 31:17) and being defeated by the challenges of life. Sometimes there are the failures of the individual, but at other times life itself causes the suffering.

Jim Sanders finds eight categories of suffering in the Old Testament: (1) retributive, (2) disciplinary, (3) revelational, (4) probationary, (5) illusory

---

3. E. S. Gerstenberger and W. Schrage, *Suffering*, trans. John E. Steely (Nashville: Abingdon, 1980), 22–102.

4. Lloyd R. Bailey criticized the same point in his "The Bible on 'Suffering,'" *Interpretation* 35 (1981): 302. He commented, "Should not one distinguish Israelite folk-religion, where demons abound, from 'official' Yahwism, which ignores them as irrelevant, reduces them to Yahweh's agents or to common nouns (demythologizes them) or treats them as intrusions from foreign cults and condemns them?"

(or transitory), (6) mysterious, (7) eschatological, and (8) meaningless. He defines them succinctly:

> The retributive solution underlies the orthodox position of the Bible. The disciplinary and revelational views are closely related and stem from the basic beliefs which underlie faith in an ethical deity. The probationary solution includes the ideas of refining and testing, often in themselves closely allied (Jer. 6:27–29; 9:6; Isa. 48:10; Zech. 13:9; Job 23:10; Ps. 66:10), and formed a part of orthodox thinking. The idea that sufferings of the righteous are but for a moment (Hab. 2:4) [sic] is frequent in the psalter. . . . The eschatological solution is found often in post-exilic thinking, while the heretical assertions that sufferings are meaningless are discernible in the books of Ecclesiastes and Job.[5]

I would offer another organization of the kinds of suffering in the Old Testament: (1) retributive suffering, (2) educational or disciplinary suffering, (3) vicarious suffering, (4) empathetic suffering, (5) evidential or testimonial suffering, (6) revelational suffering, (7) doxological suffering, and, finally, (8) eschatological or apocalyptic suffering.[6]

Eight Kinds of Suffering in the Old Testament

Retributive Suffering

One of the fundamental principles by which God governs the world is retributive or judgmental suffering. It is the most comprehensive type of distress or suffering mentioned in the Bible.

Its most basic definition is that retributive suffering is that kind of suffering that comes as a result of sin because sin must call down the judgment of God. If God is the one and only righteous and just judge of the whole world (Ps. 7:8–10; 58:10–11; 82:1–4; Prov. 16:10–11), then as surely as one man's righteousness will be rewarded, another man's unrighteousness will be punished. The choice is up to mortals: Will men and women choose good or will they choose evil? Will they choose life or death (Deut. 30:19)? The norms of life—ethically, morally, socially, doctrinally, and ritually—are set by God. When we run against the established grain of the universe and the order that God has set in the world, God must judge that rebellion.

Unrighteousness, then, whether committed by individuals or nations, must be punished in God's moral government of the world. Examples of

5. Sanders, "Suffering as Divine Discipline in the Old Testament and Post-Biblical Judaism," *Colgate Rochester Divinity School Bulletin* 28 (1955): 1.
6. This was developed as early as 1982 in my book, *A Biblical Approach to Personal Suffering* (Chicago: Moody Press, 1982), 121–30.

such retributive suffering can be seen in the judgment that came on Sodom and Gomorrah, and in the fall and destruction of Samaria, the capital of the northern ten tribes of Israel, and of Jerusalem, the capital of Judah.

H. Wheeler Robinson summarizes this aspect of retributive suffering:

> This principle, then, is not to be dismissed as one that is superseded by the doctrine of divine grace. . . . However harsh may seem the retributive principle when taken alone, and however untrue to our experience of life when the sole principle for the interpretation of suffering, it remains as much a part of the moral order of the universe as does the regularity of Nature, on its lower level.[7]

What we have labeled retributive suffering, Gordon R. Lewis names "judgmental suffering," as we have already noted above. Lewis defines this type of suffering as the one we bring on ourselves by our failure to live as God has instructed us to live. Many of these shortcomings are listed among the proverbs of Israel. For instance, a stingy person often suffers want (Prov. 11:24), an idle person suffers hunger (Prov. 19:15), and persons who keep the wrong company come to harm (Prov. 13:20). Often, in this type of suffering, the misfortune that awaits the one who is indulgent, or indolent, can be calculated from the very beginning, because his behavior goes against the order that God has established in the universe.

We cannot blame society or our parents for what happens to us in these situations. Scripture is clear that children were not to be put to death for the sins of their fathers, and fathers were not to be put to death for their children (Deut. 24:16). On the other hand, it is when children adopt the sinful ways and habits of their parents that God's judgment comes upon them. Accordingly, the children in the wilderness, who had not sinned as their fathers had, were able to enter the land, but those descendants who acted as faithlessly as their fathers had did not enter the land. Only two men of the former generation entered: Caleb and Joshua. They had a "different spirit" about them and they "followed the LORD wholeheartedly" (Num. 14:24; 32:12).[8]

Repeatedly the Bible makes it clear that "the soul who sins is the one who will die. [Therefore,] the son will not share the guilt of [his] father, mother, nor will [his] father share the guilt of [his] son" (Ezek. 18:20). But when people and nations have sinned against God and their iniquities have

---

7. Robinson, *Suffering: Human and Divine*, 31.
8. Unless otherwise indicated, Scripture quotations in this chapter are taken from *The Holy Bible: New International Version* (NIV).

piled up so that the "cup of iniquity" (e.g., Gen. 15:16) becomes full and runs over, then that nation and those people face judgmental or retributive suffering for their sins.

Thus, while retributive suffering is real, it is a type of suffering that in some ways should have been expected, since it follows an act of rebellion against God and his order. That in part is why the Torah was given, so that the individual could know from the beginning what would happen when God's rules were violated. This suffering comes as God's punishment for our outright flaunting of his instructions to us, to our families, and to our nations; it is our own fault and we often have only ourselves to blame.

Educational or Disciplinary Suffering

Another type of suffering is educational or disciplinary suffering, which does not necessarily come upon us because of our misconduct or rebellion against God and his Word; instead, it is a constructive use of suffering for our growth as believers and for the shaping of our character. It is often called the "chastening" [Hebrew: *musar*] of the Lord (Prov. 3:11). Now this form of suffering will not be received well by those who believe that the good life means the absence of, or freedom from, all pain. The God of the Bible seems to be far less concerned immediately with our comfort than he is with the building of our character.

The speeches of Elihu in the book of Job (32–37) seem to focus on this explanation for suffering. He asks, "Who is a teacher like [God]?" (Job 36:22), for it is God "who teaches more to us than to the beasts of the earth" (Job 35:11; also see Job 33:16, 19; 34:31–32; 35:11; 36:10, 15, 22). This is one way that God opens our ears to his guidance: through suffering his chastening hand.

The word *discipline* is the famous Hebrew word *musar*.[9] For example, in Proverbs 3:11 Solomon urged, "My son, do not despise the LORD's discipline [*musar*] and do not resent his rebuke." Discipline is administered only to one who is dearly loved (Prov. 13:24; 15:5). That is exactly the point that Elihu makes in Job 36:10—"[God] makes them listen to correction" [*musar*] by various means, including adversity (33:16; 36:15). God used suffering as a teaching device by which he could "open Job's ears."

Discipline is not something that is to be passively accepted, but one must also actively discipline oneself just as an athlete would vigorously

---

9. The best study on the Hebrew word *musar* is still that of Jim Alvin Sanders, "Suffering as Divine Discipline in the Old Testament and Post-Biblical Judaism," 1–135. Sanders's study of the Hebrew verb *yasar*, from which the noun *musar* is probably derived, shows that almost one-third of its occurrences (33 out of 92) indicate that God is the one teaching a lesson by means of some kind of hardship given to an individual or a nation.

train. The humble people of the land in the book of Zephaniah were those who "feared" the Lord and who were willing to accept "discipline" [*musar*] from the Lord (Zeph. 3:7).

Educational suffering is referenced in the New Testament, where Hebrews 12:7 teaches that God deals with us as sons and daughters when we are chastened, even though, as the text admits, no one enjoys the lesson while it is being administered. But the lesson does yield great dividends and peace to those who have gone through the experience.

Vicarious Suffering

A third type of suffering is called vicarious suffering. It is the enigma seen at times in the prophets, where in their roles as the messengers of God they experience suffering and abuse from the very people they want to rescue from the coming destruction. The prophet Jeremiah experienced this type of agony:

> Oh, my anguish, my anguish!
>   I writhe in pain.
> Oh, the agony of my heart!
>   My heart pounds within me,
>   I cannot keep silent.
> For I have heard the sound of the trumpet;
>   I have heard the battle cry.
> Disaster follows disaster;
>   the whole land lies in ruins.
> In an instant my tents are destroyed,
>   my shelter in a moment.
> How long must I see the battle standard
>   and hear the sound of the trumpet?
> "My people are fools;
>   they do not know me.
> They are senseless children;
>   they have no understanding.
> They are skilled in doing evil;
>   they know not how to do good." (Jer. 4:19–22; cf. Jer. 8:18–21;
>   15:15).

However, despite the reality of the pain that the prophet bore so that his people could repent and be delivered from the impending disaster, this is not the best example of a truly vicarious type of suffering.

Instead, vicarious suffering is best seen in the substitutionary nature of the roles given to the two goats on the Day of Atonement (*Yom Kippur*) in Leviticus 16. On that day, two goats were selected by lot for one sin offering to God. The High Priest would confess over the head of the first goat all the sin of all Israel (that is, of all those in Israel who truly repented of their sins). Then the goat was slain, its life given up for all in Israel whose sins had in effect brought death upon their lives. The blood of that goat was taken into the Most Holy Place this one time each year and applied to the lid of the ark of atonement, where a state of being "at one" with God could be attained. In this way, the people were depicted as being ransomed or delivered by a substitute on the basis of the declared word of God. Of course, the blood of bulls and goats could not (and did not) atone for anyone's sins, as Hebrews 10:4 affirms, but neither did any Old Testament text say that their blood was effective in doing that. The goat was only a picture of what God was announcing: the sins of the people were declared to be paid in full on the basis of a substitute. This act portrayed a life that needed to be offered up as a ransom, so serious was the weight of sin.

Then the priest confessed over the head of the second goat all the same sins, "transferring" them to the goat. A designated person led the goat away into the wilderness to ensure it got lost and would never return again. This second goat completed the picture of the one sin offering in two parts: sins were *forgiven* on the basis of a substitute and then sins were *forgotten*, never to be remembered against Israel anymore, as far as the east is from the west (Ps. 103:12).

The greatest example of the vicarious or substitutionary aspect of suffering, however, is to be found in the person of the "Servant of the LORD," who suffered on behalf of others. The most passionate description of the Servant's vicarious, expiatory, and atoning function is seen in Isaiah 52:13–53:12:

> Surely he took up our infirmities
>   and carried our sorrows,
> yet we considered him stricken by God,
>   smitten by him, and afflicted.
> But he was pierced for our transgressions,
>   he was crushed for our iniquities;
> the punishment that brought us peace was upon him,
>   and by his wounds we are healed. (Isa. 53:4–5)

The principle here is that our sins have injured and ruptured our relationship with God. So great and serious is the effect of our misconduct that our lives have been put at risk. If there is no expiation or propitiation, we will remain isolated from the God who made us, loves us, and who wishes to restore us back to his favor and presence.

Christ's work on the cross is God's answer to our predicament. It involved Christ's suffering to take the pain we should have endured but were totally unable to due to our own spiritual bankruptcy. Intimations of this great atoning act of God's Son on the cross could be seen already in Genesis 22:12–13 (the offering of Abraham's son Isaac on Mount Moriah) and Exodus 13:13–15 (the redemption of all the firstborn of the land). It could also be seen in Moses' prayer for the people of Israel as he offered to give himself in place of the people who had just sinned so grievously with the golden calf (Exodus 32).

Empathetic Suffering

Often the pain and grief that come from suffering affect not only the sufferer, but also the lives and feelings of those who know, love, and watch the sufferer. Accordingly, empathy produces another form of suffering. This was the case with the prophets who served as God's messengers and addressed audiences who were not receptive to what they had to say.

This type of suffering also affects our Lord, for "in all their distress he too was distressed . . . [yet] in his love and mercy he redeemed them . . . all the days of old" (Isa. 63:9). In Hosea 11:8 God spreads out his hands, much like a distraught parent would, and asks, "How can I give you up, Ephraim? How can I hand you over, Israel? How can I treat you like Admah? How can I make you like Zeboiim? My heart is changed within me; all my compassion is aroused." God takes no pleasure in the death of anyone (Ezek. 18:31–32), so why do we humans continue causing him pain and hurt?

Did not Naomi experience this type of pain and suffering when she considered the situation of her recently widowed daughters-in-law, saying, "It is exceedingly bitter to me for your sake, that the hand of the LORD has gone out against me!" (Ruth 1:13 ESV)? Ruth's and Orpah's pain affected Naomi as well. This is the same teaching found in the New Testament, to "mourn with those who mourn" (Rom. 12:15) and to share in the afflictions, suffering, and anguish of others, as did the apostle Paul in 2 Corinthians 2:4.

Evidential or Testimonial Suffering

The first two chapters of Job are classic examples of evidential or testimonial suffering. Despite his intense suffering, Job refused to give up the integrity of his trust in God. Job would have loved to know what had been going on behind the scenes in the conversations between God and Satan, which we readers are informed about from the start, but even without this knowledge, he still retained his faith. God had allowed Satan to test Job's loyalty by divesting him of all that he owned (Job 1:9–12), even his health (Job 2:4–6). But Job resolutely refused to cave in to bitterness or to his wife's advice to curse God and die.

Rather than viewing the situation as one in which Job was on trial, the text of Job 1–2 lets us know that it was God who was on trial. Satan had accused God of blessing Job to the point where Job could do nothing other than praise him and serve him, but Satan's wager was that if all these blessings were removed from Job, then the praise, worship, and service would disappear. Satan turned out to be wrong. Job did not crack.

Hebrews 11 is famous for its extensive list of Old Testament saints who suffered for their testimony of faith and trust in God. They were "tortured . . . faced jeers and flogging, while still others were chained and put in prison. They were stoned; they were sawed in two; they were put to death by the sword. They went about in sheepskins and goatskins, destitute, persecuted and mistreated" (Heb. 11:35–37). But they still trusted God and had faith in him. In the same way, Moses "chose to be mistreated along with the people of God [Israel] rather than to enjoy the pleasures of sin for a short time. He regarded disgrace for the sake of Christ as of greater value than the treasures of Egypt, because he was looking ahead to his reward" (Heb. 11:25–26). The text astounds us by saying that in the days of Moses he knew about the name and cause of Jesus Christ.

For contemporary Christians the message is the same: in comparison to the eternal glory of God, what are the short-lived instances of suffering we face in this life (Rom. 8:18; 2 Cor. 4:17)? We merely fill up whatever sufferings are still necessary for building up the church (Col. 1:24).

The prophet Habakkuk exhibits this same testimonial or evidential suffering. Viewing the alarming rate of the increase of evil in Judah with no evidence of God's intervening hand of judgment, he asked God to deal with this problem, for it was God himself who had made Habakkuk so sensitive to the problem in the first place. God's answer was that he would deal with Judah's sins; he would bring the Babylonians in to conquer Judah. This terrified Habakkuk all the more, for surely God knew that the Babylonians were not only brutal but were godless as well. Why would God use a more godless people to punish a relatively godlier people? To this complaint there was no immediate answer. Instead, Habakkuk would wait to see what God would do, for "the righteous shall live by his faith" (Hab. 2:4). From a human standpoint, the prospect of a Babylonian invasion tore Habakkuk apart; however, inwardly he was just as resolute: "Yet [or, Nevertheless] I will rejoice in the LORD, I will be joyful in God my Savior" (Hab. 3:18).

This "yet/nevertheless" reminds us of another "nevertheless" in Psalm 73:23–24. As the psalmist Asaph watched the wicked prosper and the arrogant grow so great, he was tempted to say, "Surely in vain have I kept my heart pure; in vain have I washed my hands in innocence" (v. 13). It was not until he "entered the sanctuary of God [that he] understood their final destiny" (v. 17). Yes, there were times when his "heart was grieved," and his "spirit embittered" (v. 21), "Yet," he declared, "I am always with you; you hold me by my right hand. You guide me with your counsel, and afterward you will take me into glory" (vv. 23–24).

In all these cases, suffering produced a strong testimony or evidence of God's faithfulness. Suffering was the means God used to point men and women to himself in a way that was so distinct that few other kinds of evidence could match.

Revelational Suffering

Often our Lord uses suffering to bring us into a deeper knowledge of himself. The best example of this type of suffering is the prophet Hosea. What he faced in his life revealed to the people of his day (and to us) the kind of God he served, just as much as his words did.

Hosea's family life was marked by the most severe test a married person could endure. The tranquility of his marriage was upset after the birth of his three children, when his wife, Gomer, suddenly decided that she wanted to experience something more. She left the prophet and their three children to earn her living by prostitution at the local cult of Baal.[10] One can only guess what an embarrassment this was for the prophet and imagine the catcalls, insinuations, and slurs made in public as he attempted to minister in the very locale where his wife was now serving everything that he stood against.

Nevertheless, Hosea affirmed that he still loved his wife, even though she had abandoned her covenant of marriage and her love for him and her children. But as he declared his love for his wife, he found a ready-made illustration of the message of God's love and the persistence of his faithfulness toward Israel. For Israel had just as audaciously abandoned her love for God, her husband, and had gone after other gods to serve them instead. Amazingly, God declared he still loved his wayward "bride" and wanted her back just as Hosea was proclaiming. It is for this reason that the book of Hosea is known as the book of the "heart and holiness of God." Here,

---

10. Some incorrectly believe that a holy God ordered Hosea to marry Gomer, who already was a practicing prostitute, but for a brief refutation of that idea, see Walter C. Kaiser Jr., et al., *Hard Sayings of the Bible* (Downers Grove, IL: InterVarsity, 1996), 322–24.

then, was a suffering that truly revealed the love and patience of a waiting God for a wayward people, both in that day and this day as well.

Doxological Suffering

Sometimes our Lord calls us to go through suffering not as a result of our own sins or to teach us some needed lesson but in order to show his own purpose and glory.

Joseph's thirteen-year separation from his family at the hands of his heartless brothers is a prime example of this type of suffering. Jealousy so consumed the brothers that their only thought was to get rid of him physically. When the prospect of selling him to some Midianite/Ishmaelite merchants suddenly presented itself, they quickly seized it, and Joseph, along with the pesky dreams that so galled his brothers, was gone—or so they thought.

Amazingly, Joseph never complained or showed the slightest bit of anger for what had so unfairly happened to him during all those years. Did the meaning of the dreams give him the stability he needed for those trials through all the years of his loneliness? In two descriptions of the whole affair, he declared that whereas the brothers had indeed meant it for evil against him (how else could it have been viewed?), it was God who had meant it for good all along (Gen. 45:4–5, 7; 50:20). It was for the glory of God. God had taken the evil purposes and methods of his brothers and had worked his eternal purpose and glory out of the whole mess. Nothing Joseph had done was the reason for his imprisonment; it had been allowed specially that the glory of God might be worked out.

A similar situation appears in the New Testament. When Jesus was asked by his disciples why the man in John 9 had been born blind, Jesus clearly indicated that it was not a result of the parents' sin or the man's own sin; rather, it happened so the glory of God might be seen in his life (John 9:3). Thus, some suffering has a special divine purpose of lifting up and magnifying the power, presence, and glory of God.

Eschatological or Apocalyptic Suffering

The historical period of this present world age ends, according to the plan of Scripture, with a period of intense suffering. The depth of the darkness and the intensity of suffering during those days will assuredly end with the triumphant appearance of the kingdom of God. Major portions of the prophets' messages are dedicated to describing the events that lead up to this glorious moment. Key texts are the "Little Apocalypse" of Isaiah 24–27, the "Book of Consolation" section of Jeremiah 30–33, the future hope of Ezekiel 33–48, Daniel's prophecies of Daniel 2–12, and Zechariah 12–14.

Israel will suffer enormously just prior to the second advent of our Lord; however, the protector of Israel will descend on the scene with unprecedented relief and victory, putting an end to all the shame, suffering, misery, and disgrace the nation has suffered for her own sin (Jer. 31:16; Ezek. 36:3, 6, 22–23). Out of this furnace of affliction will emerge a purified people ready to face a whole new day in God's eschaton (Zech. 13:9; Mal. 3:3).

How Workable Are the Old Testament's Answers to Suffering?

We have seen a multiplicity of types, experiences, and causes of suffering in the Old Testament. What we have not seen is any attempt to systematize or find a unitary explanation for all misery, suffering, or anguish in life. Every type examined takes each calamity by itself and reacts to it as it was deemed appropriate in the revelation of God.

The Old Testament is not interested, as a whole or in its parts, in a theory or a set structure that explains all of life's experiences of suffering. Thus, the question, "How could a good and powerful God allow suffering?" is answered in specific instances in each of its appearances, but no overarching theory, other than the fall of humanity in Genesis 3, is supplied as a root cause and final explanation. Of course, we must distinguish between calamity that is self-induced or caused accidentally by society or other external forces. But just as in the case of Job, these must also be permitted by God even though he is not the sponsor or source of the calamity itself.

It is a special point of note that the Old Testament surprisingly allows calamity and suffering to be brought out into the open rather than suppressing them. The Old Testament does not depict its characters as holy, faultless icons; instead it paints them in all their graphic sinfulness, warts and all. In our technological society, by way of contrast, "blame" for individuals is almost nonexistent. Instead, there are processes, agents, forces, and external drives. "Sin" is given a mechanistic interpretation so that blame is steered away from the individual. In this environment, it is no wonder that even the idea of a personal God to whom we must answer tends to get lost.

Ours is hardly the most just of all possible worlds, at least not in its present manifestation, but the hope of the world is found in the God who cares and knows about our suffering, hurts, and disgrace. Even if it has not been necessary for him to give any kind of definitive explanation as to why he ever allowed evil in this world in the first place, he has assured us that all of the misery, suffering, hurt, and pain do fit together in a plan that he is working to the honor and glory of his own name.

This plan is seen even more clearly in the New Testament, especially in the Son of God's incarnation, life, death, resurrection, and second coming. It is to the New Testament and its fuller revelation that we next turn.

4

SUFFERING AND THE GOODNESS OF GOD IN THE GOSPELS

DAN G. MCCARTNEY

The problem of the suffering of God's people is to some degree the backdrop of the entire New Testament. A thesis of the New Testament, perhaps *the* thesis, is that the answer to the problem of suffering and death lies in the suffering and death of Jesus Christ. His suffering and death is the necessary pathway to the resurrection and redemption of his people. Resurrection is the climactic conclusion of God's restoration of his people, restoring them to *shalom*, or wholeness, to the full image of God and to freedom from evil both within and without.

Jesus' announcement of the coming of God's kingdom, his "setting things to right" as promised in the Old Testament, is the opening development in God's answer to suffering. Jesus' message presupposes a situation of oppression and suffering to which the kingdom, or the hoped-for reign of God, is the answer. When the apostles proclaim the gospel after Jesus' death and resurrection, a key question is, why did God's chosen Messiah suffer and die? And the people of God are still asking a related question: why are we called to suffer? The New Testament addresses both questions by linking the suffering and restoration of believers in various ways to the suffering and resurrection of Christ. Thus suffering, far from undermining the goodness of God, is actually seen to be its most pointed and poignant expression.

In this chapter we will focus on what Jesus taught, both about his own suffering and the suffering his disciples would undergo. We will see how suffering in both cases is an expression not of the arbitrariness of suffering but of the goodness of God in redeeming his people and disciplining them. The following chapter will survey how both of these themes are further developed in Acts, the letters of Paul and certain other New Testament writers, as well as in the book of Revelation.

The Suffering of the Messiah

Jesus transformed the way people thought about suffering. While the Old Testament hinted at the notion of redemptive suffering (Isaiah 53), and spoke of a redeemer in various contexts, most Jewish thinking about suffering focused on why the people of Israel had to suffer, and what its purpose might be, or on how one should trust God in the midst of suffering. Jesus refocused the whole notion of suffering in terms of the suffering of the Christ, regarding it as a central theme of Old Testament revelation (Mark 9:12; Luke 17:25; 24:26). Christ's new christocentric way of thinking about suffering permeates the rest of the New Testament. The result is that the meaning of Israel's (or the church's) suffering, and the suffering of individual believers, is found in the suffering of the Christ.

Jewish thinking during the period of the Second Temple accepted the Old Testament teaching that suffering was often the consequence of sin. The problem of why the innocent suffered was also of intense interest, and thus a theology arose of a vicarious suffering of the righteous remnant on behalf of Israel as a whole. This is one of the most remarkable developments in Judaism, presumably stemming from Isaiah 53, and the expectation that the "righteous remnant" spoken of in Isaiah (Isa. 10:19ff., etc.) and Jeremiah (Jer. 6:9 and throughout the rest of the book) would, by enduring suffering even though they were righteous, vicariously atone for the sins of Israel. This representative suffering would then qualify Israel as a whole for redemption.

Isaiah describes the sufferings of Israel as birth pangs, through which, though at first seemingly without effect, God brings resurrection from the dead:

Like a pregnant woman who writhes and cries out in her pangs when she is near to giving birth, so were we because of you, O LORD; we were pregnant, we writhed, but we have given birth to wind. We have accomplished no deliverance in the earth, and the inhabitants of the world have not fallen. Your dead shall live; their bodies shall rise. You who dwell in the dust, awake and sing for joy! For your dew is a dew of light, and the earth will give birth to the dead. (Isa. 26:17–19)

Jewish messianic expectation therefore included a tribulation that would intensify immediately before the coming of Messiah. Hence the pre-messianic sufferings are "birth pangs of the Messiah." We also see this imagery in the New Testament, particularly in Revelation 12:1–6. But Jews regarded these messianic pangs not as suffering which the Messiah himself would undergo, but as sufferings that Israel itself would undergo in preparation for the coming of Messiah. Indeed, Israel's atonement for its sins is what would clear the way for God's blessing by sending the deliverer.

This tendency to see the suffering of the righteous as a substitute for Israel appears most clearly in 4 Maccabees. After describing in rather gruesome detail the suffering of the priestly family of Eleazar that refuses to yield to Antiochus's attempts to get them to eat pork, the author concludes:

The tyrant was punished, and the homeland purified—they having become, as it were, a ransom for the sin of our nation. And through the blood of those devout ones and their death as an expiation, divine Providence preserved Israel that previously had been afflicted. (4 Macc. 17:21–22 RSV)

Messianic "birth pangs," the suffering that the remnant of Israel would undergo in preparation for the coming of Messiah, were thus understood to be the redemptive price—the ransom—that Israel's righteous remnant would pay on behalf of the nation. Like the "great tribulation" in the Olivet Discourse that anticipates the final revelation of God's judgment in the coming of the Son of Man, Jews expected an especially intense suffering as the prelude to God's kingdom (including his sending of the Messiah). But note that in Jewish expectation, the "messianic birth pangs" were not the sufferings of *the Messiah*, but the sufferings of faithful Israelites, like Eleazar and his children in 4 Maccabees, that would usher in Messiah. The notion that the Messiah himself would suffer does not seem to have been a part of Jewish expectation, and indeed quite the opposite. So much was this the case that Isaiah 53 was either modified (as occurred in the Targum of Isaiah, an interpretive Aramaic translation) or else understood as not referring to Messiah. It was offensive to suppose that the Christ himself would suffer, for that would be to make a mockery of the messianic hope as they understood it.[1]

Jesus, however, does not directly speak of the suffering Messiah at the beginning of his ministry. It is only after Peter's confession in Matthew 16 (Mark 8 and Luke 9 parallels) that he begins to teach his disciples about his suffering. But Jesus does speak of suffering in other ways prior to this occasion.

Suffering and the Kingdom of God

The suffering of God's people is seen as the manifestation of Satan's power. Judaism in the first century viewed the oppression of Israel as in some ways the work of evil angels. Hints of this appear in Daniel 10:20–21, which speaks of the "one like a man" sent to Daniel as contending, alongside "Michael," with the "principalities" of Greece and Persia.

But Jesus sees this satanic origin of suffering as having a personal dimension, not just a national one. He identifies the suffering of the woman with an infirmity for eighteen years as oppression by Satan (Luke 13:16). And certainly the possession of human beings by evil spirits is said to be ultimately the work of Satan (Matt. 12:24–26). Thus Jesus' casting out of Satan by healing and exorcism is regarded as one of the primary indications that the promised rule of God is coming (12:28)—a coming that signifies the defeat of Satan and the end of his oppression.

In the meantime, Jesus recognizes that suffering is a universal reality, regardless of one's spiritual state. In Luke 13:2 he points out that the victims of a catastrophe are not more wicked than others, but that such incidents ought to remind everyone that life is tenuous and the need for repentance is urgent.

Jesus also indicates early in his ministry that suffering will be a mark of discipleship. In the beginning of the Sermon on the Mount, the so-called "beatitudes" end with "blessed are you when others revile you and utter all kinds of evil against you falsely on my account" (Matt. 5:11). That suffering is a characteristic feature of being a follower of Jesus Christ permeates the New Testament.

The Kingdom of God Is a Reversal

The problem of evil and the problem of suffering are tied together. If God is good, then why does he allow evil? If God is good, why do the righ-

1. Oscar Cullmann, *Christology of the New Testament*, trans. S. Guthrie (Philadelphia: Westminster, 1959), 63.

teous suffer, and not the wicked? The Old Testament writers answered this question in eschatological terms: God's judgment was coming, and when it arrived, the wicked in their ease would suffer the consequences of their sin, while the oppressed righteous would be lifted up and given relief from their suffering. Because this involves a reversal of fortunes for the wicked and righteous, the expectation is sometimes called the hope of "eschatological reversal."

Jesus also expected this eschatological reversal, and it is a hallmark of his preaching. It can clearly be seen in such parables as the rich man and Lazarus (Luke 16:19–31), in the beatitudes of Matthew 5, and even more in the blessings and woes of Luke 6:20–26. So, when John the Baptist by way of his disciples asks Jesus whether he is the expected one (Matt. 11:3), John is in effect asking, "So where is the reversal?" Jesus answers the question in verse 5: The deaf hear, the blind see, the dead are brought back to life, and the poor receive good news. A counterpart to this is that those who hear do not hear, those who see do not see (13:13), and the rich receive bad news (Luke 6:24). In other words, the reversal is happening.

Indeed eschatological reversal lies at the heart of the notion of the kingdom of God.[2] The phrase "kingdom of God" does not mean a geographic territory, nor does it mean "heaven" as it is usually understood; it means the actuated reign of God, the time when God will set things to right. So, when Jesus declared that the kingdom of God is near, he was in effect saying that the expected time of eschatological reversal is at hand. However, the way he sees this reversal being initiated is something of a surprise.

Transforming Expectations of Eschatological Reversal

After Peter's confession that Jesus is the Christ (Mark 8:29–30 and parallels), Jesus begins to explain how he will usher in the eschatological reversal. He will first do so through encompassing suffering and glory, the humiliation and the exaltation, *in himself;* then by his disciples undergoing the same pattern; then finally in judgment when the Son of Man applies the reversal to the whole world. But the first stage is that Jesus, the Messiah, the Son of Man whom Jews regarded as a figure of glory,[3] must undergo humiliation and suffering. Jesus thus stands in the place of his people by undergoing

---

2. "Kingdom of heaven" is Matthew's preferred phrase for what Mark and Luke call "kingdom of God." Compare Matt. 4:17 with Mark 1:15; Matt. 13:11 with Mark 4:11 and Luke 8:10; and Matt. 13:31 with Mark 4:30 and Luke 13:18. Also see Herman Ridderbos, *The Coming of the Kingdom* (Philadelphia: Presbyterian and Reformed, 1962), 18–19.

3. The one "like a Son of Man" in Daniel is the one who comes on the clouds and receives dominion from the Ancient of Days (Dan. 7:13–14). The phrase "Son of Man" was taken up in *1 Enoch* to refer to the glorious heavenly redeemer figure (e.g., *1 En.* 46:1–3; 48:2–7).

the suffering they as sinners deserve, and then manifesting the vindication and exaltation that he as the righteous sufferer deserves.

In the Gospel of Mark, Jesus announces the necessity of his suffering to his disciples four times: 8:31; 9:12; 9:31; and 10:33–34.[4] Note that Jesus' intention is specifically *suffering* many things, as well as dying and rising. The way God's anointed king, the Christ, brings the kingdom is not, as so many Jews thought, by driving out the Romans or overthrowing the Herodian dynasty, but through achieving the eschatological reversal in his own person—first by undergoing humiliation, rejection, and death, followed by resurrection, ascension, and enthronement.

Mark 8:31 marks a turning point in Jesus' ministry, because it is at this point that he begins to tell his disciples of the necessity of his suffering, rejection, death, and resurrection. The great theme of eschatological reversal, whereby God turns the world upside down by exalting the lowly and humbling the proud, has its focal point in that quintessential reversal brought about by the glorious Son of Man being humiliated, rejected and killed, and then raised from the dead. It is interesting that Peter, like those around him, could not conceive of a suffering Messiah and tried to rebuke the man he had just declared to be the Christ. The irony is huge. Peter apparently could not even hear the "resurrection" part—the humiliation of the Christ was just too intolerable a thought. But the path to exaltation is a path first of suffering and death. Peter's inability to cope with that notion is met with Jesus' stern rebuke: "Get behind me, Satan! For you are not setting your mind on the things of God, but on the things of man" (8:33).

Jesus then goes on to apply that same path, the path of humiliation and service, to his disciples. Here too he introduces the notion of the cross, though not at this point saying that his own death would be by crucifixion. Instead, he mentions the cross as that which the disciples must embrace in order to follow him, which is a stark indication of the extreme self-sacrifice and abnegation that he would require. His disciples know that crucifixion is the most extreme humiliation and the harshest execution of the Roman judicial system. Yet it is this suffering that the Christ and those who follow him must take up on the way to resurrection.

4. In addition, some of Jesus' parables also suggest this expectation of suffering, e.g., Mark 12:1–12. Note how in this parable (v. 10) Jesus connects the killing of the vineyard owner's son with the "stone that the builders rejected" of Ps. 118:22. Psalm 118 is traditionally understood to have been about how David was rejected by the leaders but chosen by God. Jesus is thus equating the rejected "son" of the parable with the rejection of David when he was anointed but still suffering in the wilderness.

Jesus' prediction of his suffering, death, and resurrection, is repeated three more times in Mark. Each of these follows a moment when the disciples have their minds on glory: right after the transfiguration (Mark 9:12), immediately after the healing of the demoniac boy who could not be healed by the disciples (9:31), and as they were coming near Jerusalem (10:33–34). That the disciples were having trouble hearing the message about suffering is evident from the surrounding text. In Mark 9:11 the disciples ask about the Jewish expectation of a coming of Elijah before the Christ, possibly because they had just seen him on the Mount of Transfiguration. The disciples want some judgment action, and Elijah of course is best known for manifesting the power of God in the fire on Mount Carmel. The incident with the demoniac boy suggests that the disciples who were not at the transfiguration also want to see some power plays. But Jesus responds again by pointing to the way of suffering, humiliation, and lowly servanthood, not lordly power (9:33–37; 10:31–45). In these reiterations he also says, "The last shall be first, and the first last," a summary proverb that encapsulates the notion of eschatological reversal.

The point of all this is that suffering and death is *necessary* (Gk. *dei*) in order to win through to resurrection life, both on the part of Jesus the Christ and on the part of his disciples. As we will see in the book of Acts, this is why the disciples declare it is *necessary* for anyone entering the kingdom of God to take the path of suffering (Acts 14:22). The reality of the kingdom—the application of its eschatological reversal—*had* to begin with Christ's suffering, and now *must* continue in the suffering of his disciples.

So then, if suffering truly is necessary, it is not arbitrary or haphazard but purposeful. Therefore, while the proximate cause of suffering may be evil, its presence in the overall scheme of things is for biblical writers not something that calls God's goodness into question; rather, it is the means by which God's goodness is expressed. All true redemption is via suffering—first the suffering of God's own Son, and then by application the suffering of the disciples as they are linked to the Son.

Luke 9:22; 17:25; and Mark 8:31 also link the suffering of Christ to *rejection* by leaders as well as to death. Luke 17:25 in particular speaks of rejection by "this generation" before the Son of Man comes in power. Again, it appears that this is a purposeful path. The eschatological reversal requires the Son to plummet to the most extreme depths of humiliation, suffering, and death in order to destroy their power.

Again, this path of suffering servanthood as the way to resurrection is not without precedent. We saw already how Isaiah 53 undergirds Jesus' understanding of his ministry, and Mark 10:34 further makes this connection in that it specifically mentions mocking, spitting, and scourging (cf. Isa. 53:3–5).

Ransomed Life

Amazingly, right after Jesus' clear announcement that he came to give his life as a ransom, the disciples again begin to jostle for position. In Mark 10:43–45, which is the climax of Jesus' rebuke of his disciples, he teaches that service, not power, is what makes one great in the kingdom. Thus, he, their teacher, the Son of Man, "came not to be served but to serve, and to give his life as a ransom for many." The ultimate purpose of Jesus' suffering, then, is not only to function as an example of humiliation and service; it is the climactic moment of God's redemption, the means by which he would save his people.

The term *ransom* or *redemption* can refer to a "buy-back" price for redeeming land or an item that had been pawned (Lev. 25:29), to liability coverage in an accidental injury or death (Ex. 21:30), or to the price of buying someone out of slavery (Lev. 25:48). Someone who had "pawned himself" to pay off debt in the Old Testament was effectively a slave, and to be "ransomed" he had to pay off his purchase price or else wait for the sabbatical year. Since sin incurred a liability to death, the term was also used to refer to the atonement offerings that Israelites brought to the Lord as a symbolic "ransom" for their sins (Ex. 30:12).[5] (In the Mediterranean world, of course, many slaves simply had the misfortune to have been on the wrong side of a conflict with Rome.) Moreover, Israel as a nation had been successively conquered by Babylonians, Persians, Greeks, and Romans, largely as a result of its past disobedience, and so thought of itself as in a kind of slavery, in need of "ransoming," not just to be free to return to the land (e.g., Ex. 6:6; Mic. 4:10) but to be free of pagan domination within it.

Thus when Jesus declares himself to be giving his life as a ransom, he indicates that his life is the "buy-back" price that covers on behalf of many their liability for sins. As R. T. France has definitively shown,[6] the roots of this notion lie in Isaiah 53, which speaks extensively of the substitutionary suffering of the Servant of the Lord, and declares it to be a guilt offering (v. 10).

---

5. The recognition that the ransom offering was only symbolic and not an actual redemption for sin is evident in Ps. 49:7–8. The psalmist recognizes that it is only God who can ransom one's soul from the power of the grave (Ps. 49:15).

6. R. T. France, "The Servant of the Lord in the Teaching of Jesus," *Tyndale Bulletin* 19 (1968): 32–37.

France elsewhere points out that the context of Mark is that of reminding the disciples that they are not called to lord their authority over the church but to serve the church, as Jesus did.[7] And as Jesus' service culminates in suffering *for* his people, the foundation is laid for the application by other New Testament writers of the principle to believers suffering *for* each other. Again we see the principle of eschatological reversal—Christ expresses his rule not by dominating but by serving, and that is also how the disciples will "rule" the church.

Suffering Is the Prelude to the Coming of the Son of Man

Jewish expectation did not anticipate the suffering of the Christ, but it did see a time of increased suffering prior to the hoped-for climactic intervention by God. This expectation may be reflected in Jesus' comments on the "great tribulation" recorded in Mark 13 and Matthew 24, known as the Olivet Discourse.[8] While the interpretation of the Olivet Discourse is complex, there is little doubt that at least part of it on some level is predicting the events of the Jewish War in A.D. 66–70, which climaxed in the siege of Jerusalem and the destruction of the temple. Although the Christians of Jerusalem, who had fled to Pella,[9] did not directly experience the final climactic horror, they did suffer in the times leading up to that event, as seen in the book of Acts. And the suffering of the Jews remaining in Jerusalem during the siege was horrific, according to Josephus,[10] and could be well described as a "great tribulation."

But the discourse also has elements in it that seem to point beyond the events of A.D. 70.[11] If it be understood as on some level descriptive of the final *parousia* (what we, following Heb. 9:28, usually call the "second coming"), then the text refers as well to the final great suffering of the people of God, which culminates in deliverance through the Lord's appearing. Whatever interpretation of the discourse is correct, it does appear that Jesus was warning his disciples that they would face severe trials as an

7. R. T. France, *Gospel of Mark* (NIGTC; Grand Rapids, MI: Eerdmans, 2002), 421.
8. The parallel passage in Luke 21 does not mention a great tribulation, but there Jesus also warns the disciples of much suffering to come.
9. Eusebius, *Church History* III.5. A few scholars have questioned the reliability of this tradition, e.g., S. G. F. Brandon, *The Fall of Jerusalem and the Christian Church*, 2nd ed. (London: SPCK, 1957), but there is little reason to doubt it. See the critical review of Brandon's book by F. F. Bruce in *Evangelical Quarterly* 24 (1952): 115–16.
10. Josephus, *Jewish War*, Books V and VI.1–8, describes the misery in some detail.
11. For example, the warnings against anything that is not an unambiguous *parousia* in Matt. 24:23–27 and the expectation that the gospel would first be preached to all the nations (Matt. 24:14; Mark 13:10), suggest to many interpreters that the Olivet Discourse looks to something beyond A.D. 70.

aspect of their calling to bear testimony to the gospel (Mark 13:9–13). Just as the vocation of Jesus was to suffer, it is the vocation of those who follow him to suffer as well. And just as Jesus' own sufferings were a fulfillment of the messianic birth pangs, so the suffering of the disciples functions in that way as well.

Jesus' frequent references to the Son of Man as the one who will suffer is also indicative of what is to come. As Jesus himself eventually makes clear (Mark 13:26; 14:62 and parallels), the roots of the self-referential title "Son of Man" lie in Daniel, in particular Daniel 7, where "one like the son of man" comes before the Ancient of Days to receive dominion. Given this exalted description in Daniel, it seems strange that Jesus would speak so consistently of the Son of Man as *suffering*. Yet several of Jesus' comments, which we will look at shortly, speak of the Son of Man having to suffer many things.

In the first century AD Daniel was a highly regarded figure, and the book of Daniel appears to have been a favorite of groups with high eschatological expectation such as the Qumran covenanters.[12] Interestingly, the figure known as the Righteous Teacher (or Teacher of Righteousness) in the Dead Sea Scrolls is described both in terms of the quintessential wise man, Daniel, and as the one who suffers unjustly (1QpHab. 11:4–8). Did the Qumran community make the connection between the Danielic "Son of Man" and the "Suffering Servant" of Isaiah 53? Whether or not they did, it appears Jesus did, and thus again drew attention to the fact that his lordship and dominion were accomplished by way of vicarious suffering on behalf of his people.

The Lord's Supper as an Appropriation of Christ's Suffering

We noted earlier that in Mark 10:45 (Matt. 20:28 parallel) Jesus declared that his mission is "to give his life as a ransom for many." Later, when he celebrates his last Passover meal with his disciples, he tells them: "This is my blood of the covenant, which is poured out for many" (Mark 14:24). The blood is the physical representation of the life (Gen. 9:4; Lev. 17:11–14; Deut. 12:23) and thus the pouring out of blood is the giving of life. The Lord's Supper, then, is for the disciples the symbolic appropriation of the ransoming act of Jesus.

According to Matthew 26:28, Jesus also understood his suffering, and the supper that represented it, as being "for the forgiveness of sins." The

---

12. At least eight copies of the book of Daniel, from three different caves, have been identified among the Dead Sea Scrolls (1Q71–2, 4Q112–16, and 6Q7pap). In addition there are several similarities and allusions that may be due to Danielic influence.

Lord's Supper was, of course, the celebration by Jesus and his disciples of the Jewish feast of Passover (Luke 22:15). The Passover was a reenactment of God's deliverance of Israel in Egypt from the plague that fell on the firstborn. The blood of the lamb was plastered on the lintels and doorposts so that the angel of death would pass over that house. Later Jewish interpreters rightly understood this to be a special sacrifice, where the death of the lamb was substituted for the death of the firstborn, and since human life generally was forfeit because of sin, the Passover lamb also came to represent God's judgment passing over those who were "under the blood." When Jesus identified his own shed blood with the Passover wine, he was in effect identifying himself as the Passover lamb who would suffer in place of those people who were covered by it.

But the participation in the Lord's Supper by his disciples calls for more than just their willingness to be covered by the ransoming sacrifice of Jesus. It also hints that they would *share* in Christ's sufferings in their own experience. Right before Jesus' declaration regarding his giving his life as a ransom in Mark 10, Jesus tells the disciples, "The cup that I drink you will drink, and with the baptism with which I am baptized, you will be baptized," indicating that they will indeed suffer for the kingdom (10:39). To be sure, Jesus' suffering remains unique—he is the only true "righteous remnant" that suffers on behalf of the whole people.[13] Yet as people are connected with Jesus they also participate in his suffering, and not just symbolically.

There may also be a hint in the Synoptic Gospels of the suffering that believers would undergo for each other. The most direct reference Jesus makes to giving his life as a ransom (Mark 10:45) is in the context of instructing the disciples that following him means following the path of serving, not ruling. The Son of Man's death is the primary instance of Jesus' serving. It could be, then, that here in Mark 10:42–45 Jesus is guiding the disciples toward an awareness that they will need to suffer for each other.

Finally we should note that when Jesus explains his teaching and sums it up for his disciples after his resurrection, he again describes his suffering as a *necessary* part of the plan of redemption that God promised in the Old Testament Scriptures. To the disciples on the road to Emmaus he says: "O foolish ones, and slow of heart to believe all that the prophets have spoken! Was it not necessary that the Christ should suffer these things and

---

13. This uniqueness of Jesus' own suffering may be reflected in the fact that in the Gospels Jesus uses the word *suffer* (Gk. *pascho*) or its noun form (*pathema*) only ever with reference to his own sufferings. The sufferings of his disciples, like those of the prophets in the Old Testament, are called persecution, beatings, or tribulation but never "suffering." Other books of the New Testament, however, do refer to the "suffering" of believers.

enter into his glory?" (Luke 24:25–26). A little later to the Twelve (minus one) he says, "Thus it is written, that the Christ should suffer and on the third day rise from the dead" (24:46). Thus Jesus indicates once again that the suffering of the Christ was no unfortunate accident; it was no unanticipated setback that God had to overcome. It was God's purpose from the beginning, because it *had* to be that way, and was a central message of the Old Testament.

Suffering in the Gospel of John

In John, Jesus' predictions of his suffering are expressed in the ironic language of the "lifting up" (exaltation) of the Son of Man. "Lifting up" has a double reference: first, the lifting up on a cross, which is the ultimate humiliation, and second, the resurrection and exaltation that eventuated from the cross. By the cross God glorified and exalted Jesus, thereby drawing all people to himself (John 12:32). Thus Jesus' "lifting up," both in suffering and death *and* in resurrection and ascension, becomes the nexus of God's relation to mankind. It is therefore not surprising that, just as Jesus expresses his suffering as a *necessity* in the Synoptics, here in John as well, "the Son of Man *must* be lifted up" (3:14, 12:34). It is an indispensable and inevitable event in God's plan for redeeming his people.

Using a different metaphor, Jesus in John 10:11, 15 says, "I lay down my life for the sheep." A shepherd is the "ruler" of his sheep, but he exercises his rule by serving them, and even laying down his life for them. Again it is by going down that Jesus is able to rise up and take the humble up with him (cf. John 3:13–14). God turns humiliation into exaltation, and death into life, thus accomplishing the "eschatological reversal." This is especially observable in John 12:23–24: "And Jesus answered them, 'The hour has come for the Son of Man to be glorified. Truly, truly, I say to you, unless a grain of wheat falls into the earth and dies, it remains alone; but if it dies, it bears much fruit." Jesus then goes on to apply this to people generally, saying, "Whoever loves his life loses it, and whoever hates his life in this world will keep it for eternal life" (12:25). These words come shortly after the raising of Lazarus, which Jesus also connects to his own death and resurrection. Just as Jesus serves and suffers for his people, so also must his disciples.

Likewise the representative unity of Jesus with his people is explicit in John. Jesus repeatedly speaks of his own unity with the Father (e.g., John 10:30), as well as his unity with his people (17:21). His suffering is echoed in their suffering (17:14), but commensurately his glory becomes their glory (17:22).

The suffering of Jesus again becomes the suffering of the disciples in John 16:21, and once more sorrow is reversed to joy at the end of the day:

> "Truly, truly, I say to you, you will weep and lament, but the world will rejoice. You will be sorrowful, but your sorrow will turn into joy. When a woman is giving birth, she has sorrow because her hour has come, but when she has delivered the baby, she no longer remembers the anguish, for joy that a human being has been born into the world. So also you have sorrow now, but I will see you again, and your hearts will rejoice, and no one will take your joy from you." (John 16:20–22)

Even after the resurrection of Jesus, the disciples must now undergo tribulation in the world:

> "Behold, the hour is coming, indeed it has come, when you will be scattered, each to his own home, and will leave me alone. Yet I am not alone, for the Father is with me. I have said these things to you, that in me you may have peace. In the world you will have tribulation. But take heart; I have overcome the world." When Jesus had spoken these words, he lifted up his eyes to heaven, and said, "Father, the hour has come; glorify your Son that the Son may glorify you." (John 16:32–17:1)

Thus in John, as in the Synoptics, Jesus has transformed the Jewish notion of vicarious suffering of the righteous remnant by giving it a specifically Christological focus. It is as the Christ suffers and dies that he brings relief and life to his people, even eternal life. In this life (this *aiōn*, this age or this world) his disciples still have sorrow, because this world hates them.

There is yet another way we discussed earlier in which the suffering of Jesus is applied to believers—through his symbolic reminder of his giving his body and blood. In the Synoptics we noted that this is explicitly presented in the Passover meal Jesus ate with his disciples just prior to his death. In John, however, instead of describing the Passover meal itself, he expounds upon the meaning of this symbolic act through an extended application; the demonstration of mutual humble service (foot washing) and the communion of the disciples with Jesus and with each other through the Holy Spirit (John 14–17).

Using two metaphors, John symbolically calls attention to the effectiveness of the Supper in uniting the believer with Christ's suffering. The first is the "bread from heaven" discourse that follows shortly after the miracle of feeding the five thousand (John 6). Not all exegetes accept this connection, but John specifically connects the feeding of the five thousand to the time of Passover (6:4; this detail is not mentioned in the other Gospels). Moreover, the highly metaphorical character of much material in John's Gospel (especially "eating my flesh" and "drinking my blood" in 6:53) gives credibility to the notion that here John is making a connection between the sacrificial giving of Jesus' body and the provision of eschatological bounty (the "bread from heaven"). The spiritual "feeding" on Christ that happens in the Lord's Supper not only unites the believer to Christ's suffering, but also gives meaning to the believer's own suffering.

The other way in which, at least in this writer's opinion, John's Gospel makes this connection with the Lord's Supper is in the miracle at Cana, where Jesus turns the water to wine. When his mother informs him that they are out of wine, Jesus enigmatically says to her, "O woman, what have you to do with me? My hour has not yet come" (John 2:4 RSV). This has a certain shock value—"What have you to do with me?" (literally, "What to me and to you?") is the same phrase by which the demons address Jesus in Mark 5:7. It has the force of, "What do we have to do with each other? Leave me alone!" Commentators have pointed out that the introductory vocative "Woman" is probably not as brusque as it is in English, but there is no escaping the fact that by addressing her as "Woman" (*Gynē*) rather than "Mother" (*Mētēr*), Jesus is in some degree distancing himself from his mother's request. The key, however, lies in the following phrase, "My hour has not yet come." In John's Gospel, Jesus' "hour" is a cipher for his crucifixion, i.e., the time of his "lifting up," his humiliation and exaltation (John 7:30; 8:20; 12:27; 13:1; 16:32; 17:1). The implication of Jesus' statement, then, is that he is making a connection between the request for wine and his death, symbolized by his blood. Most exegetes recognize that, whatever the precise character of the symbolisms in John 2, the abundant provision of wine—far more than would be needed for a village wedding feast—is indicative of the eschatological bounty promised in the Old Testament (Joel 2:24; Amos 9:13–14).

So then the simple observation of Jesus' mother that they have no wine is, in John's framework, a comment that they have no redemption. Indeed, to run out of wine at a wedding feast was a social travesty of the first order, so even on the literal level, Mary was saying the hosts were in deep trouble. But Jesus uses this potential social catastrophe to point to the bigger problem—it is not just literal wine that they lack; they lack the means of redemption. Even though Jesus' hour to lay down his life for his people has not yet come, the fruit of that coming redemption breaks through, and the water in the jars ordinarily used for external purification (John 2:6) is transformed into a symbol of that which truly purifies, the eschatological wine of Jesus' blood. Thus does the astonished master of ceremonies declare, "You have kept the good wine until now!" (v. 10).

Whether or not the "bread of life" discourse and the miracle at Cana are intended to point to the Lord's Supper, and the consequent connection of the disciples' suffering to Christ's suffering, it remains true that for John, as for the Synoptic Gospels, being a disciple of Christ means following the same path of suffering. Just as the world hated Christ, so it will hate his disciples (John 15:18–19, cf. 17:14). Just as for Jesus the path of glory lay through suffering, so also for his disciples (12:24–25).

Conclusion

Jesus transformed people's thinking about suffering, and his words should transform our thinking too. Most Old Testament thought on the subject concentrated on Israel's suffering or on sufferers' trusting God. In the four Gospels Jesus refocused the whole notion of suffering on the suffering of the Christ, regarding it as a central theme of the Old Testament. After Peter's confession that Jesus is the Christ, Jesus begins to explain how he will usher in the eschatological reversal. He will first do so through encompassing suffering and glory, *in himself*, then by his disciples' undergoing the same pattern, then finally in judgment when the Son of Man applies the reversal to the whole world.

On the cross Jesus stands in the place of his people by undergoing the suffering they as sinners deserve, and then in the resurrection manifesting the exaltation that he as the righteous sufferer deserves. The words of Jesus must impact the way we view suffering. Suffering—the suffering on the cross (and resurrection) of our Lord and Savior Jesus Christ—is the most important event in history. God does not exempt himself from suffering but enters into it fully in the person of his Son. And, mysteriously, the suffering of God incarnate accomplishes our salvation! As a result, it is no wonder that our worship as the people of God is consumed with Jesus' suffering and vindication. We worship the crucified and risen One. How can we, as his beloved people, saved by his suffering, refuse to drink when he offers us the cup of suffering?

Given the realities of the fall and God's plan to rescue sinners, the Gospels show that suffering and death are *necessary* in order to gain resurrection life, both on the part of Jesus the Christ and on the part of his disciples. So then, if suffering truly is necessary, it is purposeful. Therefore, while the immediate cause of suffering may be evil, its presence in God's overall plan is not something that calls God's goodness into question; rather, it is the way that God expresses his goodness. All true redemption is via suffering—first the suffering of God's own Son and then by application the suffering of his disciples. For all four Gospels, being a disciple of Christ means following the same path of suffering. Just as the world hated Christ, so it will hate his disciples. Let us, then, not shrink from the path of suffering when our Savior calls us to follow that path. And just as for Jesus the path of glory lay through suffering, so also for his disciples. Let us, therefore, fix our eyes more firmly on his triumphant resurrection which—after we have suffered a little while—guarantees our own!

Jesus' new Christocentric way of thinking about suffering permeates the rest of the New Testament. The result is that the meaning of the suffering of both the church and individual believers is found in the suffering of the Christ. These themes are developed in the next chapter.

5

SUFFERING IN THE TEACHING OF THE APOSTLES

DAN G. MCCARTNEY

As noted at the end of chapter 4, Jesus' new Christocentric way of thinking about suffering permeates the rest of the New Testament, and now we take our consideration of that fact from the Gospels to the book of Acts.

The Book of Acts

The Gospels record Jesus teaching that the prophets foretold great sufferings for the Christ. Although in the Gospels the apostle Peter initially struggled to accept this type of "suffering Messiah," the book of Acts shows us a Peter who had come to understand Jesus' words and was now even preaching the same message himself: "But what God foretold by the mouth of all the prophets, that his Christ would suffer, he thus fulfilled" (Acts 3:18, cf. 1 Pet. 1:11). Likewise, Paul's preaching as reported in Acts finds the suffering of Christ as the theme of Scripture: "And Paul went in [to the synagogue], as was his custom, and on three Sabbath days he reasoned with them from the Scriptures, explaining and proving that it was necessary for the Christ to suffer and to rise from the dead, and saying, 'This Jesus, whom I proclaim to you, is the Christ'" (Acts 17:2–3). Notice that the eschatological *necessity* of the suffering and resurrection of Christ, which Jesus spoke of in the Gospels, is here echoed in Paul's preaching.

The suffering of Christ is, as it was in the Gospels, the key to God's redemptive purpose. But that suffering is something in which those who have faith in Christ also must share. Acts records how Paul was stoned and left for dead but miraculously lived. As he then traveled through Asia Minor he encouraged the disciples that suffering is necessary for entry into the kingdom of God: "When they had preached the gospel to that city and had made many disciples, they returned to Lystra and to Iconium and to Antioch, strengthening the souls of the disciples, encouraging them to continue in the faith, and saying that through many tribulations we must enter the kingdom of God" (Acts 14:21–22). Note the word *must* again. We can therefore understand why the disciples, having been hauled before the Sanhedrin, were "rejoicing that they were counted worthy to suffer dishonor for the name" (5:41). They deemed themselves honored to be counted with Christ in his sufferings.

Although suffering is a calling for all disciples, it is particularly a calling for the apostles, who were Christ's primary representatives to the church. We see suffering "for Christ" as an apostolic calling in Acts 9:16, where the Holy Spirit tells Ananias the disciple regarding Paul: "I will show him how much he must suffer for the sake of my name." Suffering is the means by which Paul will bear the name of Christ to the world (v. 15).[1] Hence it is Paul's conviction, "in every city . . . imprisonment and afflictions await me" (20:23).

Acts also hints at the fact that tribulation is sometimes the means by which God both sanctifies his people and readies them for service. In Acts 11:19 the "scattering" of the church due to persecution is actually the means God uses to spread the gospel outside of Jerusalem.

The Letters of Paul

It is not surprising, therefore, that we see these themes reappear in Paul's letters.[2] For Paul, as for other New Testament writers, the starting point for understanding the meaning of Christ's suffering is that its purpose is the redemption, or "ransom," of his people. First Timothy 2:5–6 echoes

---

1. Cf. W. Michaelis, *TDNT* 5:919.
2. Though many scholars have doubts regarding the authorship of the Pastoral Letters, here I will simply assume Paul is their author and moreover will assume that the letters of the New Testament are authored by those named as such. Cf. Donald Guthrie, *New Testament Introduction*, 2nd ed. (Downers Grove, IL: InterVarsity, 1990) for detailed arguments.

Mark 10:45: "There is one mediator between God and men, the man Christ Jesus, who gave himself as a ransom for all."[3]

When dealing with Christ's redemptive work, Paul most frequently focuses on the *death* of Christ rather than his suffering broadly considered. Of course, his death is the climax of his suffering, but it is the imposition of that ultimate punishment (death by torture on a cross) that is the manifestation of the true cost of forgiveness for sin against God. When Paul does speak of the sufferings of Christ, it most often is in terms of the believer's *sharing* in Christ's suffering (2 Cor. 1:4–5; Phil. 3:10; Col. 1:24). The existential drive for thinking both about the suffering of Christ and that of his people is the fact that in the ancient world, as in our own day, such suffering seemed incongruous with the favor of God.

In 1 Corinthians 1 and 2, Paul forcefully argues that the Christ he preaches is a crucified Christ and that the gospel is the "word of the cross" (1 Cor. 1:18). The cross, the ultimate symbol of suffering and humiliation, was a problem for both Jews and Greeks. For Jews, the Messiah (Christ) was the symbol of God's deliverance of his people from their suffering, as well as the supreme evidence of God's blessing and approval. The kingdom of God was therefore purely an *exaltation* of the Messiah. To speak of a humiliated and suffering Messiah was, in their eyes, an insult. It was to say that God had failed or that Israel's hope was futile. They expected to see the Christ as a manifestation of power and glory, thinking that they themselves would then also be exalted along with the Christ. To be sure, Jesus' resurrection and ascension was indeed a manifestation of God's power and glory, but that was not publicly visible—the suffering of Israel continued unabated. So a crucified Christ, a publicly humiliated and executed Christ, was the ultimate symbol of degradation.

On the other hand a crucified, suffering Christ was also a problem for Gentiles (or "Greeks"). Although Greek playwrights wrote plays warning against *hubris* (presumptuousness), the favor of a god was marked by earthly success, and the quintessential mark of divine favor was wisdom, understood as the ability to achieve balance and success in life. A crucified, humiliated Christ was looked on as absurd and unreasonable—not a figure to attract important, wise, and successful Gentiles.

Paul indicates, however, that contrary to Jews who want *power* and Greeks who want *wisdom*, the gospel of Jesus emphasizes God's favor as manifest

3. As noted in the previous chapter, *ransom* is the term used for the price of rescuing someone from a condition of slavery or imprisonment.

through weakness, humiliation, and even death. Suffering, far from being a mark of God's rejection, is actually a mark of his favor and blessing.

Suffering as Christian (and Apostolic) Vocation

We noted that Paul in Acts 14:22 understood that suffering is part of the "package" of faith in Christ. He is there echoing the teaching of Jesus in Matthew 5:11, John 16:33, and elsewhere. This conviction is also evident in Paul's letters. In 2 Timothy 1:11–12 and 3:11 Paul sees his own sufferings this way, as part of his calling as both a teacher and an apostle. Suffering is therefore what validates the apostle as a chosen vessel (2 Cor. 11:23–24). Similarly, ministers of Christ are shown to be such by the fact that they suffer. Paul includes the necessity of suffering in his preaching, as he reminds the Thessalonians: "For when we were with you, we kept telling you beforehand that we were to suffer affliction, just as it has come to pass, and just as you know" (1 Thess. 3:4).

But Paul also applies the necessity of suffering to Christians generally, because suffering is that which serves to qualify all believers for the kingdom of God:

> Therefore we ourselves boast about you in the churches of God for your steadfastness and faith in all your persecutions and in the afflictions that you are enduring. This is evidence of the righteous judgment of God, that you may be considered worthy of the kingdom of God, for which you are also suffering. (2 Thess. 1:4–5)

Sharing in Christ's suffering is therefore the pathway to the glorious resurrection, and thus Paul actually embraces it:

> Indeed, I count everything as loss because of the surpassing worth of knowing Christ Jesus my Lord. For his sake I have suffered the loss of all things ... that I may know him and the power of his resurrection, and may share his sufferings, becoming like him in his death, that by any means possible I may attain the resurrection from the dead. (Phil. 3:8–11)

This eschatological orientation, then, also puts present suffering into perspective. Since suffering is "preparing for us an eternal weight of glory beyond all comparison," Paul can consider it a "light momentary affliction" (2 Cor. 4:17) and conclude that "our present sufferings are not worth comparing with the glory that will be revealed in us" (Rom. 8:18 NIV). Suffering is thus a pointer to future glory.

Sharing in Christ's Suffering and Death

Paul declares in 2 Corinthians 1:5 that "as we share abundantly in Christ's sufferings, so through Christ we share abundantly in comfort too." A believer's suffering thus marks him as belonging to Christ and as an heir of Christ who will also be glorified with him: ". . . if children, then heirs—heirs of God and fellow heirs with Christ, provided we suffer with him in order that we may also be glorified with him" (Rom. 8:17). Hence, suffering is regarded as a "gift" for believers: "For it has been granted to you that for the sake of Christ you should not only believe in him but also suffer for his sake" (Phil. 1:29).

Just as Christ's suffering was for the benefit of the church, so also is the suffering of both Paul as an apostle and believers for other believers. Since suffering links believers with Christ, it also links suffering believers with other suffering believers. One result is a "communion of suffering," as it were, where sufferers may comfort one another.

> If we are afflicted, it is for your comfort and salvation; and if we are comforted, it is for your comfort, which you experience when you patiently endure the same sufferings that we suffer. Our hope for you is unshaken, for we know that as you share in our sufferings, you will also share in our comfort. (2 Cor. 1:6–7)

Paul can say this because he sees all Christians as linked together as part of a body so that "if one member suffers, all suffer together; if one member is honored, all rejoice together" (1 Cor. 12:26). But Paul means more than just having a capacity for sympathy. He regards himself as suffering *for* other believers and therefore advancing the positive effects of the gospel: "So I ask you not to lose heart over what I am suffering for you, which is your glory" (Eph. 3:13). Paul's suffering serves to advance the gospel in part because non-Christians notice how Christians suffer, and also because it encourages other believers to boldly proclaim the gospel.

> I want you to know, brothers, that what has happened to me has really served to advance the gospel, so that it has become known throughout the whole imperial guard and to all the rest that my imprisonment is for Christ. And most of the brothers, having become confident in the Lord by my imprisonment, are much more bold to speak the word without fear. (Phil. 1:12–14)

The story of the growth of the church through the suffering of its early members is widely known. Tertullian famously pointed out that "the blood of the martyrs is the seed of the church,"[4] and even the skeptical historian Will Durant acknowledged that the real power of the church came from its endurance of suffering:

> There is no greater drama in human record than the sight of a few Christians, scorned or oppressed by a succession of emperors, bearing all trials with a fierce tenacity, multiplying quietly, building order while their enemies generated chaos, fighting the sword with the word, brutality with hope, and at last defeating the strongest state that history has known. Caesar and Christ had met in the arena, and Christ had won.[5]

Since believers suffer for one another, and since believers' suffering is a sharing in Christ's suffering, Paul is even so bold as to say his sufferings are "filling up" what is "lacking" in the sufferings of Christ (Col. 1:24). Obviously, as Paul makes clear throughout his writings, he does not mean that his sufferings redeem people from sins, because redemption is solely the act of Christ. The context of his statement in Colossians 1 is the recognition that his own sufferings serve as a testimony and encouragement to other believers, even the Colossians whom he had not personally met.

Suffering thus has many dimensions, especially in its unique character as that which links the believer to Christ, not only in manifesting the "dying" to sin and "attaining" to the resurrection, but also in giving the church an opportunity to participate in the great vocation to suffer *for* others, thus bringing others to faith and comforting and encouraging others in their endurance of suffering, and all as a testimony for the gospel. But there is also an existential, personal benefit from suffering. Paul says it produces endurance and endurance character and character hope, and hope does not disappoint. More than that, however, suffering has the effect of increasing the believer's awareness of his dependence on Christ. Paul testifies to an aspect of his own suffering in 2 Corinthians 12:

> To keep me from becoming conceited because of the surpassing greatness of the revelations, a thorn was given me in the flesh, a messenger of Satan to harass me, to keep me from becoming conceited. Three times I pleaded with the Lord about this, that it should leave me. But he said to me, "My grace is sufficient for you, for my power is made perfect in weakness." Therefore I will boast all the more gladly of my weaknesses, so that the power of Christ may rest upon me. For the sake of Christ, then, I am content with weaknesses,

4. *Apologeticum* 50.
5. Will Durant, *Christ and Caesar* (New York: Simon & Schuster, 1944), 652.

insults, hardships, persecutions, and calamities. For when I am weak, then
I am strong. (2 Cor. 12:7–10)

It appears God gave Paul this suffering in order that he might know God's
power more fully. And therefore Paul actually rejoiced in his suffering and
weakness.

Hebrews: Suffering as Perfecting

The people to whom the book of Hebrews was written had experienced real
suffering (Heb. 10:32–34). For them suffering was not hypothetical, and the
author writes to encourage them to persevere in faith. He does so both by
warning against failure to endure and by reminding them that there is great
reward for those who continue in faith (10:35–39). In order to do that, the
author first develops a theology of Christ's priestly suffering, wherein Christ
understands and can sympathize with sufferers and has won the victory by
endurance in suffering. The author then applies that theology to believers.
The book of Hebrews views suffering as the path to learning obedience.
Although discipline is unpleasant (12:11), it is a mark of God's love (12:6)
and of our sonship (12:7–8), as well as the path to holiness (12:10).

Amazingly, even the sinless Son Jesus Christ is said to have "learned
obedience through what he suffered" (Heb. 5:8). This is a remarkable statement for many reasons. Why did the Son have to learn obedience? Surely
he was obedient always and did not have to learn it, especially by suffering. Further, the phrasing in the Greek is striking: ἔμαθεν ἀφ' ὧν ἔπαθεν
(*emathen aph' hōn epathen*)—a phrase similar to some Greek sayings that
are akin to our proverbs about "having to learn things the hard way."[6] The
shocking character of the phrase underscores both the depth of Jesus'
self-humiliation and the radical character of his suffering. This was not an
intellective knowledge of obedience Jesus lacked, nor was it moral knowledge. This was the experiential knowledge of what it meant to obey in the
midst of a fallen world, surrounded by sin and tempted at every point in
the same way as others. Jesus suffered in order to experience obedience in
the worst possible environment.

He thus becomes qualified to be the trailblazer of the path of suffering,
as he has tasted death on behalf of all the people, and by suffering has been
made "perfect":

6. As one example, Aeschylus, *Agamemnon*, strophe 3, demonstrates in the opening chorus: "by
suffering comes learning."

> But we see him who for a little while was made lower than the angels, namely
> Jesus, crowned with glory and honor because of the suffering of death, so
> that by the grace of God he might taste death for everyone. For it was fitting
> that he, for whom and by whom all things exist, in bringing many sons to
> glory, should make the founder of their salvation perfect through suffering.
> (Heb. 2:9–10)

This uniquely qualifies Jesus then to give comfort to others when they are
undergoing the test of suffering, "for because he himself has suffered when
tempted, he is able to help those who are being tempted" (2:18). More
than that, though, is the fact that suffering has perfectly qualified Jesus to
become a merciful and faithful high priest to represent mankind (2:17).
In representing the people, a priest must actually be chosen from among
them (5:1) and able to sympathize with their weakness (4:15).

Not only does Christ's suffering qualify him to be a sympathetic high
priest, however; it actually makes him the acceptable and perfect sacrifice:

> He has appeared once for all at the end of the ages to put away sin
>   by the sacrifice of himself. (Heb. 9:26)

> So Jesus also suffered outside the gate in order to sanctify the people
>   through his own blood. (Heb. 13:12)

The author of Hebrews does not draw very much on the suffering of
believers as a link to Christ's suffering, but he does, as noted already, see
suffering as necessary because of the need for discipline. In Hebrews 12
he applies his teaching on the priesthood and sacrifice of Christ by first
pointing to Christ as having run the race ahead of us, and then encouraging
believers to run the same race:

> Therefore, since we are surrounded by so great a cloud of witnesses, let us
> also lay aside every weight, and sin which clings so closely, and let us run
> with endurance the race that is set before us, looking to Jesus, the founder
> and perfecter of our faith, who for the joy that was set before him endured
> the cross, despising the shame, and is seated at the right hand of the throne of
> God. Consider him who endured from sinners such hostility against himself,
> so that you may not grow weary or fainthearted. (Heb. 12:1–3)

For our sake Jesus endured both suffering and the hostility of the world.
If it was fitting for Jesus to suffer, it is fitting for believers in him to suffer
as well. The author goes on in Hebrews 12 to point out that suffering is of
great benefit to believers. The passage deserves to be quoted fully:

In your struggle against sin you have not yet resisted to the point of shed-ding your blood. And have you forgotten the exhortation that addresses you as sons?

"My son, do not regard lightly the discipline of the Lord,
    nor be weary when reproved by him.
For the Lord disciplines the one he loves,
    and chastises every son whom he receives."

It is for discipline that you have to endure. God is treating you as sons. For what son is there whom his father does not discipline? If you are left without discipline, in which all have participated, then you are illegitimate children and not sons. Besides this, we have had earthly fathers who disciplined us and we respected them. Shall we not much more be subject to the Father of spirits and live? For they disciplined us for a short time as it seemed best to them, but he disciplines us for our good, that we may share his holiness. For the moment all discipline seems painful rather than pleasant, but later it yields the peaceful fruit of righteousness to those who have been trained by it.

Therefore lift your drooping hands and strengthen your weak knees, and make straight paths for your feet, so that what is lame may not be put out of joint but rather be healed. (Heb. 12:4–13)

The situation of the original readers of Hebrews was one of persecu-tion. They had not yet been killed for their faith (Heb. 12:4), but they had suffered enough to begin to wonder whether God had forsaken them. The author of Hebrews reminds them that God disciplines his children, and the suffering Christians must undergo is to "yield the peaceful fruit of righteousness" (12:11).

James: Suffering as the Pathway to Maturity[7]
The book of James takes a special interest in suffering as a trial or test. One scholar has identified James as generically a "theology of suffering,"[8] a subtype of Jewish wisdom literature. This may be an overstatement, since James is concerned with far more than suffering.[9] But certainly suffering appears to be at least one of the driving concerns that James addresses both at the beginning and at the end of his letter. However, suffering itself is not

---

7. This section is adapted from my chapter "Suffering in James" in *The Practical Calvinist: An In-troduction to the Presbyterian and Reformed Heritage in Honor of Dr. D. Clair Davis*, ed. P. Lillback (Fearn, Ross-shire, Scotland: Mentor, 2002), 477–86.

8. Peter Davids, "Theological Perspectives on the Epistle of James," *JETS* 23 (1980): 97.

9. The overarching concern of James is *genuine faith*, and that profession of faith in Christ (2:1) must result in a faithful life, whether in trials (as in 1:2, 12), use of the tongue (chap. 3), social relations within the church (2:1–13 and 4:1–12), business (4:13–17) or in caring for the destitute, the sick, and those burdened with sin (1:26–27; 2:15–16; 5:13–20).

the primary focus of James; rather, he is concerned with the Christian's *response* to suffering, just as he is concerned with the Christian's response to other matters. In the course of addressing various issues, we see three aspects to suffering in James: (1) suffering is a characteristic trait of God's people; (2) suffering is a trial or test meant to lead Christians to maturity; and (3) suffering is a call to faithful living.

Suffering Is Characteristic of God's People

Just as Jesus, Paul, and the other disciples describe suffering as a necessary dimension of discipleship, so James regards suffering as characteristic of faith in Christ.

> Listen, my beloved brothers, has not God chosen those who are poor in the world to be rich in faith and heirs of the kingdom, which he has promised to those who love him? (James 2:5)

> Blessed is the man who remains steadfast under trial, for when he has stood the test he will receive the crown of life, which God has promised to those who love him. (James 1:12)

Notice how in both passages "those who love him" are identified with those who are suffering but remain steadfast.

Since the believers in Christ are those who are suffering now, they can rejoice in affliction, partly because such sufferings serve to bring maturity (James 1:3–4) but also because the "eschatological reversal" is soon to begin (1:9–10). The community of faith is the community of those who endure suffering and humiliation; it is those who humble themselves and are exalted by the Lord (4:10).

The notion of the community of faith being the poor has its roots in the Old Testament (cf. Ps. 86:1 where it is the poor who are deeply aware that they are dependent on God). The Qumran community also regarded itself as the community of the poor (1QH 2:5; 1QpHab 12:3, 6, 10, 4QpPs37 2:9; 3:10). It is precisely because the community is the poor that they deserve respect (James 2:1–7) and why dishonoring them is so contrary to true faith (2:6, an echo of Prov. 14:31, which declares dishonoring the poor man to be an insult to his Maker).

Suffering Leads People to Maturity

James has no explicit development of the idea of redemptive suffering. Rather it is the believer's fortitude in the trial, his endurance, that is given positive theological value in James.[10] This is different from 1 Peter (see below), where Christ's suffering is redemptive, and where the believer's suffering is a means of identification with Christ. First Peter encourages the believer to persevere because of what *suffering* does in the believer, uniting him to Christ's suffering. James, however, regards *endurance* as the primary function of suffering in the believer's life. He sees suffering as an opportunity to let endurance do its job of "perfecting" or maturing the believer. For James, the Christian who endures is the Christian who matures.

The background to suffering as the path to maturity lies in Jewish wisdom literature. Suffering was a test that gave one an opportunity to endure heroically and thus bring glory to God. In the literature of the intertestamental period we see the patriarchs and heroes of the Old Testament presented as examples of endurance, such as Abraham (*Jub.* 19:8) or Joseph (*Test. Jos.* 2:7). In the Testament of Job (e.g., *Test. Job* 1:5; 4:5–6; 27:6–7), Job is presented as a model of endurance. James also speaks of Job's endurance (or "steadfastness" as ESV renders it) as an example: "Behold, we consider those blessed who remained steadfast. You have heard of the steadfastness of Job, and you have seen the purpose of the Lord, how the Lord is compassionate and merciful" (James 5:11). Since testing is an opportunity for endurance, particularly endurance in faith, and endurance brings completeness or maturity, James even says it is reason for joy: "Count it all joy, my brothers, when you meet trials of various kinds, for you know that the testing of your faith produces steadfastness. And let steadfastness have its full effect, that you may be perfect and complete, lacking in nothing" (1:2–4).

Count it *all* joy, says James, i.e., *entirely* a matter of joy, when you meet trials, because that is how we grow up into the men and women God wants us to be. Again, it is not the trial itself that produces maturity but the faithful endurance or steadfastness, staying the course, that brings one to completeness. Suffering, or trials, is the means of "proving,"[11] which provides occasion for endurance, which leads to maturity.

10. The term for *endurance* is a common one in Greek moral literature, especially among the Stoics. There it refers to the patient endurance of whatever comes, without allowing distress to influence one's convictions, thinking, or lifestyle (cf. F. Hauck, *TDNT* 6:582). Endurance is a particularly desirable characteristic of a soldier. James, like other New Testament writers, has taken the term and applied it to the Christian's faithfulness in staying the course in the face of opposition. It is therefore not a little related to the biblical notion of faith—real faith trusts Jesus even when it is hard to do so.

11. The Greek word *dokimion* here does not mean the *result* of the test (as in 1 Pet. 1:7 where it means "genuineness") but the *means* of testing, as for example in the Septuagint translation of Prov. 27:21 where the furnace is a *dokimion* for silver and gold.

This sequence or chain of maturity in James 1:3–4 is further developed in verse 12: endurance of trials (*hypomone peirasmon*) is the proof (*dokimos*) that results in the crown of life.[12] The "crown of life" is the victor's wreath, which for the Christian who has finished the race is eternal life with God (cf. Rev. 2:10). This chain of life in James 1:12 stands in opposition to a chain of death in 1:13–15, where trials lead to desires that give birth to sin, which brings forth death. Again, this shows that it is not the trial itself that produces maturity and life, for a trial can result in non-endurance, in the giving in to desire, and in the birthing of sin and death.

Trials and testing of all kinds, including suffering, thus have a purpose, and James says we should not defeat that purpose through impatience, by abandoning obedience for the sake of comfort, or by attempting an inappropriate escape from testing.

Suffering Is a Call to Faithful Living

James connects suffering with faithful living because suffering drives one to eschatology, the motivation for ethical faithfulness.[13] As we noted, the appropriate response to suffering is patient endurance because of an eschatological hope. James compares it to a farmer's patience: "Be patient, then, brothers, until the Lord's coming. See how the farmer waits for the land to yield its valuable crop and how patient he is for the autumn and spring rains" (James 5:7 NIV). The sufferer waits patiently because of the expectation of judgment (5:1–5) at the *parousia* of the Lord (5:8–9). Moreover, the response of the prophets to suffering, in particular Elijah and Job, is given as a pattern for believers to be patient in suffering (5:10–11, 17–18).[14]

---

12. We can compare both of these to a similar chain in Romans 5:3–5, though hope stands at the end of that list rather than "perfection": *thlipsis* → *hypomone* → *dokime* → *elpis*. In both cases the treatment of suffering is driven by Christological eschatology. This is one of the many surprising points of contact between James's and Paul's letters, which suggests that the book of Acts is accurately portraying things when it presents Paul and the Jerusalem church as ultimately harmonious. However, Paul goes on to add the dimension of the Holy Spirit: "Hope does not put us to shame, because God's love has been poured into our hearts through the Holy Spirit who has been given to us." James on the other hand, with the possible exception of 4:5 (in my view unlikely), never mentions the Holy Spirit.

13. See A. Chester and R. P. Martin, *The Theology of the Letters of James, Peter and Jude* (Cambridge: Cambridge University Press, 1994), 16–17, 30–31.

14. Anyone who has read the book of Job may want to object to this example, since Job was hardly a model of what we typically regard as patience. But this example may clue us in to the fact that true patience, as James uses the term, is not passive acceptance but an unremitting appeal to God for help and the certain hope of eventual vindication. Cf. R. P. Martin, *James*, WBC (Waco: Word, 1988), 16.

But James is even more interested in how the Christian responds to the suffering of others. Just as genuine faith endures trials, so a Christian must respond to the suffering of others as a fellow sufferer. Hence he says true religion[15] is to care for sufferers (James 1:27). Because real faith (2:14–17) is faith that God will exalt the humble (1:9), the works that proceed from true faith will involve showing mercy to those who suffer. Of particular concern to James are the truly destitute, such as "orphans and widows" (1:27), or the man in filthy garments (2:2), who in that social environment were often the most marginalized and powerless people. The church is the community that anticipates the eschatological reversal by caring for and respecting the poor.

Therefore James has little tolerance for those who show favoritism to the rich. This kind of favoritism is offensive first because it violates the law of love and misrepresents the character of God, who cares about the poor. Note that the context of the law of love in Leviticus 19 specifically condemns partiality (Lev. 19:15).[16] Second, partiality belies the eschatological nature of the community, which ought to display in advance God's exaltation of the poor. James 2:1–17 thus teaches us that faithful living does not just pity the poor, but it *respects* the poor. This is a difficult concept for most of us who are not poor, especially because suffering, poverty, and destitution can make a person appear repulsive, which in turn has the effect of increasing that person's suffering.

For James, however, it is precisely those who suffer who are to rejoice in trials; it is those who are poor who are rich in faith; it is those who are humble who will be exalted. "Perfection" and wholeness in the gospel runs counter to the world's notion of wholeness. The world's view of completeness, the *goal* (*telos*) of worldly life and worldly wisdom (James 3:15), is success and the achievement of domination. But the "wisdom from above" is good behavior in a humble wisdom (3:13).

Finally, a faithful response to suffering is prayer, both by the sufferer and for the sufferer. In 5:13 James tells his hearers: "Is anyone among you suffering? Let him pray." Verse 14 expands this responsibility to the church leaders, for whom prayer is a major calling. The "anointing" of the sick commanded here is not the establishment of some sacrament of unction,

---

15. The term used here for *religion* (*threskeia*) means not one's overall faith commitments but religious practice, acts of piety, or cultic activity. By "true religion," therefore, James does not mean "the essence of true Christian faith" but "the essence of true Christian religious activity."
16. The love command of Lev. 19:18 is shared throughout the New Testament as definitive for Christian life. Its widespread use as the basis of ethics is probably due to the fact that it was promulgated by Jesus himself (Mark 12:29–31 and parallels). James's point is that showing favoritism violates the most basic ethic of God and, hence, violates the whole law.

nor is it simply medicinal anointing. Rather, it is symbolic of the anointing with the oil of gladness. Isaiah 61:3 speaks of the messianic "eschatological reversal," reminding us that the Messiah has been anointed "to grant to those who mourn in Zion—to give them a beautiful headdress instead of ashes, the oil of gladness instead of mourning." Suffering is once again, as in James 1:2, linked with joy. Like other forms of suffering, sickness is a trial, and trials are opportunities for endurance, which leads to maturity.

1 Peter: Suffering and the Path to Redemption

Like the book of James, 1 Peter sees suffering as necessary (1 Pet. 1:6) because it is the proving ground of faith (1:7), and because it is therefore cause for joy (1:8). But 1 Peter goes further than James by seeing suffering not just as something to be endured because it brings maturity, but as the means by which the redemption obtained by Christ's suffering is applied to the believer. In other words, suffering identifies the believer with Christ.

The addressees of 1 Peter are actually suffering. For the most part their suffering is verbal, like being slandered or misrepresented (1 Pet. 2:12; 3:16; 4:14), but in 4:12 it appears that the potential for the persecutions becoming deadly is real ("fiery trials"), and slaves had already experienced "stripes" unjustly. At the very least, these Christians have experienced isolation within their surrounding culture so that they are "strangers and exiles" (an echo of the experience of Abraham in Gen. 23:4). This actual suffering of believers is therefore a central existential concern of 1 Peter, and it drives the theology of the entire epistle. Suffering is the key connection between the believer and Christ. Christ, by suffering, identified with his people; Christians, by suffering, are identified with Christ.

Peter carries on this idea of Christ's vicarious suffering with and for his people as it is found in the book of Isaiah. This is particularly clear in his allusion to Isaiah 53 in 1 Peter 2:24: "He himself bore our sins in his body on the tree, that we might die to sin and live to righteousness. By his wounds you have been healed." Indeed, 1 Peter shares Jesus' conviction that the suffering of the Christ is a central theme of the Old Testament. Jesus' instruction in Luke 24:46 is echoed in 1 Peter 1:10–11: "The prophets who prophesied about the grace that was to be yours searched and inquired carefully, inquiring what person or time the Spirit of Christ in them was indicating when he predicted the sufferings of Christ and the subsequent glories." The translation obscures an interesting oddity in the Greek. First Peter actually says that the prophets predicted the sufferings that were *unto* the Christ. Since he is speaking of the Old Testament writers' attempt to understand what God would do, he seems to be referencing to the fact that certain sufferings were things God had planned for the Christ and were designated as his. Apparently Peter, who so vehemently rejected the idea that the Christ would suffer and die (Mark 8:31–32), finally saw the importance of this truth. He understood that his role as an apostle was primarily as a witness to those sufferings (1 Pet. 5:1).

But it is not just Christ who suffers for the Christian; the Christian must suffer for Christ. Although one might suffer for doing wrong (1 Pet. 2:20; 3:17), such suffering does not mean anything other than that these are the consequences of doing wrong. But if one suffers as a Christian, i.e., for the "name" (4:14, 16), then he or she is blessed, because the Spirit of God rests on him or her.

Peter addresses this theme of suffering "as a Christian," first, with respect to a group that was intimately familiar with suffering—those who were slaves. Slaves, who were the lowest social stratum in the social world of the New Testament, had been responsive to the gospel message of hope for an eschatological reversal. But they were still slaves, and they still suffered. Peter tells slaves that they may indeed suffer unjustly, but if they do so it is a gift, because it identifies them with Christ who also suffered unjustly.

> For this is a gracious thing, when, mindful of God, one endures sorrows while suffering unjustly. For what credit is it if, when you sin and are beaten for it, you endure? But if when you do good and suffer for it you endure, this is a gracious thing in the sight of God. For to this you have been called, because Christ also suffered for you, leaving you an example, so that you might follow in his steps. (1 Pet. 2:19–21)

The *actual* suffering of slaves is thus identified with the suffering of Christ, who knew what it was like to be beaten.

But it is not only slaves who are identified with Christ in their unjust suffering; this is the character of discipleship in general (1 Pet. 2:21). Indeed, Peter says that Christians everywhere are experiencing suffering: "Resist [the Devil], firm in your faith, knowing that the same kinds of suffering are being experienced by your brotherhood throughout the world" (5:9). We will return to this mention of the satanic origins of suffering. Before we turn to that matter, however, we should point out that 1 Peter vividly develops the theme of suffering as the means of identification for all Christians, both of Christ with his people and of the people with Christ, in the remarkable passage sometimes called the "stone catena" (or chain of verses about the "stone") in 2:4–8.

The Living Stone and the Living Stones

This passage connects three Old Testament passages that speak of a person as a "stone": Psalm 118:22, Isaiah 28:16, and Isaiah 8:14. Jesus, in his parable of the vineyard tenants (Matt. 21:33–44), identified himself as the "stone" of Psalm 118:22, citing it with regard to the tenants' rejection of the son in the parable, a clear reference to the fact that the Jewish leadership would kill Jesus. Psalm 118 probably originally referred to the fact that David, though anointed king (i.e., "christ"), was for a long time "rejected" by the leaders of Israel; yet God had chosen him. Jesus the Anointed, who was the greater David, was likewise rejected, but God exalted him and made him the head of the corner, that is, the cornerstone which guides the shape and orientation of the whole building. First Peter 2:6 also says Jesus is the "stone" of Isaiah 28:16, which God called his "chosen, precious cornerstone." But the Jewish leaders "stumbled" at God's stone, so he became for them a stumbling stone and a rock of offense (Isa. 8:14). Hence the stone was rejected by his own people but was eventually exalted by God and is the One chosen by God to guide his people.

The interesting thing about this passage is the way in which Peter applies it to believers. Just as Jesus is a living stone (1 Pet. 2:4), so Christians are "living stones" (2:5) being built up into a spiritual house, i.e., the true temple of God, so that they may offer up spiritual sacrifices acceptable to God and be a holy priesthood. Though Peter mixes metaphors slightly here, his image speaks powerfully. Just as Jesus became a rejected stone, so believers will be rejected stones; but as God exalted the stone, so he will exalt the stones. God builds his household; he constructs a suitable priesthood to worship him rightly by the agency of a *suffering* Messiah who brings in his train a multitude of other sufferers to be his special inheritance. First Peter 2:9–10 then continues the line of thought in naming this people by the terms applied to Israel in the Old Testament: a chosen race (Isa. 43:20), a royal priesthood and holy nation (Ex. 19:6), a people for God's own possession to declare his praises (Isa. 43:21), and a people who were once not a people but are now the people of God (adapting Hos. 1:6, 9; 2:23). The point is that when believers suffer rejection it marks them as stones belonging to the rejected but chosen Stone.

As mentioned earlier, much of the suffering experienced by the original readers of 1 Peter was in the form of slander, verbal abuse, and false accusations. It is worth noting that Peter is quite familiar with the sting of such verbal assaults. He recognizes that slander can escalate into violence and even turn deadly, as we see in his change of tone in 4:12. Whereas earlier Peter asks, "Who is going to hurt you for doing good?" but acknowledges it might happen, here in 4:12 he may have gotten word that Christians were being killed, as they were undergoing "fiery trials." This could be a reference to the literal burning of some Christians in the reign of Caesar Nero, which probably began sometime in the late 60s. But since the letter was not written to Christians in Rome but in northern Asia Minor (1 Pet. 1:1), it is not clear that a Roman reference is intended. Regardless, Peter is certainly aware that certain forms of suffering may be not only imminent but deadly. Yet even if it turns deadly, the Christian has no cause for fear:

> But even if you should suffer for righteousness' sake, you will be blessed. Have no fear of them, nor be troubled, but in your hearts honor Christ the Lord as holy, always being prepared to make a defense to anyone who asks you for a reason for the hope that is in you; yet do it with gentleness and respect, having a good conscience, so that, when you are slandered, those who revile your good behavior in Christ may be put to shame. For it is better to suffer for doing good, if that should be God's will, than for doing evil. For Christ also suffered once for sins, the righteous for the unrighteous, that he might bring us to God, being put to death in the flesh but made alive in the spirit. (1 Pet. 3:14–18)

Thus in suffering the believer is being patterned after Christ, who came to resurrection by way of death, who did good and yet suffered, and who is blessed above all. Since believers share in Christ's sufferings, they therefore also share in his glory. "But rejoice insofar as you share Christ's sufferings, that you may also rejoice and be glad when his glory is revealed" (1 Pet. 4:13). This verse occurs in the midst of a passage dealing with another way that suffering functions in 1 Peter: it leads believers away from sin. This too is connected with suffering "in Christ."

Suffering, Judgment, and Blessing
In chapter 4, Peter declares that those who suffer for doing good are blessed. He then goes on to explain why suffering for Christ brings blessing, but the reason may seem a little cryptic to us:

> For it is time for judgment to begin at the household of God; and if it begins with us, what will be the outcome for those who do not obey the gospel of God? And
>   "If the righteous is scarcely saved,
>   what will become of the ungodly and the sinner?"
> Therefore let those who suffer according to God's will entrust their souls to a faithful Creator while doing good. (1 Pet. 4:17–19)

"Judgment begins with the household of God" is an echo of some Old Testament texts where God says that his judgment will begin with his people (Ezek. 9:6 and Jer. 25:29). But these Old Testament prophecies speak of judgment due to the sin of the people, not for their faithfulness. So why does Peter indicate that this suffering "as a Christian, for the name" is the beginning of God's judgment?

We get a clue to answering this a little earlier in the chapter, in another difficult text. First Peter 4:1 makes the strange claim that the one who has suffered in the flesh has ceased from sin: "Since therefore Christ suffered in the flesh, arm yourselves with the same way of thinking, for whoever has suffered in the flesh has ceased from sin." It seems unlikely that Peter would claim that someone's suffering indicates that they have stopped sinning, because he has just observed in chapter 2 and will again later in chapter 4 that some people suffer because of wrongdoing. So this verse has been a bit of a conundrum.

Some scholars have suggested that the second half of the verse, like the first, is still talking about Christ, and that "ceased from sin" should be translated "has finished with sin."[17] It would mean something like this: "Since therefore Christ suffered in the flesh, arm yourselves with the same way of thinking, for the one who suffered (i.e., Christ) has made an end of sin." The problem with this view is that the word translated "ceased" (*pauomai*) followed by an accusative noun indicating an action (in this case "sin") always means to stop doing that action. Since Peter shares the conviction of the rest of the New Testament that Jesus never committed sin (1 Pet. 2:22), it follows that he could not "cease from doing sin." Also, the next verse indicates that the *purpose* of the suffering/ceasing is so that the sufferer, i.e., the Christian, might live out the rest of his life by the will of God rather than according to the lusts of the flesh.

Other scholars suggest that because 1 Peter consistently speaks of Christ's *suffering* when referring to his *death*, and because here the aorist participle (*pathon*) is used instead of a progressive participle, this verse is a reference to the symbolic death of the person, by virtue of his union with Christ in baptism, along lines found in 2:24.[18] This only works, however, on the supposition that the letter of 1 Peter is about the symbolic "death" of baptism. While 1 Peter does speak of baptism a few verses earlier in 3:20–21, it is there described not as a suffering but as a washing and is mentioned in passing as that for which the great flood was a precursor, in that Noah and

17. A. Strobel, "Macht Leiden von Sunde frei? Zur Problematik von 1 Petr, 4:1f.," *Theologische Zeitschrift* 19 (1963): 412–25.
18. E.g., W. Michaelis, *TDNT* 5:921.

his family were saved through water. In fact, whereas baptism is sometimes described as a symbol of "death" (Romans 6), this construction requires that baptism and suffering, both metaphors for death, be somehow connected. Yet baptism is never identified directly as a symbol of suffering. More importantly, Peter's driving existential concern in this epistle is the fact that his hearers are undergoing actual suffering. If Peter is using the word *suffered* to mean "baptized" in 4:1, he certainly chose a very obscure way to speak of it.

The solution is to see these two conundrums (1 Pet. 4:17 and 4:1) as stemming from the same source, the fact that just as Paul regards the believer as united to Christ's *death*, Peter regards the believer as united to Christ's *suffering*. Just as for Paul death is judgment (Rom. 5:16), and that Christ by dying underwent that judgment in place of his people (5:8) that they might live to righteousness (5:19), so for Peter suffering is judgment, and Christ underwent *suffering* on behalf of his people (1 Pet. 3:18) so that they might live to righteousness (2:24). As Paul speaks of the believers who have died as being "dead in Christ" (1 Thess. 4:16), so Peter speaks of the believers who have actually suffered as having fellowship with Christ's sufferings (1 Pet. 4:13). And just as Paul describes his experience as a "dying daily" (1 Cor. 15:31) and the body being "dead" (Rom. 8:10), so Peter sees the believer's experience as a life of "suffering" in the flesh, so as no longer to live according to human lusts (1 Pet. 4:2). In a unique way then, the believer's actual experience of suffering links him or her to Christ. The believers, the "house of God," thus undergo, as it were, the judgment of God but in Christ, not alone, and so can entrust themselves to their faithful Creator by doing good (4:19).

Suffering and the Angelic Powers

In the Gospels, as we noted earlier, Jesus attributed the suffering of human beings, even physical infirmities, to Satan (Luke 13:16). Peter, addressing people who are facing suffering of various kinds, tells his readers, "Your adversary the devil prowls around like a roaring lion, seeking someone to devour" (1 Pet. 5:8). Therefore the appropriate response to suffering is to "Resist him [the Devil], firm in your faith, knowing that the same kinds of suffering are being experienced by your brotherhood throughout the world" (5:9). Thus Peter, like Jesus, sees suffering as the work of the Devil.

This has weighty implications for how we understand suffering. In particular, the victory of Jesus described in 1 Peter 3:18–22 includes in it the defeat of the evil powers, and thus gives hope to the sufferer. The passage is a notorious one and has been understood in various ways. Although it may seem a little strange to our Western way of thinking, it probably is not talking about Jesus going into the netherworld to preach the gospel, nor is it describing how Christ effectively preached the gospel through the lips of Noah to the generation of the flood. Rather, it describes Christ's proclamation of victory over the "spirits in prison," who are the "angels, authorities, and powers" of 3:22 who have all been made subject to the resurrected Christ. The comfort for the suffering readers of 1 Peter is that, although Satan still "roams around like a lion seeking to devour someone," he and his emissaries have already been defeated and are in a sense already "in prison" and awaiting sentencing at the last judgment.

This enables us to answer the question, then, about what sort of suffering counts. It may seem that 1 Peter regards only suffering that is explicitly persecution for being a Christian as suffering that links a person with Christ. But since suffering and trials are something brought on not ultimately by an imperial officer or an angry neighbor but by the Devil, all the trials and sufferings he is permitted to send our way are ultimately a testing that identifies us with Christ's suffering.

Peter finally closes the body of his letter by once more connecting the future calling to glory and the present experience of suffering: "And after you have suffered a little while, the God of all grace, who has called you to his eternal glory in Christ, will himself restore, confirm, strengthen, and establish you" (1 Pet. 5:10).

Revelation

The book of Revelation by John the Seer is often seen as a mysterious guidebook to future events, but its primary purpose was to encourage those who were facing various pressures not to compromise their Christian faith. Some, like the Christians in Smyrna (Rev. 2:9–10) were, or would soon be, suffering for Christ, possibly even to the point of death (cf. 13:9–10). John reminds them that Jesus will ultimately prevail, and indeed in some ways has already prevailed, and that those who stay firm in the severest persecution will receive the "crown of life" (cf. James 1:12). In common with 1 Peter, John sees the suffering of believers as the last vicious throes of Satan as he attempts again and again to destroy the people of God (Rev. 12:13), though in Revelation Satan's efforts are as much by way of deceit and falsehood within the people of God as by direct persecution from the outside world. John presents a series of visions that go deeper into what is really going on when we see the church being tried and suffering. While there are several different ways of understanding the whole of Revelation, this is not the context for dealing with them. However, whatever one's view of the structure and meaning of the specific symbols of Revelation, some things are clear, particularly with regard to suffering.

First, the suffering of God's people is temporary. The "eschatological reversal" begun in the resurrection of Jesus will be totally implemented, and God will wipe every tear from the eyes of those who have suffered in his name (Rev. 7:17; 21:4). Hence those who are suffering and poverty-stricken now, like the church in Smyrna, should recognize that they are actually rich (cf. James 2:5). On the other hand, those who think they are rich, like the church in Laodicea (Rev. 3:17) are actually poor, and their so-called riches will be short-lived.

Second, suffering now is a reminder of the reality of eschatological justice. One day suffering will be returned upon the heads of those who are now causing God's people to suffer—whether that be other humans or, more significantly, Satan and his angels, they will be cast into the lake of fire (Rev. 19:20; 20:10, 14). Those who have suffered, even those who have been killed for their faith, will therefore be "given a white robe and told to rest a little longer, until the number of their fellow servants and their brothers should be complete, who were to be killed as they themselves had been" (6:11).

Third, suffering is a "test," an opportunity for the believer to endure and become "one who conquers" (*ho nikōn*, to whom is given a promise at the end of each of the seven letters in chapters 2 and 3) by resisting the Devil, overcoming by persevering in the midst of false teaching and persecution. Revelation shares the notion of Jesus and 1 Peter that the suffering of God's people, as well as false religion, have their origins in demonic scheming. In Revelation 2:10 it is the Devil who is "about to throw some of you into prison, that you may be tested." Of course, the suffering of God's people is not the only evil Satan is responsible for—much more important is his authorship of deceit and his leading so many people astray (Rev. 12:9)—but even his deceit fosters the oppression of the faithful. Hence God's ultimate solution to suffering lies in his final destruction of Satan (20:10).

Fourth, at least some suffering is, as in Hebrews, the Lord's discipline: "Those whom I love, I reprove and discipline" (Rev. 3:19). The "great tribulation" can therefore be seen as a positive discipline that leads to salvation: "These are the ones coming out of the great tribulation. They have washed their robes and made them white in the blood of the Lamb" (7:14). But the great tribulation can be seen also as a negative discipline to punish a church for consorting with false teaching and thus lead it to repentance: "Behold, I will throw her [the false prophetess "Jezebel"] onto a sickbed, and those who commit adultery with her I will throw into great tribulation, unless they repent of her works" (2:22).

Fifth, Christians are called to suffer because that is the pattern of the "slaughtered Lamb" or "the Lamb who was slain" (e.g., Rev. 5:6, 12). The Lamb has become victorious over Satan and worthy of praise because it suffered unto death (5:9). Therefore the people that belong to the Lamb may also expect to suffer under the power that the Devil and his angels deploy, for belonging to the kingdom of Jesus means sharing in his tribulation (1:9). But those who do share in Jesus' tribulation also share in the Lamb's victory because "they loved not their lives even unto death" (12:11).

Finally, the reward for persevering in suffering to the end is glory, glory unimaginable, glory so overwhelming that John in Revelation 20 and 21 can only describe it in fantastic pictures, borrowing from the language of Isaiah and Ezekiel, who themselves were having to search for words to describe what they saw. The conclusion then—and not only for Revelation but for Acts to the end of the New Testament—is that the suffering that God's people now endure is not pointless, nor is it endless. But the glories that come after never end. Even as Paul said in Romans 8:18, "Our present sufferings are not worth comparing with the glory that will be revealed in us" (NIV).

6

SUFFERING AND THE BIBLICAL STORY

CHRISTOPHER W. MORGAN
AND ROBERT A. PETERSON

The last four chapters have examined what many Old and New Testament passages say about suffering. In this chapter we will build on the insights of the preceding ones and look at suffering from a wider angle, particularly from the Bible's overall plotline of creation, fall, redemption, and consummation.

Creation and Suffering

The story of the Bible begins: "In the beginning, God created the heavens and the earth" (Gen. 1:1). God, already in existence prior to matter, space, or time, created the universe and all that exists. He is the eternal, self-existent, uncreated Creator. Bruce Waltke introduces Genesis 1:1–2:3:

> The creation account is a highly sophisticated presentation, designed to emphasize the sublimity (power, majesty, and wisdom) of the Creator God and to lay the foundation for the worldview of the covenant community.
>
> Creation is divided into six days or "panels," each following a basic process of creation. The key words—"said," "separated," "called," "saw," "good"—as actions of God emphasize his omnipotent and omniscient presence in cre-

ation. The process of creation typically follows a pattern of announcement, commandment, separation, report, naming, evaluation, and chronological framework.[1]

The chief character in the creation account is God (*elohim*), who "creates, says, sees, separates, names, makes, appoints, blesses, finishes, makes holy, and rests."[2] God is the transcendent Creator who creates the totality of that which exists. He transforms the initially unformed, empty, dark, and watery cosmos into something good—carefully crafted, filled, and blessed with light and land. God creates out of nothing, tames the chaos, forms it according to his purposes, and fills it with plants and animals. The account makes it clear that the God of Israel is not like others in the ancient Near East. Gordon Wenham observes: "God is without peer and competitor. He does not have to establish his power in struggle with other members of a polytheistic pantheon. The sun and moon are his handiwork, not his rivals."[3] The true God is not the sky, sun, moon, land, water, trees, animals, human, or anything else created; God created them, and they are subject to him. The creation is neither God nor a part of God; he is absolute and has independent existence, and creation has derived existence from him and continually depends on him as its sustainer (cf. Acts 17:25–28).

The transcendent Creator is depicted as sovereign. He possesses amazing authority and power, like a human king, only infinitely greater. By his very word, he brings things into being (Gen. 1:3; cf. Heb. 11:3). He displays his authority over all creation by his calling and naming the elements (Gen. 1:5).

Although many would not automatically think of a transcendent, sovereign, *and* personal Creator, this rare combination in a deity is exactly how the creation account describes God.[4] On each day God is personally involved in every detail of the creation, crafting it in a way that pleases him and benefits his creatures. In a dramatic fashion, on the sixth day, he personally created man in his own image, breathing life into him. The personal God has made us personal as well, with the ability to relate to him, live in community with one another, and have dominion over creation. As D. A. Carson reminds, "We are accorded with an astonishing dignity" and have

1. Bruce K. Waltke, *Genesis: A Commentary* (Grand Rapids, MI: Zondervan, 2001), 56.
2. C. John Collins, *Genesis 1–4: A Linguistic, Literary, and Theological Commentary* (Phillipsburg, NJ: P&R, 2006), 71.
3. Gordon J. Wenham, *Genesis 1–15*. Word Biblical Commentary (Waco: Word, 1987), 37–38.
4. D. A. Carson, *The Gagging of God: Christianity Confronts Pluralism* (Grand Rapids, MI: Zondervan, 1996), 223.

"implanted within us a profound capacity for knowing God intimately."[5] By creating us in his image, God distinguishes us from the rest of creation and establishes that he is distinct from us—we are not gods, but creatures made in his image.

Genesis 1 also stresses God's goodness, which is reflected in the goodness of his creation and reinforced in the steady refrain, "And God saw that it was good" (1:4, 10, 12, 18, 21, 25). On the sixth day creation is even described as "very good" (1:31). The inherent goodness of creation leaves no room for a fundamental dualism between spirit and matter such that spirit is good and matter is bad. Indeed material creation reflects God's goodness, which is also evident in his generous provisions of light, land, vegetation, animals, fish, birds, livestock, and even "creeping" things. These are blessings given for humanity's benefit, as are the ability to relate to God, fertility to procreate, and authority to use the abundant provisions for their good.

Although creation reaches its summit in God creating man in his image, Genesis 1:1–2:3 culminates in the resting of God. On the seventh day, God finishes his creative work, rests, and blesses and sanctifies the day as holy, as a Sabbath to be kept. In doing so, God displays his joy and satisfaction in his creation and his celebration of completion, and he commemorates this special event so that his people would remember that "God, by his powerful Word, transforms the chaos into a holy and blessed creation."[6]

Whereas Genesis 1:1–2:3 centers on God's creation of the world in six days and the inauguration of the Sabbath, Genesis 2:4–25 focuses on God's formation of man and woman and his provision of the garden of Eden as a place [for them] to live and work.[7] Or as Allen Ross summarizes, "God has prepared human beings, male and female, with the spiritual capacity and communal assistance to serve him and to keep his commands so that they might live and enjoy the bounty of his creation."[8]

This section commences with Genesis's typical structural introduction: "These are the generations of" (2:4) but atypically references God as "the Lord God." Wenham notes:

> Usually one or the other name is used, but here the two are combined, suggesting no doubt that this story reveals both God's character as sovereign creator of the universe (God) and his intimate covenant-like relationship with mankind (the Lord).

5. Ibid., 205.
6. Allen P. Ross, *Creation and Blessing: A Guide to the Study and Exposition of Genesis* (Grand Rapids, MI: Baker, 1996), 114.
7. Collins, *Genesis 1–4*, 39, 101.
8. Ross, *Creation and Blessing*, 127.

Both traits are prominent in the first scene (2:5–17) which shows the LORD God creating man and a perfect environment for him. It discloses God's sovereignty over man his creature and his loving concern for his well-being.[9]

In Genesis 2:4–19, "the LORD God" is "the sole actor, as he forms the man, plants the garden, transports man there, sets up the terms of a relationship with man, and searches for a helper fit for the man, which culminates in the woman."[10] Man is formed from the dust of the ground but is more than dust—his life comes directly from the very breath of God (2:7)! In planting the garden and moving man there, the Creator and covenant Lord provides a delightful and sacred space for humans to enjoy a harmonious and intimate relationship with him, each other, the animals, and the land. Waltke observes, "The Garden of Eden is a temple-garden, represented later in the tabernacle."[11] As such the garden highlights God's presence with man.

Living in God's presence comes with strings attached, however. God displays his sovereignty and holiness by demanding obedience to his will and commands. He establishes the terms for living in his presence and graciously puts forward only one prohibition: man shall not eat from the tree of the knowledge of good and evil. Contrary to what might be expected, man is allowed to eat of the Tree of Life, which confers immortality, but not the Tree of the Knowledge of Good and Evil, which gives access to wisdom, "for that leads to human autonomy and an independence of the creator incompatible with the trustful relationship between man and his maker which the story presupposes."[12] Because God's generosity to man is so abundant, his prohibition would not seem to be difficult to accept.

God's generosity to Adam is further depicted as he notices that "it is not good that the man should be alone" and meets man's need by creating woman as a complementary and intimate companion united with him for life together. Chapter 2 of Genesis ends happily and, given the beliefs of ancient Israel, surprisingly: "And the man and his wife were both naked and not ashamed." In the garden, nakedness is not reason for shame, but points to their innocence and the pristine delight they have in each other.[13]

At first glance, one might conclude that this first epoch of the biblical story has little to contribute to our understanding of suffering. After all, suffering is not even mentioned. Ah, but that silence speaks volumes!

9. Wenham, *Genesis 1–15*, 87.
10. Collins, *Genesis 1–4*, 132.
11. Waltke, *Genesis*, 85.
12. Wenham, *Genesis 1–15*, 87.
13. Ibid., 88; Collins, *Genesis 1–4*, 139.

Understanding Genesis's teaching about God's creation sheds light on our understanding of suffering in two important and related ways. First, we discover that suffering is not something created or authored by God. Rather, God created a good universe and good human beings. Second, we learn that there was a time when there was no suffering. Suffering is not original; it has not always existed.

Suffering Is Not Created by God

As we have seen, Genesis 1–2 shows the Creator to be transcendent, sovereign, personal, immanent, and *good*. God's goodness is displayed in his turning the chaos into something good—the heavens and the earth. His goodness is even more clearly reflected in the goodness of his creation, evidenced by the steady refrain, "And God saw that it was good" (1:4, 10, 12, 18, 21, 25), a goodness accentuated on the sixth day: "Behold, it was very good" (1:31). God's generous provisions of light, land, vegetation, and animals are blessings given for man's benefit, as are the abilities to know God, work, marry, and procreate. God blesses man with the Sabbath, places him in the delightful garden of Eden, gives him a helper, and establishes only one prohibition, given not to squelch man but to promote his welfare.

The conclusion is clear: God is good and did not create suffering or evil. He created a good world for the good of his creatures. Humans too were created good and blessed beyond measure, being made in God's image, with an unhindered relationship with God and with freedom. As a result, casting blame for suffering on the good and generous God is unbiblical and unfounded.

Suffering Has Not Always Existed

A related but distinct principle we learn from the biblical account of creation is that suffering has not always existed. From a theological standpoint, God's creation of the universe out of nothing shows that he alone is independent, absolute, and eternal. Everything else has been created. Further, the inherent goodness of creation precludes a fundamental dualism between spirit and matter. Contrary to some philosophical and religious traditions, the Bible teaches that matter is a part of God's creation and is good.

From a historical standpoint, the story of creation unmistakably recounts that there was a time when there was no suffering. Suffering is not original. Indeed, the very fact that our world now includes suffering testifies that it is not now the way it was, and therefore, as Cornelius Plantinga helpfully states, "It is not the way it is supposed to be."[14]

14. Cornelius Plantinga Jr., *Not the Way It's Supposed to Be: A Breviary of Sin* (Grand Rapids, MI: Eerdmans, 1995), 2.

The Fall and Suffering

We know from the biblical account of creation that suffering is not created by God and that there was a time when there was no suffering. We also know from experience, however, that evil exists and suffering occurs. The world is now not the way it was, and it is no longer the way it is supposed to be. What went wrong?

In a nutshell, "the fall" happened. Carson observes:

> The Bible begins with God creating the heavens and the earth (Gen. 1–2). Repeatedly, God's verdict is that all of his handiwork is "very good." There is no sin and no suffering. The garden of Eden brings forth food without the sweat of toil being mixed into the earth. But the first human rebellion (Gen. 3) marks the onset of suffering, toil, pain, and death. A mere two chapters later, we read the endlessly repeated and hauntingly pitiful refrain, "then he died . . . then he died . . . then he died . . . then he died."[15]

We saw from Genesis 1–2 that God creates Adam and Eve in his image, as good, and with wonderful privileges and significant responsibilities in the garden of Eden. They experience an unhindered relationship with God, intimate enjoyment of each other, and delegated authority over creation. They are given only one prohibition: they must not eat of the Tree of the Knowledge of Good and Evil.

Sadly, Genesis 3 informs us that they do not obey God's command but "fall." The account begins with a tempter who calls into question God's truthfulness, sovereignty, and goodness. The tempter is "crafty" and deflects the woman's attention from the covenantal relationship God has established, as Collins points out:

> It is interesting to note that, though the deity throughout Genesis 2:4–3:24 is "the LORD God," the serpent only calls him "God," and he and the woman use only that title in their conversation (3:1b–5). Now, as many have observed, the name God designates the deity in his role of Cosmic Creator and Ruler (its use in 1:1–2:3), while "the LORD" ("Yahweh") is particularly his name as he enters into covenantal relationship with human beings. By dropping the covenant name, then, the serpent is probably advancing his program of temptation by diverting the woman's attention from the relationship the Lord has established. The woman's use of it shows that she is trapped, and we begin to have a clue as how she could be led into disobedience by forgetting the covenant.[16]

15. Carson, *How Long, O Lord? Reflections on Suffering and Evil* (Grand Rapids, MI: Baker Academic, 1991), 41.
16. Collins, *Genesis 1–4*, 171.

In verses 6–8, the central scene in the story of the fall reaches its climax. The fatal sequence is described rapidly in 3:6: "she saw," "she took," "she ate," "she gave," and culminates in "he ate." Wenham observes that the midpoint of 3:6–8, "and he ate," employs the key verb of the narrative—*eat*—and is placed between the woman's inflated expectations in eating (good to eat, delight to the eyes, and giving insight) and the actual effects: eyes opened, knowing they were nude, and hiding in the trees.[17] The contrast is striking: the forbidden fruit did not deliver what the tempter promised but brought new and dark realities warned of by the good and truthful covenant Lord.

Allen Ross notes that this initial act of human rebellion brings divine justice: "The oracles thus all reflect talionic justice: they sinned by eating, and so would suffer to eat; she led her husband to sin, and so would be mastered by him; they brought pain into the world by their disobedience, and so would have painful toil in their respective lives."[18] The effects, though appropriate, are devastating.[19] The couple immediately feels shame, realizing they are naked (3:7). They sense their estrangement from God, even foolishly trying to hide from him (3:8–10). They are afraid of God and how he might respond (3:9–10). Their alienation from each other also emerges as they begin the pastime of "passing the buck"; the woman blames the serpent, the man blames the woman, and by intimation even God (3:10–13)! Pain and sorrow also ensue. The woman experiences pain in childbirth, the man toils in trying to grow food in a land with pests and weeds, and both discover dissonance in their relationship (3:15–19). Even worse, the couple is banished from Eden and God's glorious presence (3:22–24).

How they wish they would have listened to God's warning: if you eat of the Tree of the Knowledge of Good and Evil, "you shall surely die" (2:17)! And die they did. Upon eating the forbidden fruit, they do not immediately

---

17. Wenham, *Genesis 1–15*, 75.

18. Ross, *Creation and Blessing*, 148. C. John Collins (*Genesis 1–4*, 169) is also helpful: "There are small ironic wordplays in this pericope, some of which can be obscured in English versions. For example, in Genesis 3:5 the serpent promises that the humans' eyes will be *opened* and they will *know* something, while in verse 7 it is fulfilled: their eyes were *opened* and they *knew* something—but it was just that they were naked! Since they already knew that in 2:25 (and knew it blissfully), we may conclude that their dispositional stance toward that knowledge is different, as becomes obvious right away when they try to cover themselves. Similarly, there is a play between the use of the root *r-b-h* in 3:16 ("I will surely *multiply* your pain in childbearing") and its use in the commission of 1:28 ("Be fruitful and *multiply*"). Whereas procreation had previously been the sphere of blessing, now it is to be the area of pain and danger" (italics his).

19. For more on the effects of sin on the sinner's relationship to God, himself, and others, see Millard J. Erickson, *Christian Theology* (Grand Rapids, MI: Baker, 1985), 601–19.

fall over and die from something like cardiac arrest. Yet they died spiritually, and their bodies also began to experience gradual decay that ultimately led to their physical deaths (as God predicts: "to dust you shall return"; 3:19).

Most devastating of all is that these consequences did not only befall Adam and Eve but extend to their descendents as well. Robert Pyne describes the scene:

> Standing together east of Eden [Adam and Eve] each felt alone—betrayed by the other, alienated from God, and confused about how it had all come apart so quickly. . . .
>
> The children were all born outside of Eden. . . . None of them ever saw the tree of life or had a chance to taste or reject the forbidden fruit. At the same time, none of them enjoyed marriage relationships without some degree of rivalry or resentment, and they inevitably ate bread produced by the sweat of their brow. Born in a fallen world, they knew only the curse, never Eden. Still they knew that this was not the way life was supposed to be. . . .
>
> Adam and Even sinned alone, but they were not the only ones locked out of the Garden. Cut off from the tree of life, they and their descendents were all destined to die.[20]

In sum, sin disrupted their relationship to God, to each other, and to creation. Even more, although sin originated in the garden, it did not stay there. Its contaminating effects spread to all people.

The biblical account of the fall helps us understand suffering in three important ways. First, we see that suffering is a consequence of sin. Second, we learn that suffering is not natural to God's good creation but is an intruder. Third, we realize that suffering contains an element of mystery.

Suffering Is a Consequence of the Fall
God is the author of neither sin nor suffering. He creates a good world and good human beings who reflect his goodness. Henri Blocher wisely warns, "We cannot be too radical here. The perfect goodness of God's creation rules out the tiniest root, seed, or germ of evil."[21] Suffering is not a part of God's creation but rather a byproduct of sin, as Carson states so clearly:

20. Robert A. Pyne, *Humanity and Sin.* Swindoll Leadership Library (Dallas: Word, 1999), 162.
21. Henri Blocher, *Original Sin: Illuminating the Riddle. New Studies in Biblical Theology* (Grand Rapids, MI: Eerdmans, 1997), 56.

Between the beginning and the end of the Bible, there is evil and there is suffering. But the point to be observed is that from the perspective of the Bible's large-scale story line, the two are profoundly related: evil is the primal cause of suffering, rebellion is the root of pain, sin is the source of death.[22]

Genesis 3 makes it clear that as sin enters through Adam so do its consequences—estrangement from God, shame, alienation from others, suffering, banishment, and death. Paul in Romans 5:12–21 confirms this: sin entered the world through one man's sin, and condemnation and death through sin.

On a cosmic scale, therefore, all suffering is an effect of the fall.[23] Indeed, because we live in this fallen world, we will suffer and "reap sin's consequences in the home, the workplace, and the cemetery."[24]

Suffering Is an Intruder

As a consequence of sin, suffering is also an intruder into God's good creation. Michael Williams observes: "By beginning with the story of creation rather than the Fall, Scripture proclaims categorically that sin is an intruder. It is not the product of God's creativity. It does not belong."[25] Sin is not the only intruder, but its evil children—suffering and death—have intruded as well.

We intuitively know this but often do not consider its significance. When we encounter suffering, something inside us often cries out: "This is wrong! The world should not be like this! Children should not be abused, senior adults should not get Alzheimer's, missionaries should not be tortured!" Or on a more personal level we might protest: "Why me? What did I do to deserve this?" Such instincts are valid because they recognize that this world is not the way it is supposed to be. We know this when we consider sin; we know to hate rape, murder, bigotry, and child abuse. We oppose sin and refuse to be at ease with it. In the same way, we are not to be comfortable with the reality of suffering, although we are to be at peace with God in the midst of it, and should do our best to alleviate it.[26] Like sin, suffering is an intruder and cannot be welcomed as

22. Carson, *How Long, O Lord?* 42.
23. This is not to suggest that particular instances of suffering can be or should be traced back to particular sins. In some cases, that is possible, but in other instances it is unfounded. The point is that all suffering results from Adam's sin.
24. Pyne, *Humanity and Sin*, 160.
25. Michael D. Williams, *Far as the Curse Is Found: The Covenant Story of Redemption* (Phillipsburg, NJ: P&R, 2005), 64.
26. For more on this theme, see William Edgar's essay on oppression on pages 165–82 of this volume.

natural.[27] The horror of suffering's intrusion points to the horror of sin, its fundamental source.

Suffering Is Mysterious

Suffering is not only a consequence of sin and an intruder, but it is also mysterious. Theologians speak of "the riddle of sin." For example, Anthony Hoekema asserts:

> The fact that we can discern these stages in the temptation and fall of our
> first parents, however, does not mean that we have in the Genesis narrative
> an explanation for the entrance of sin into the human world. What we have
> here is the biblical narrative of the origin of sin, but not an explanation for
> that origin. One of the most important things we must remember about
> sin . . . is that it is inexplicable. The origin of evil is . . . one of the greatest
> riddles of life.[28]

The riddle centers on the question: why would Adam and Eve sin? Augustine helpfully taught that Adam was able not to sin and able to sin, so that there was an inherent possibility to sin in him. We agree, but as Hoekema advises: "How this possibility became actuality is a mystery that we shall never be able to fathom. We shall never know how doubt first arose in Eve's mind. We shall never understand how a person who had been created in a state of rectitude, in a state of sinlessness, could begin to sin."[29]

The difficulty remains: "How could a sinless will begin to will sinfully?"[30] Adam and Eve were created good and did not initially have a corrupt heart to lead them astray. They had a close relationship with the Lord, enjoyed intimacy with each other, and retained authority over creation. It would seem that they had everything in Eden they could possibly want; they lived, after all, in paradise! Collins notes:

> In 3:6, as [the woman] regards the tree and sees that it is "good for food, a
> delight to the eyes, and desirable for giving insight," the irony of the parallel
> with 2:9 (there was already "every tree desirable to the sight and good for
> food" in the garden) should not escape us. She already had everything she

---

27. It is important to coordinate the emphasis on the intrusion of suffering with a robust view of God's sovereignty. The fall does not fall outside God's design for history.
28. Anthony A. Hoekema, *Created in God's Image* (Grand Rapids, MI: Eerdmans, 1986), 130–31.
29. Ibid., 131.
30. Ibid.

could possibly want, and she even had the resources to get everything she thought the tree had to offer.[31]

The first couple had everything they could ever want, and yet history records that, in unfaithfulness to God and disobedience to his one prohibition, they threw it all away for a piece of fruit! How absurd! As Augustine noted, trying to determine reasons for such foolishness is like trying to see darkness or hear silence. Or as Cornelius Plantinga describes, sin is like sawing off a branch that supports us—it cuts us off from our only help.[32] We cannot make sense out of such folly or find clear-cut explanations for the irrationality of this Original Sin.[33]

If the origin of evil is one of the greatest mysteries of life, then it should come as no surprise that the existence of its byproduct—suffering—likewise remains a mystery. Paul's words "now I know in part" (1 Cor. 13:12; see also v. 9) show that for at least some matters even apostolic revelation is partial; and suffering is one of those matters. God has revealed much about suffering (and hence this book!), but our knowledge is limited, and some mystery concerning suffering will remain.[34]

While its source, nature, extent, and effects are themselves enigmatic enough, the primary mystery related to suffering concerns how and why a sovereign and good God chooses to decree/permit suffering in general, as well as to distribute it so seemingly inequitably. We know that sin, suffering, and death are results of the fall, but if God is sovereign, why would he do it this way? And why do some seem to live in relative ease while others are consistently pounded with heavy blows? And why does this particular circumstance happen to this person—or worse, to me or my family? At its core, this aspect of the mystery of suffering is really the mystery of providence: why does God run his universe the way he does?[35]

Scripture's account of the fall tells us that sin and its corollaries suffering and death are not created by God; they do not belong. Yet through the rebellion of Adam, they have intruded. The world is not the way it was, but thankfully, as Genesis 3:15 hints and the rest of the Bible makes

31. Collins, *Genesis 1–4*, 172.
32. Plantinga, *Not the Way It's Supposed to Be*, 123.
33. Not everything about sin is mysterious, however, and sometimes theologians too quickly appeal to mystery. For a helpful response to such approaches, see Blocher, *Original Sin*, 107–9.
34. Carl F. H. Henry, *God, Revelation, and Authority* (Waco: Word, 1976–1983; repr., Wheaton, IL: Crossway Books, 1999), 6:302.
35. After Job raises this and other questions to God, God turns the tables and poses the question back to Job (see Job 38:1–41:34), asking essentially: Do you know enough to run the world? Do you really believe you have some insights to offer me on how to guide history? Job learned that God's providence is good, sovereign, wise, and mysterious.

increasingly clear, the world will not always be this way. In this interval between God's initial good creation and final re-creation, sin, suffering, and death exist. But somehow the good, sovereign God guides history in such a way that he plans that evil occurs and even utilizes it to bring about his intended purposes for creation. He plans it, guides it, restrains it, and uses it.[36] In doing so, he will glorify himself and benefit his creatures. So suffering may be mysterious, but it is not utterly pointless. A biblical view of the providence of God "affirms that all things ultimately have purpose, even evil acts which appear to be completely senseless."[37]

Christ's Redemption and Suffering

Sin and suffering, then, were not parts of God's original good creation, but intruded into the scene as a result of Adam's fall. Admittedly, there is great mystery here. But no greater mystery than that surrounding God's remedy for sin and suffering. Nothing less was involved than the Creator's becoming one of his creatures so he could suffer and die for them that he might overcome sin and suffering forever.

Christ's life was marked by suffering. Hundreds of years before his birth, Isaiah predicted that he would be "a man of sorrows, and acquainted with grief" (Isa. 53:3). And so he was. It is for good reason that theologians have designated the period of time from his birth to his burial as "the state of humiliation." After his baptism, "the Spirit immediately drove him out into the wilderness" (Mark 1:12), where he fasted forty days and was tempted by Satan. In response to a scribe's pledge to follow him, Jesus replied, "Foxes have holes, and birds of the air have nests, but the Son of Man has nowhere to lay his head" (Matt. 8:20). At that time the Lord of all and Savior of the world was a homeless person.

Sorrow assailed the Son of God from all directions. Did the leaders of the covenant people whom he came to redeem humbly receive his ministry of grace and truth? To the contrary, they opposed him from the beginning (Mark 2:6–7), claimed that he cast out demons by "Beelzebul, the prince of demons" (Matt. 12:24), rejected his teaching (John 7:47–49), and resolved to put him to death (John 11:53).

Sadly, his heart was also broken by his closest followers. The twelve never seemed to understand his purposes (John 11:16; 14:8) and they found his parables opaque (Matt. 13:10, 36). Their lack of confidence in his ability

36. See Erickson, *Christian Theology*, 387–432.
37. Pyne, *Humanity and Sin*, 203.

to protect them provoked him to say: "Why are you afraid, O you of little faith?" (Matt. 8:26).

When he predicted that he "must suffer many things and be rejected by the elders and the chief priests" (Mark 8:31), die, and rise again, they would not believe him. Instead, immediately after hearing his prediction, two of his innermost circle and their mother asked for the best places in his coming kingdom, and the rest were indignant at them (Matt. 20:20–21, 24). Once, his follower with the greatest leadership abilities rebuked him for speaking of going to the cross at all (Matt. 16:22)! Clearly, his disciples generally were not a source of comfort to him. Rather, they increased his sorrow, so that he exclaimed in frustration: "O faithless and twisted generation, how long am I to be with you? How long am I to bear with you?" (Matt. 17:17).

But his worst suffering still lay ahead. He agonized in the garden of Gethsemane as he contemplated drinking the cup of God's wrath for sinners: "My soul is very sorrowful, even to death" (Matt. 26:38). One of the twelve betrayed him to a terrible fate (Matt. 26:47–50). Some Christians picture a divine Jesus who was not really human and therefore above suffering. The real Jesus was certainly divine but took to himself genuine humanity, so that: "In the days of his flesh, Jesus offered up prayers and supplications, with loud cries and tears, to him who was able to save him from death, and he was heard because of his reverence. Although he was a son, he learned obedience through what he suffered" (Heb. 5:7–8). How was he heard by the Father? Not by being spared the cross, but by being raised from the dead.

The epitome of Christ's sufferings lies in his arrest, sham trials, beatings, mocking, scourging, crucifixion, more mocking, death, and burial. Succinctly Peter sums up all of this as "the sufferings of Christ" (1 Pet. 1:11; 5:1) or by the words "Christ suffered" (2:21, 23; 3:18; 4:1). Indeed, he did.

The great news, however, is that God raised him from the dead, and thereby routed all of our enemies, including the Devil, sin, hell, the world, the grave, and suffering itself. Because Jesus the victor lives triumphant, a day is coming when "death shall be no more, neither shall there be mourning, nor crying, nor pain anymore" (Rev. 21:4).

Although Jesus' resurrection put an end to his suffering, it did not end his ministry. In all four Gospels, John the Baptist predicts that the Messiah (the Anointed One) will baptize people with the Holy Spirit (Matt. 3:11; Mark 1:8; Luke 3:16; John 1:33). But Jesus does not do this in any of the Gospels. Instead, he reminds his followers of John's prophecy in Acts 1:5 and fulfills it in Acts 2, when he pours out the Holy Spirit upon the church.

Jesus' story contributes to our understanding of suffering in at least three ways.

Christ's Suffering Saves Us Forever

Paul summarizes the saving message that he preaches in 1 Corinthians 15:3–4: "For I delivered to you as of first importance what I also received: that Christ died for our sins in accordance with the Scriptures, that he was buried, that he was raised on the third day in accordance with the Scriptures." As we saw above, the fact that Christ died for our sins meant terrible suffering for him. Peter underscores the redemptive character of that suffering: "For Christ also suffered once for sins, the righteous for the unrighteous, that he might bring us to God" (1 Pet. 3:18).

But the author who most emphasizes it is the writer to the Hebrews. Christ came to rescue the sons and daughters of fallen Adam through the suffering of death. "We see him who for a little while was made lower than the angels, namely Jesus, crowned with glory and honor because of the suffering of death, so that by the grace of God he might taste death for everyone" (Heb. 2:9). If Christ were like the Old Testament priests who repeated the same sacrifices, "then he would have had to suffer repeatedly since the foundation of the world. But as it is, he has appeared once for all at the end of the ages to put away sin by the sacrifice of himself" (Heb. 9:26). The unique suffering of our Great High Priest, Jesus, who offered himself in sacrifice, both propitiates God's wrath and expiates our sins (Heb. 2:17; 9:26). As a result, "by a single offering he has perfected for all time those who are being sanctified" (Heb. 10:14).

Christ's suffering unto death constituted a single priestly offering to God, an offering that he presented in heaven by sitting at God's right hand after his resurrection and ascension. This offering was finished, perfect, and therefore effective to save completely all who come to God through him (Heb. 1:3; 7:24–25; 10:12–14). As a result, his blood, his violent death, purifies his people: "So Jesus also suffered outside the gate in order to sanctify the people through his own blood" (Heb. 13:12). Moreover, he continues his high priestly ministry by interceding for his own, granting them grace to aid them: "For because he himself has suffered when tempted, he is able to help those who are being tempted" (Heb. 2:18; see also 4:14–16).

In Christ's suffering on the cross divine love and justice meet. The cross is the supreme manifestation of God's love for sinners. Rarely will a human being give his or her life for another and then only for a friend; no one would die for an enemy, "but God shows his love for us in that while we were still sinners, Christ died for us" (Rom. 5:8). To define love, the biblical starting point is not below but above: "In this is love, not that we have loved God but that he loved us and sent his Son to be the propitiation for our sins" (1 John 4:10).

The cross also displays the justice of God as nothing else. The Old Testament sacrifices depicted the gospel but did not really put away sin. Rather, in his mercy God forgave Old Testament believers on the basis of the work of Christ that was still future. In that way, "he had passed over former sins" (Rom. 3:25). When Christ died on the cross, however, God definitively dealt with sin by putting him "forward as a propitiation by his blood" (v. 25). God satisfied his wrath by giving Christ to die, "to show his righteousness at the present time, so that he might be just and the justifier of the one who has faith in Jesus" (v. 26).[38] The cross is thus the supreme revelation of both God's love and justice.

Christ's Suffering Drives the Christian Life

The nexus between Christ's suffering and ours is our spiritual union with him brought about by the Holy Spirit. Although Christ accomplished the work of salvation in the first century, his work does not benefit us until we are united to him. Calvin said it famously: "As long as Christ remains outside of us, and we are separated from him, all that he has suffered and done for the salvation of the human race remains useless and of no value for us."[39] But because Jesus has fulfilled his office as the One anointed with the Holy Spirit par excellence ("the Christ") by pouring out that Spirit upon the church, Christ does not remain outside of us. Rather, the Spirit has joined us to him, our Savior and living head, for that is the Spirit's main ministry (1 Cor. 12:13; Rom. 8:9). As a result we are no longer "separated from Christ . . . having no hope and without God in the world. But now in Christ Jesus [we] have been brought near by the blood of Christ" (Eph. 2:12–13).

The words "in Christ Jesus" are Paul's favorite way of indicating union with Christ. No longer are we apart from him; henceforth we are "in him," spiritually joined to him so that all of his saving benefits become ours. We died with him so that the stranglehold of sin's power over us was broken (Rom. 6:2, 6–11); we have been raised with him to newness of spiritual life now and in the future bodily resurrection (Rom. 6:4–5).

Through union with Christ we have a share in his sufferings. When believers suffer communally now "the Father of mercies and God of all comfort"

---

38. For a defense of the traditional Reformational understanding of propitiation, see D. A. Carson, "Atonement in Romans 3:21–26," in *The Glory of the Atonement*, ed. Charles E. Hill and Frank A. James III (Downers Grove, IL: InterVarsity, 2004), 119–39.
39. *Institutes* 3.1.1. McNeill/Battles 1:537.

gives them great comfort (2 Cor. 1:3). As he comforts them in their affliction, he equips them to share that comfort with others who are afflicted. Here is the Pauline principle: "For as we share abundantly in Christ's sufferings, so through Christ we share abundantly in comfort too" (2 Cor. 1:5).

Our union with Christ defines and embraces our whole existence. That is why Paul can say: "It is no longer I who live, but Christ who lives in me" (Gal. 2:20). Believers are so united to Christ that he lives in them. And that is why John writes: "Blessed are the dead who die in the Lord from now on" (Rev. 14:13). Even death does not separate us from Christ, for we die in union with our Lord Jesus.

After many years of walking with Christ, Paul expresses his life's goal, "that I may know him and the power of his resurrection, and may share his sufferings, becoming like him in his death" (Phil. 3:10). Because Jesus died and arose, true believers are joined to his death and resurrection. We are God's children and heirs, Paul teaches, "provided we suffer with him in order that we may also be glorified with him" (Rom. 8:17). Thus our suffering with Christ assures us of present sonship and of sharing future glory with him.

God uses our suffering with Christ as a means to bring us to maturity in grace and holiness (Rom. 5:3–4; James 1:2–4; 1 Pet. 5:12–19). Even as we struggle, God reminds us, "My grace is sufficient for you, for my power is made perfect in weakness" (2 Cor. 12:9; cf. 1 Cor. 10:13). In fact, God's allowing his children to endure the discipline of suffering is a sign of his love for them and a means to teach them holiness and contentment (Heb. 12:3–11). Moreover, we follow Christ's example in suffering; he does not ask us to undergo something from which he shrank (Heb. 12:1–3; 1 Pet. 2:21–23; 4:1). He suffered to make us his children; we suffer because we are spiritually joined to him our Lord, Savior, and example.

We suffer with Christ in hope, joy, faith, and prayer. Present suffering handled in a godly manner produces endurance, character change, and hope, because seeing God at work in us now breeds hope for the unseen future (Rom. 5:4). Moreover, God grants us joy in suffering as the testing of our faith glorifies him (1 Pet. 1:6–7). Though Christ is at present invisible, we walk by faith and love him who first loved us. Thus, "though you do not now see him, you believe in him and rejoice with joy that is inexpressible and filled with glory" (v. 8).

Peter cautions his readers, when suffering, not to "repay evil for evil," but instead to bless. He then quotes Psalm 34, including: "For the eyes of the Lord are on the righteous, and his ears are open to their prayer" (1 Pet. 3:12). It is not difficult to understand that suffering for Christ drives us to him in prayer. God uses suffering providentially to remind us of our need for him and to draw us close to him.

Suffering for Christ also points us to future salvation, for, as we suffer, "we ourselves, who have the firstfruits of the Spirit, groan inwardly as we wait eagerly for adoption as sons, the redemption of our bodies" (Rom. 8:23).

Christ's Suffering Guarantees Our Future Glory

The Old Testament prophets predicted and Jesus himself confirms that the Christ had to suffer before entering into his glory (1 Pet. 1:11; Luke 24:26). Peter says much about Christians suffering. And he knows whereof he speaks because he writes as "a witness of the sufferings of Christ, as well as a partaker in the glory that is going to be revealed" (1 Pet. 5:1). He urges Christians not to shrink from suffering: "If you are insulted for the name of Christ, you are blessed, because the Spirit of glory and of God rests upon you" (1 Pet. 4:14). And again: "If anyone suffers as a Christian, let him not be ashamed, but let him glorify God in that name" (1 Pet. 4:16).

Peter explains his underlying confidence: "But rejoice insofar as you share Christ's sufferings, that you may also rejoice and be glad when his glory is revealed" (1 Pet. 4:13). As surely as we share in Jesus' sufferings now, we shall share in his glory then. That confidence is based on the excellence of Christ's saving work.

Speaking of his consecration as priest to sacrifice himself on the cross, Jesus prays: "And for their sake I consecrate myself, that they also may be sanctified in truth" (John 17:19). Jesus' offering of himself in death results in believers' being made holy. And this final holiness involves glory, because before his suffering on the cross, Jesus asked the Father to bring his people to heaven to be with him and see his glory (John 17:24).

How can we be sure of eventual glory? Because Jesus' "suffering of death" not only results in his being "crowned with glory and honor," but also results in God's "bringing many sons to glory" (Heb. 2:9–10). Jesus' suffering obtains future glory for believers. Therefore, as Hafemann reminds us: "Sin and sickness are not the last word! Suffering is the pathway toward the believer's final redemption."[40] It is to that final redemption that we now turn our attention.

The Consummation and Suffering

"The evil and suffering in this world are greater than any of us can comprehend. But evil and suffering are not ultimate. God is. Satan, the great lover

---

40. Scott J. Hafemann, *The God of Promise and the Life of Faith: Understanding the Heart of the Bible* (Wheaton, IL: Crossway Books, 2001), 128.

of evil and suffering, is not sovereign. God is," as John Piper reminds us.[41] It is time for us to consider what is ultimate, that is, God. And that brings us to the last act in the biblical story in which God's final resolution of the problem of suffering brings about believers' final salvation.

Suffering Will End: God's Final Resolution Will Be Great

God will triumph gloriously. Although Jesus accomplished all that was needed to vanquish sin and suffering in the first century, God's glorious victory will not be manifest until Jesus comes again. Isaiah predicted the newness and joy of that day: "For behold, I create new heavens and a new earth, and the former things shall not be remembered or come into mind. But be glad and rejoice forever in that which I create" (Isa. 65:17–18).

The new heavens and earth will be characterized by peace: "'The wolf and the lamb shall graze together; the lion shall eat straw like the ox, and dust shall be the serpent's food. They shall not hurt or destroy in all my holy mountain,' says the LORD" (Isa. 65:25).

Furthermore, God's glorious victory will be characterized by a universal knowledge and worship of God: "'The time is coming to gather all nations and tongues. And they shall come and shall see my glory. . . . And they shall declare my glory among the nations. . . . All flesh shall come to worship before me,' declares the LORD" (Isa. 66:18, 19, 23). Habakkuk is more succinct: "For the earth will be filled with the knowledge of the glory of the LORD as the waters cover the sea" (Hab. 2:14).

Romans 8 speaks of the groaning of creation, of believers, and of the Holy Spirit himself, as they long for the future day of deliverance (Rom. 8:22, 23, 26). That day will mean glory, freedom, and bodily redemption for the children of God (Rom. 8:18, 21, 23). It will mean deliverance for the creation too—for it will "be set free from its bondage to corruption and obtain the freedom of the glory of the children of God" (Rom. 8:21).

All of this is God's glorious victory for his creation and his people. But that victory will not be painless for all of humanity.

God will judge justly. For as the prophets foretold, on the Day of the Lord God will punish wickedness and exalt righteousness. And that means deliverance for believers but wrath for unbelievers.

> For behold, the day is coming, burning like an oven, when all the arrogant and all evildoers will be stubble. The day that is coming shall set them ablaze, says the LORD of hosts, so that it will leave them neither root or

---

41. John Piper and Justin Taylor, eds., *Suffering and the Sovereignty of God* (Wheaton, IL: Crossway Books, 2006), 29.

branch. But for you who fear my name, the sun of righteousness shall rise with healing in its wings. You shall go out leaping like calves from the stall. (Mal. 4:1–2)

Here Malachi contrasts the destruction of the wicked with the Christ ("the sun of righteousness") healing and blessing the righteous, whose joy is compared to that of frolicking young animals. Daniel speaks starkly of the resurrection of the godly and ungodly to their respective eternal destinies: "And many of those who sleep in the dust of the earth shall awake, some to everlasting life, and some to shame and everlasting contempt" (Dan. 12:2).

Jesus delivered the same message as the prophets. He spoke of his glorious second coming, all the nations being gathered before him, and his separating the saved from the lost "as a shepherd separates the sheep from the goats" (Matt. 25:31–32). At that time King Jesus will say to the saved, "Come, you who are blessed by my Father, inherit the kingdom prepared for you from the foundation of the world" (v. 34). That day will mean blessing and a great inheritance for the people of God. By contrast, Jesus will say to the lost, "Depart from me, you cursed, into the eternal fire prepared for the devil and his angels" (v. 41). That day will mean everlasting suffering for the unsaved, the same suffering reserved for the devil himself (cf. Rev. 20:10). Tersely, Jesus sums up: "And these will go away into eternal punishment, but the righteous into eternal life" (v. 46).

Jesus' apostles reinforce his teachings on heaven and hell. The last judgment will be a "day of wrath when God's righteous judgment will be revealed" (Rom. 2:5). Paul depicts the returning Christ bringing deliverance to God's persecuted people but woe to enemies of the gospel:

God considers it just to repay with affliction those who afflict you, and to grant relief to you who are afflicted as well as to us, when the Lord Jesus is revealed from heaven with his mighty angels in flaming fire, inflicting vengeance on those who do not know God and on those who do not obey the gospel of our Lord Jesus. They will suffer the punishment of eternal destruction, away from the presence of the Lord and from the glory of his might, when he comes on that day to be glorified in his saints, and to be marveled at among all who have believed. (2 Thess. 1:6–10)

The Old Testament prophets, Jesus, and his apostles bring the same message: the last judgment will mean everlasting suffering at the hands of almighty God for the wicked and everlasting bliss at the hands of the same God for the righteous.

God will reign eternally. Some claim that for God to reign forever all must be saved; otherwise the joy of heaven would be ruined.[42] Others, knowing the Bible does not teach universalism (the view that all will be saved), claim that God will punish the wicked according to their desserts and then annihilate them, so they exist no more.[43] Both of these views run counter not only to the passages on hell discussed in the last section but to the Bible's portrait of the end.

When Scripture speaks of "a new heaven and a new earth," it tells of the bliss of the righteous—"The one who conquers will have this heritage, and I will be his God and he will be my son"—but does not eliminate the wicked. To the contrary, the next verse says, "But as for the cowardly, the faithless, the detestable, as for murderers, the sexually immoral, sorcerers, idolaters, and all liars, their portion will be in the lake that burns with fire and sulfur" (Rev. 21:7–8). It is not true that God's vision of the end involves the extermination of the lost.

Revelation 22 paints another picture of the end, and it too includes the just and unjust. The former are described as happy, cleansed, and enjoying eternal life within the holy city of God, the New Jerusalem: "Blessed are those who wash their robes, so that they may have the right to the tree of life and that they may enter the city by the gates" (Rev. 22:14). But not so the wicked: "Outside are the dogs and sorcerers and the sexually immoral and murderers and idolaters, and everyone who loves and practices falsehood" (v. 15). Notice that here again the wicked are not omitted as nonexistent, but are alive and excluded from God's salvation.

The preoccupation of the eternal state is not with the wicked, but with the presence of the Father, Son, and Holy Spirit with the people of God. "Behold, the dwelling place of God is with man. He will dwell with them, and they will be his people, and God himself will be with them as their God" (Rev. 21:3). And death and suffering will be things of the past because God "will wipe away every tear from their eyes, and death shall be no more, neither shall there be mourning, nor crying, nor pain anymore, for the former things have passed away" (v. 4).

42. John Hick argues for universalism in *Evil and the God of Love* (London: Macmillan, 1966); *Death and Eternal Life* (New York: Harper & Row, 1976); and *God Has Many Names* (London: Macmillan, 1980). See J. I. Packer's criticism of universalism in *Hell Under Fire* (Grand Rapids: Zondervan, 2004), 169–94.
43. For arguments for and against annihilationism (conditionalism), see Edward William Fudge and Robert A. Peterson, *Two Views of Hell: A Biblical and Theological Dialogue* (Downers Grove, IL: InterVarsity, 2000); and for a critique of it, see Christopher Morgan in *Hell Under Fire*, 195–218.

Suffering Will End: Believers' Final Salvation Will Be Magnificent

Although it may be difficult for terribly persecuted or incurably ill saints to fully believe, Scott Hafemann speaks God's truth: "Sin and sickness are not the last word! Suffering is the pathway toward the believer's final redemption."[44] Because of the excellence of Christ's saving work, creation's paradise, lost in the fall, will be restored when Jesus returns and ushers in the new heaven and the new earth. But what does this salvation look like for God's people? Scripture gives at least four answers to this question.

We will be in God's perfected image. The image of God in human beings, a gift of creation (Gen. 1:26) tarnished in the fall yet renewed in Christ (Col. 3:10; Eph. 4:24), will be fully restored in the resurrection. Paul contrasts the first man, Adam, with the last man, Christ, the second Adam: "Just as we have borne the image of the man of dust, we shall also bear the image of the man of heaven" (1 Cor. 15:49). Paul means that even as believers have felt the results of Adam's fall in their bodily weakness and mortality, so shall they know the benefits of Christ's resurrection in their bodies. Specifically, God will conform them to the risen Christ; their mortal bodies will be raised "imperishable . . . in glory . . . in power" (vv. 42–43). Furthermore, their resurrection bodies will be "spiritual" (v. 44), that is, dominated by the Spirit of God.

The goal of God's foreloving and choosing his people for salvation will be realized on that day: they will "be conformed to the image of his Son, in order that he might be the firstborn among many brothers" (Rom. 8:29). We will be made like Christ, our older Brother, in glory and holiness.

We will know true freedom. True freedom is not merely the ability to make choices, which human beings have always had. It is the ability to love and serve God unhindered by sin. And that freedom, enjoyed by Adam and Eve at creation, was forfeited in the fall. True freedom, although regained now in Christ, will be perfected only after the resurrection of the dead. On that day we will know, love, and enjoy God and fellow believers as our first parents did before the fall. "The throne of God and of the Lamb will be in it [the New Jerusalem], and his servants will worship him" (Rev. 22:3). What will occupy their time? "They are before the throne of God, and serve him day and night in his temple" (Rev. 7:15).

In fact, things will even be better than they were before the fall because, unlike Adam and Eve, as "the spirits of the righteous made perfect" (Heb. 12:23) we will be unable to sin. Then we will supremely glorify God and

---

44. Hafemann, *The God of Promise and the Life of Faith*, 128.

enjoy him forever. Indeed, we will serve God in the unhindered true freedom for which we were created.

We will share incomparable glory. Both Testaments portray believers'
final salvation in terms of radiance and glory:

> And those who are wise shall shine like the brightness of the sky above; and
> those who turn many to righteousness, like the stars forever and ever. (Dan.
> 12:3)

> Then the righteous will shine like the sun in the kingdom of their Father
> (Matt. 13:43)

> We rejoice in hope of the glory of God. (Rom. 5:2)

> For I consider that the sufferings of this present time are not worth compar-
> ing with the glory that is to be revealed to us. (Rom. 8:18)

> For this light momentary affliction is preparing for us an eternal weight of
> glory beyond all comparison. (2 Cor. 4:17)

> To this he called you through our gospel, so that you may obtain the glory
> of our Lord Jesus Christ. (2 Thess. 2:14)

> Therefore I endure everything for the sake of the elect, that they also may
> obtain the salvation that is in Christ Jesus with eternal glory. (2 Tim. 2:10)

> And after you have suffered a little while, the God of all grace, who has called
> you to his eternal glory in Christ, will himself restore, confirm, strengthen,
> and establish you. (1 Pet. 5:10)

Scripture's testimony concerning our glorification is incredible. Resurrected
saints will see Jesus' glory (John 17:24), be transformed by that vision (1 John
3:2; Phil. 3:21), and actually partake of his glory (1 Pet. 5:2). It is no wonder
that the Bible says that God, who "prepared [us] beforehand for glory"
(Rom. 9:23), will bring his "many sons to glory" (Heb. 2:10).

We will experience enduring joy. Old Testament saints saw the joy of the
new heavens and new earth dimly and "from afar" (Heb. 11:13). David spoke
of the joy of Christ and believers: "You make known to me the path of life;
in your presence there is fullness of joy; at your right hand are pleasures
forevermore" (Ps. 16:11). Isaiah predicted the joy of the godly on resurrection day: "Your dead shall live; their bodies shall rise. You who dwell in
the dust, awake and sing for joy!" (Isa. 26:19; cf. 55:12). After promising a

"new heavens and a new earth" (Isa. 65:17), the prophet urges: "But be glad and rejoice forever in that which I create; for behold, I create Jerusalem to be a joy, and her people to be a gladness" (Isa. 65:18). God's new creation is filled with joyous people.

Jesus, who suffered death on the cruel cross "for the joy that was set before him" (Heb. 12:2), also speaks of final salvation in terms of joy. Twice in the parable of the talents he says: "Well done, good and faithful servant. You have been faithful over a little; I will set you over much. Enter into the joy of your master" (Matt. 25:21, 23). The reward for faithful service to Christ is the joy of being with him.

Jude, in his concluding doxology, praises "him who is able to keep you from stumbling and to present you blameless before the presence of his glory with great joy" (Jude 24). Once more the presence of God, this time characterized by glory, means joy for his victorious people.

Near the end of the Bible's story are two beatitudes promising blessing to those who believe in Christ and persevere (Rev. 22:7, 14). What is the source of their joy? It is the presence of God who fulfills his covenanted promise to dwell with his people. He who "will be with them as their God . . . will wipe away every tear from their eyes, and death shall be no more, neither shall there be mourning, nor crying, nor pain anymore, for the former things have passed away" (Rev. 21:3–4). Suffering, sorrow, and death will be things of the past in that day, when the joy of God's people is complete. Hallelujah!

In this book we have focused attention on the teaching concerning suffering and God's goodness in Holy Scripture because that is where we find God's wisdom. It is also important, however, not to neglect thorny questions associated with suffering and evil. In the next chapter, therefore, theologian and philosopher John Frame carefully explores the problem of evil.

7

THE PROBLEM OF EVIL

JOHN M. FRAME

The problem of evil is probably the most difficult problem in all of theology, and for many atheists it is the Achilles' heel of the theistic worldview.[1] In a nutshell, the problem is this: how can there be any evil in the world, if God exists? Or to put it more formally:

1) If God is omnipotent, he is able to prevent evil.
2) If God is good, he wants to prevent evil.
3) But evil exists.
   Conclusion: either God is not omnipotent, or he is not good.

As I have formulated it, the argument assumes that God exists. But the conclusion is often taken as a *reductio ad absurdum*[2] of that assumption.

---

1. I have discussed the problem of evil in *The Doctrine of God*, vol. 2, in "A Theology of Lordship" (Phillipsburg, NJ: P&R, 2002), 160–82; *Apologetics to the Glory of God* (Phillipsburg, NJ: P&R, 1994), 149–90; *Cornelius Van Til: An Analysis of His Thought* (Phillipsburg, NJ: P&R, 1995), 83–86.
2. "*Reductio ad absurdum* is a mode of argumentation that seeks to establish a contention by deriving an absurdity from its denial, thus arguing that a thesis must be accepted because its rejection would be untenable." http://www. iep.utm.edu/r/reductio.htm.

To say that God is not omnipotent or not good is to say that the God of the Bible does not exist.

The above syllogism is sometimes called "the logical problem of evil," for it accuses the theistic worldview of logical inconsistency. The charge is that theists believe in an omnipotent, good God but also believe, inconsistently, that evil exists. Often, of course, the problem of evil is felt rather than argued. "The emotional problem of evil" is simply the agony we feel when we experience tragedy in life, and we cry out, "Why, Lord?"

Another distinction that we should initially make is between natural and moral evil. The former includes anything that brings suffering, unpleasantness, or difficulty into the lives of creatures. Earthquakes, floods, diseases, injuries, and death are examples of natural evil. Moral evil is the sin of rational creatures (angels and men). According to Scripture, moral evil came first. Satan's temptations and the disobedience of Adam and Eve led to God's curse upon the earth:

> "Cursed is the ground because of you;
> through painful toil you will eat of it
> all the days of your life.
> It will produce thorns and thistles for you,
> and you will eat the plants of the field.
> By the sweat of your brow
> you will eat your food
> until you return to the ground,
> since from it you were taken;
> for dust you are,
> and to dust you will return." (Gen. 3:17–19)[3]

God will remove this curse only on the final day, the consummation of Jesus' redemption, when he executes his final judgment and this world is replaced by a new heaven and a new earth. In the meantime, the whole creation "has been groaning as in the pains of childbirth" (Rom. 8:22), "in eager expectation for the sons of God to be revealed" (v. 19).

Scripture, therefore, gives us an explicit answer to the problem of natural evil. Natural evil is a curse brought upon the world because of moral evil. It functions as punishment to the wicked and as a means of discipline for those who are righteous by God's grace. It also reminds us of the cosmic dimensions of sin and redemption. Sin brought death to the human race

3. Unless otherwise indicated, Scripture quotations in this chapter are taken from *The Holy Bible: New International Version* (NIV).

but also to the universe over which man was to rule. God has ordained that the universe resist its human ruler until that ruler stops resisting God. So in redemption, God's purpose is no less than "to reconcile to himself all things, whether things on earth or things in heaven" (Col. 1:20). The unanswered question is the problem of moral evil: how can sin exist in a theistic universe? I shall therefore focus on moral evil for the rest of this chapter.

Before I do, however, I need to clarify my views related to God's sovereignty and goodness.[4] First, I hold to a strong concept of divine sovereignty, which I view as efficacious and universal. By efficacious I mean that it always accomplishes its purpose. God never fails to accomplish what he sets out to do. Nothing is too hard for him (Jer. 32:27); nothing seems marvelous to him (Zech. 8:6); with him nothing is impossible (Gen. 18:14; Matt. 19:26; Luke 1:37). His purposes always prevail (Isa. 14:24–27; Job 42:2; Jer. 23:20). When God expresses his eternal purposes in words, through his prophets, those prophecies will surely come to pass (Deut. 18:21–22; Isa. 31:2). God sometimes represents his word as his active agent that inevitably accomplishes his bidding (Isa. 55:11; Zech. 1:6). Creatures may oppose him, to be sure, but they cannot prevail (Isa. 46:10; Dan. 4:35). For his own reasons, he has chosen to delay the fulfillment of his intentions for the end of history and to bring about those intentions through a complicated historical sequence of events. In that sequence, his purposes appear sometimes to suffer defeat, sometimes to achieve victory. But each apparent defeat actually makes his eventual victory all the more glorious.

God's sovereignty is also universal; it encompasses everything that happens in the world. God's rule extends to his creation, the natural world. He has made it according to his own wisdom, his own plan. He knows it inside and out and has planned all the laws and principles by which it operates. The biblical writers do not hesitate to ascribe the events of the natural world directly to God (Gen. 8:22; Job 38–40; Ps. 65:9–11; 135:6–7; 147:15–18; Jer. 5:22; 10:13; 31:35; Jonah 4:6–7; Nah. 1:3; Acts 14:17). His sovereign control extends to those events that appear to be most random (Prov. 16:33), to the smallest details (like feeding birds, clothing lilies, and the falling of sparrows; cf. Matt. 6:26–30; 10:29–30), to human history (Acts 17:26), governments (Ps. 33:10–11), leaders (Gen. 45:5–8; 50:20), individual human lives (Jer. 1:5; Ps. 139:13–16), and human decisions. These include even sinful decisions (Gen. 45:5–8; Isa. 44:28; Luke 22:22;

4. My subsequent comments on God's sovereignty and goodness summarize my chapters 4 and 20 in *The Doctrine of God*, 47–79, 402–45. For more on my view of God's omnipotence, see ibid., 513–42.

Acts 2:23–24; 4:27–28; 13:27; Rev. 17:17). Given what the Bible teaches about God's sovereignty, then, the various attempts to show that God is too weak to prevent evil do not seem promising.[5]

Second, I also hold to the goodness of God. Goodness is a general term that summarizes many moral, kind, and generous features of God's character. God's goodness describes his righteousness, benevolence, love, grace, patience, covenant faithfulness, and compassion. Scripture is saturated with texts expounding the goodness of God. Exodus 34:6 reveals that God is "The LORD, the LORD, the compassionate and gracious God, slow to anger, abounding in love and faithfulness." Deuteronomy 32:4 asserts, "He is the Rock, his works are perfect, and all his ways are just." God does not take pleasure in evil (Ps. 5:4). His eyes are too pure to look on evil; he cannot tolerate it (Hab. 1:13).[6] Furthermore, God commends goodness to us because he is himself supremely good. His commands to us are based on what he himself is. So it is true to say that goodness is what God says it is, and it is also true to say that God commends the good because it is good.

I will not consider solutions to the problem of evil that call into question God's sovereignty and goodness but will examine the three general types of common defenses[7] against the problem. The first focuses on the nature of evil, the second on the ways in which evil contributes to the overall good of the universe, and the third on God's agency with regard to evil. I shall consider these in succession.

The Nature of Evil

The Christian Science sect and some forms of Hinduism maintain that evil is an illusion. If it is, of course, then the problem of evil disappears. But this claim is easily refuted. Even if evil does not exist in the real world, it certainly exists in our own minds and feelings. Even Christian Scientists and Hindus will concede that much. If it is an illusion, it is a deeply troubling one, and the very pain of it raises the problem of evil again. How can a good and omnipotent God allow us to be troubled by such illusions? So this proposal merely shifts the problem of evil to another level and therefore fails as a

5. As in the book by Harold Kushner, *When Bad Things Happen to Good People* (New York: Schocken, 1981), but also in the literature of process theology. See David Ray Griffin, *God, Power, and Evil* (Philadelphia: Westminster, 1976), and his *Evil Revisited* (Albany: State University of New York Press, 1991), reviewed by me in *Calvin Theological Journal* 27 (1992): 435–38.
6. Of course, Habakkuk brings up this principle in order to ask God why he *has* been tolerating evil. In effect, Habakkuk is raising the problem of evil.
7. Alvin Plantinga, in *God, Freedom, and Evil* (Grand Rapids, MI: Eerdmans, 1974), makes a useful distinction between a "defense" and a "theodicy." The latter has the goal of justifying God's ways to men, of demonstrating the goodness of all his actions. The former merely seeks to show that the problem of evil does not disprove the God of the Bible.

solution. It also fails as a claim about the world, for illusions are, after all, themselves real evils. The fact that human beings often fail to distinguish between illusion and reality is itself an evil that must be dealt with. So if evil is an illusion, it is not an illusion. The illusionist view refutes itself.

Another view that attempts to put evil into a shadowy metaphysical category is that evil is a privation. This view is far more widespread within Christendom than the previous one, having been advocated by Augustine, the Catholic and post-Reformation scholastic traditions, and many modern apologists and theologians. To say that evil is a privation is not to say that it is an illusion. It is rather to say that it is not something positive. It is a lack, a defect in a good universe. It is an absence of good rather than the presence of something not good. Further, it is an absence of good where good should be. We do not consider it evil that a tree is unable to see, but we do pity a human being who lacks sight. Evil is, therefore, not a mere absence of good, but a privation or deprivation.

Those who hold this view begin with the biblical premise that all being is good (Gen. 1:31; 1 Tim. 4:4). So evil is nonbeing, not a substance or object. It is a lack of being, a deprivation of being. It is "negative and accidental."[8]

Étienne Gilson, the Thomist scholar, expounds the concept as follows:

> It is very certain that all things God has made are good; and no less certain that they are not all equally good. There is the good, and the better; and, if the better, then also the less good; now in a certain sense the less good pertains to evil.[9]

Later he adds:

> But what we must especially note is that these very limitations and mutabil-ities for which nature is arraigned, are metaphysically inherent in the very status of a created being as such. . . . Things, in short, are created *ex nihilo*, and because created they are, and are good; but because they are *ex nihilo* they are essentially mutable. . . . [T]he possibility of change is a necessity from which God Himself could not absolve his creation; for the mere fact of being created is the ultimate root of that possibility. . . . [E]verything that exists in virtue of the creative action and endures in virtue of continued cre-ation, remains radically contingent in itself and in constant peril of lapsing

---

8. Étienne Gilson, *The Spirit of Medieval Philosophy* (New York: Scribner's, 1940), 113. Karl Barth's view of sin and evil as "nothingness" (*das Nichtige*) is similar, except that for Barth nothingness is an aspect of *Geschichte*, that highest reality shared by God and man in Christ, in which alone God is truly God and man is truly man. See my *Cornelius Van Til*, 359–65.

9. Gilson, *The Spirit of Medieval Philosophy*, 113.

back into nothingness. Because creatures are apt not to be they tend, so to speak, towards nonbeing.[10]

On Gilson's view, natural evil consists of the defects in the lesser goods that God has made in creating a many-valued universe and the "mutability" of creation, which is the tendency of all good things to "lapse back into nothingness," a kind of metaphysical entropy. Remember that Gilson equates being with goodness. Since God created all things good, everything is good insofar as it has being. But as things slip back into nonbeing, they lose their goodness as well as their being. So this metaphysical lapse means that things tend to lose their perfections unless God acts to sustain them.

What of moral evil? Gilson argues that rational beings, angels, and men are also mutable:

> The whole problem now stands on a new footing: all that needs to be made in order that it may be, is always tending to unmake itself, so much so that what now permanently threatens the work of creation is literally, and in the full rigour of the term, the possibility of its *defection*. But only a possibility, be it noted, nothing more; a possibility without real danger as far as concerns the physical order which has no control over itself, but a very real and practical danger indeed in the moral order, that is to say when men and angels are concerned; for in associating them with his own divine government, their Creator requires them also to keep watch with Him against their own possible defection.[11]

Rational beings, like other creatures, tend to slip into nonbeing, to "unmake" themselves, and therefore to become less perfect than God made them to be. The difference between rational and nonrational beings is that rational beings have some control over their own metaphysical stability. They can keep themselves from losing their perfections. Gilson goes on to explain that God gave to man free will (apparently in a libertarian[12] sense) to maintain himself in perfection. But man used his free will wrongly and fell into sin.

> For all evil comes of the will; this will was not created evil, nor even indifferent to good or evil; it was created good, and such that it needed only an effortless continuance in good to attain to perfect beatitude. The only danger threatening such a nature lies therefore in that metaphysical contingence

10. Ibid., 113–14.
11. Ibid., 114–15.
12. Libertarian freedom is defined on page 148.

inseparable from the state of a created being, a pure *possibility*, without the least trace of actual existence, a possibility that not only could have remained unactualized but ought to have done so. . . . [So] it seems we may justly claim for Christian thought that it has done everything necessary to reduce [evil] to the status of an avoidable accident, and to banish it to the confines of this fundamentally good universe.[13]

What is God's relation to evil in this view?

Lastly, we may proceed to this final conclusion to which we must hold firmly, however strange it may appear: viz., The cause of evil lies always in some good, and yet, God, who is the Cause of all good, is not the cause of evil. For it follows clearly from the preceding considerations, that, when evil is reducible to a defect in some act, its cause is always a defect in the being that acts. Now in God there is no defect, but, on the contrary, supreme perfection. The evil caused by a defect in the acting being could not, therefore, have God for its cause. But if we consider the evil which consists in the corruption of certain beings, we must, on the other hand, assign its cause to God. . . . [W]hatever being and action is observable in a bad act, is attributable to God as to its cause, but whatever defectiveness is contained in the act, is attributable to the defective secondary cause, and not to the almighty perfection of God.

Thus, from whatever angle we approach the problem, we always come back to the same conclusion. Evil as such is nothing. It is, therefore, inconceivable that God could be its cause. If asked, further, what is its cause, we must reply that it reduces itself to the tendency of certain things to return to nonbeing.[14]

To some extent, Gilson's reply to the problem of evil is a form of the free will defense, which I shall mention briefly later. He tries, however, to get behind human freedom to show how a wrong use of it is grounded in a metaphysical principle: the tendency of creatures to become less perfect. Every creature has this tendency. Rational creatures can guard against it, but they do not necessarily succeed. And when they do not, they are responsible for allowing themselves to become imperfect. God does not cause moral evil, but he does cause the existence of corruptible beings. He creates corruptible beings because he intends for them to add to the overall perfection of the universe. But he is not responsible for the failures of rational beings to guard against their own corruption. Evil is nonbeing, and God does not create nonbeing.

13. Gilson, *The Spirit of Medieval Philosophy*, 121–22.
14. Étienne Gilson, *The Philosophy of St. Thomas Aquinas*, trans. Edward Bullough (New York: Arno Press, 1979), 161–62.

I do not find this to be a cogent response to the problem of evil, for the following reasons:

1) It seems to assume libertarian freedom, which I reject. R. K. McGregor Wright defines this view as

> the belief that the human will has an inherent power to choose with equal ease between alternatives. This is commonly called "the power of contrary choice" or "the liberty of indifference." This belief does not claim that there are no influences that might affect the will, but it does insist that normally the will can overcome these factors and choose in spite of them. Ultimately, the will is free from any necessary causation. In other words, it is autonomous from outside determination.[15]

Libertarianism is sometimes called incompatibilism, because it is not compatible with God's absolute sovereignty. It emphasizes that our choices are not determined in advance by God; he may be the first cause of the universe in general, but in the sphere of human decisions, we are the first causes of our actions. According to the libertarian view, our character and our immediate desires may influence our decisions, but we always have the freedom to choose contrary to our character and desires, however strong. This position assumes that there is a part of human nature that we might call the will, which is independent of every other aspect of our being, and which can, therefore, make a decision contrary to every motivation. Libertarians maintain that only if we have this kind of radical freedom can we be held responsible for our actions.

Although the libertarian view of freedom is subject to several severe criticisms, I shall briefly mention five.[16] First, libertarianism is inconsistent with a biblical view of God's sovereignty, which I outlined earlier. Scripture makes clear that our choices are governed by God's eternal plan, even though we are fully responsible for them. Second, Scripture does not explicitly teach the existence of libertarian freedom. There is no passage that can be construed to mean that the human will is independent of God's plan and of the rest of the human personality. Third, Scripture never grounds human responsibility (in the sense of accountability) in libertarian freedom. We are responsible because God has made us, owns us, and has a right to evaluate our conduct. Fourth, Scripture depicts that in heaven,

15. R. K. McGregor Wright, *No Place for Sovereignty* (Downers Grove, IL: InterVarsity, 1996), 43–44.
16. For a more developed critique of libertarianism, see my chapter, "Human Responsibility and Freedom," in *The Doctrine of God*, 119–59.

the consummate state of human existence, we will not be free to sin. So the highest state of human existence will be a state without libertarian freedom. Fifth, Scripture actually condemns some people for acts that clearly were not free in a libertarian sense (e.g., Pharaoh, Judas, and those putting Jesus to death).

The better alternative is compatibilism. It bears its name because it views freedom as compatible with absolute divine sovereignty. According to this view, we have the freedom to do what we want to do. We speak and act according to our character. We follow the deepest desires of our heart. As Jesus emphasizes, a good tree bears good fruit, and a bad tree bears bad fruit (Matt. 7:15–20; Luke 6:43–45). To my knowledge, Scripture never refers to this moral consistency as a kind of freedom, but the concept of heart-act consistency is important in Scripture, and theologians and philosophers have often referred to it as freedom. In everyday life, we regularly think of freedom in this way—as doing what we want to do. When we do not do what we want, we are either acting irrationally or being forced to act against our will by someone or something outside ourselves.

Our decisions are not only tied to our character; they also are compatible with and stand under the efficacious and universal sovereignty of God. Scripture often shows that God brings about the free decisions of people, such as Joseph's brothers (Gen. 45:5–8), Cyrus (Isa. 44:28), and Judas (Luke 22:22; cf. Acts 2:23–24; 3:18; 4:27–28; 13:27). So we should not be prejudiced by the unbiblical but popular notion that God never foreordains our free decisions. Indeed, Scripture portrays human decisions as compatible with divine sovereignty. Our freedom is genuine, and God is in control. We make real choices, and God predestines everything according to the counsel of his will, although Scripture never fully explains this mystery.

It should be noted that some Reformed thinkers have held the privation theory while rejecting libertarian freedom: God is the efficient cause of everything good, but only the "effectually permissive cause of evil." He "merely permits" evil, because it "has not true being at all."[17] But I do not see any real difference between effectual permission and efficient causation, and I do not know why God should be responsible for what he causes efficiently, but not for what he permits effectually. I will have more to say on this later.

2) When someone freely chooses to allow himself to become imperfect, that choice (assuming it is libertarian) is not itself the product of meta-

17. Polan, cited in Heinrich Heppe, *Reformed Dogmatics* (Grand Rapids, MI: Baker, 1950, 1978), 143.

physical entropy. That choice itself is evidently something other than a privation of good, for on Gilson's account it is prior to the privation; it is a choice to make the privation happen. But then the privation theory is quite irrelevant, an unnecessary complication to the argument. Why not simply adopt a conventional free will defense and say that free will itself explains moral evil, rather than free will plus privation?

3) If God cannot prevent the corruption of rational beings, then how is he able to make some creatures incorruptible (angels and glorified saints)? If he can, but chooses not to, then the problem of evil recurs at a different level: why did he choose not to prevent the fall?

4) Should we regard evil as "nothing," a mere limitation or privation of goodness? Many seem to think it obvious that we should, but I am not persuaded. Long could be seen as the negation of short, but one could also say that short is the negation of long; the same could be said for straight and crooked. It seems to be a good general practice to regard opposites on the same ontological level. Males and females are opposites, but neither is a mere negation of the other. Both are substantial beings. Why should good and evil be any different?

It is true that good is prior to evil in some ways. First, good came first in history, as Creation preceded the fall. Second, good has positive value in itself; evil has positive value only to the extent that it enhances good. Third, good receives God's blessing; evil receives his curse. But it is not clear that any of these require us to say that evil is nonbeing, or a mere negation or privation. Is there some other asymmetry between good and evil that requires us to regard evil as nonbeing? I have not been able to find suggestions of that sort in the literature. Without them, I must assume that good and evil, though opposite, are both forms of being.[18]

5) There is no biblical reason to assert that created things by nature tend to slip into nonbeing, to lose their being, or to become corrupt.[19] Scripture says nothing of the kind, and in the absence of scriptural war-

18. The relation between being and nonbeing has, of course, been a difficult philosophical issue since Parmenides. It is difficult to describe nonbeing or even refer to it without making it look like a kind of being. But if evil is not an illusion but something real, then what other conditions must it fulfill to be regarded as being? I do not believe that question has been answered. It may be, as one of my correspondents suggests, that Augustine's adoption of the privation theory was a reaction to his original Manichaeism. The Manichees saw good and evil as equally powerful realities, in constant warfare. When Augustine became a Christian, he saw clearly that, in God's world, good is ultimate and evil is not. But what is it? Perhaps Augustine thought he could best reject the ultimacy of evil by denying to it the status of being. I find this move understandable but not persuasive.

19. One can of course discuss the concept of physical entropy in this connection, but the arguments for that are scientific rather than biblical, and the concept has little to do with the moral corruption we are concerned with here.

rant, I know of no other reason to say such a thing. It assumes that there are degrees of being, and that created things can slip from higher degrees to lower degrees. The idea that being admits of degrees comes from the philosophy of Plato, in which the Forms or Ideas are "real," with the Form of the Good being the most real entity and others being less real entities. It also fits Aristotle's view that things in the world are combinations of form and matter, but that matter is essentially a kind of nonbeing that inhibits form in various degrees. But in the Bible there is no hint that some things have more being than others. God and his creations exist; everything else does not exist—and that is the end of it. God is not more real than created beings, although he is very different from them in other ways. Further, in a biblical worldview there is no reason to suppose that things have an inherent tendency to become less perfect, less good, or less real.

6) But even granting Gilson's view that evil is a lack or privation of being, a kind of nonbeing, why would that absolve God of blame for evil? As presented by Gilson, God is crudely analogous to a maker of doughnuts. The doughnut maker shapes the dough into the familiar O-shape. When someone says, "I see what ingredients you use for the doughnut, but what do you make the holes out of?" the baker takes it as a bad joke. There are no ingredients for holes. The hole is simply an emptiness in the dough that appears when the pastry is created. When the baker makes one, behold, the hole is there too! Making doughnuts is not a two-step procedure in which one first makes and shapes the dough, and then makes the hole; at least, it does not have to be. The hole is not something one must make in addition to the solid doughnut; it is only a lack or privation of dough.

Agreed. But doughnuts do, after all, have holes. The doughnut maker could have made his dough into a solid pastry without a hole, but he chose to include a hole. Should he not receive blame for a hole that is too small, too large, or misshapen, or credit for one that is just the right size? Should he not take responsibility for his choice to make doughnuts rather than solid pastries?

Similarly, if God is the Creator of all the being in the universe, is he not also the source of whatever lacks or privations or negations of being there may be in the world? We have seen that God's sovereignty extends to human decisions, even sinful human actions. It does not seem to me to matter much whether we regard these sins as being or nonbeing. If they come from God, they come from God, and the problem of evil remains.

7) What is evil, on a biblical view? Natural evil is God's curse, the pains brought into the world by the fall. Moral evil is sin, the transgression of God's law (1 John 3:4). Scripture does not speculate as to whether these

evils are "being" or "nonbeing," or where they fit into the metaphysical structure of the world.

Indeed, from a biblical point of view, there are dangers in reducing evil to metaphysics, in reducing the righteousness-sin relation to the being-nonbeing relation.[20] Cornelius Van Til often warned against "reducing ethics to metaphysics," or "confusing sin with finitude,"[21] for such reduction depersonalizes sin. In such reduction, sin becomes a defect in creation itself (ultimately, contra Gilson, a defect in God's creative act), rather than the rebellion of created persons against their Creator. And this conception grants sinners a new excuse for their sin, the finitude and mutability with which God created them.

Further, this view encourages views of salvation in which the goal is to get rid of our finitude and become divine rather than to become obedient. These dangers are not at all hypothetical. They represent a definite tendency in the history of thought, especially in systems like those of Plotinus, the Gnostics, medieval and Eastern mysticism, and much modern New Age thought. Such systems replace the biblical Creator-creature distinction with a continuum of divinity, and salvation is viewed as ascent toward the top of the ontological continuum, toward divinity.

Some Good Things about Evil
Another approach to the problem of evil is to claim that the presence, or at least the possibility, of evil in the world is good, when seen from a broader perspective. Even human beings are sometimes called upon to inflict pain for a good purpose: surgery to heal, punishment of children to discipline them. So perhaps God has a good purpose in permitting evil, one which outweighs the suffering and pain—one which, in the end, makes this a better world than it would have been without the intrusion of evil. Such observations have been called "the greater-good defense" against the problem of evil.

Some have argued that the possibility of evil is necessary to have an orderly universe.[22] An orderly universe, in this view, is a universe governed predictably by natural law. But natural laws are impersonal. The law of gravity, for example, takes no account of persons. If someone jumps from a high cliff, he will be hurt, whether he is righteous or wicked. If God miraculously protected everybody (or those otherwise righteous) who took foolish chances, it would be difficult to predict natural events. So if we are

20. In one sense, the privation theory seeks to avoid this very problem. It tries to remove evil from the metaphysical sphere by removing it from the sphere of being. But it actually encourages the metaphysicalizing of sin.
21. These two formulations are more or less synonymous.
22. Ronald Nash, *Faith and Reason* (Grand Rapids, MI: Zondervan, 1988). He cites F. R. Tennant, Michael Peterson, and Richard Swinburne as advocating this approach.

to have an orderly, predictable universe, so the argument goes, we must be willing to accept a certain amount of pain and suffering.

Others have argued that a certain amount of evil in the world is necessary for "soul making." For example, John Hick argues that we are born morally immature and that we need some hard knocks to gain moral fiber.[23]

The most common form of the greater-good defense is the free will defense, which argues that God rightly risks the possibility of evil in order to allow human beings libertarian freedom of choice. See the previous section for my negative response.

Some have noticed that there are virtues that could not exist or manifest themselves except as responses to evil: compassion, patience, courage, seeking justice, and the redemptive love by which one dies for his friends (John 15:13). Sometimes these have been called "second-order goods," which are dependent on "first-order evils."[24]

We can think of other positive uses of evil. In Scripture, God uses evil to test his servants (Job; 1 Pet. 1:7; James 1:3); to discipline them (Heb. 12:7–11); to preserve their lives (Gen. 50:20); to teach them patience and perseverance (James 1:3–4); to redirect their attention to what is most important (Psalm 37); to enable them to comfort others (2 Cor. 1:3–7); to enable them to bear powerful witness to the truth (Acts 7); to give them greater joy when suffering is replaced by glory (1 Pet. 4:13); to judge the wicked, both in history (Deut. 28:15–68) and in the life to come (Matt. 25:41–46); to bring reward to persecuted believers (Matt. 5:10–12); and to display the work of God (John 9:3; cf. Ex. 9:16; Rom. 9:17).

The thrust of all these arguments is that although evil is to be deplored in and of itself, there are some respects in which it makes the world a better place. Some have argued, therefore, that evils contribute to a greater good. Some have even argued that this world, with all its evil, is "the best possible world." The philosopher G. W. Leibniz, for example, argued that an omnipotent, omniscient, omnibenevolent God could create no less.[25]

It is certainly true that when God brings pain and suffering upon people, he has a good purpose. "You intended to harm me," Joseph explains to his brothers, "but God intended it for good" (Gen. 50:20). And in a context dealing with the sufferings of Christians, Paul says that "in all things God works for the good of those who love him" (Rom. 8:28). Recognizing and affirming this principle is an essential element in any Christian response

23. John Hick, *Evil and the God of Love* (London: Collins, 1966). He cites the church father Irenaeus as the source of his approach.
24. And the latter, of course, are ultimately the abuses of first-order goods.
25. G. W. Leibniz, *Theodicy* (New Haven, CT: Yale University Press, 1952).

to the problem of evil. It is essential to realize that even though God does bring evil into the world, he does it for a good reason. Therefore, he does not *do* evil in bringing evil to pass.

I would quarrel with some of the arguments mentioned above in this connection. The idea that some human pain must be endured in any orderly universe does not take account of the biblical teachings about the pre-fall world and about the post-consummation heaven, in which God "will wipe every tear from their eyes. There will be no more death or mourning or crying or pain, for the old order of things has passed away" (Rev. 21:4). Certainly heaven will be an orderly place, and that order will be maintained without human suffering.

Hick's soul-making theodicy overlooks the fact that Adam was created good, not morally immature with a need to develop character through suffering. It is true that God uses evil to sanctify us, but the true making of souls, both in old and new creations, is by divine grace.

As for Leibniz's theory, many have doubted whether there could be such a thing as a "best possible world." Given any possible universe, can we not always imagine another that includes one more good or one less evil? Indeed, Scripture tells us explicitly that the present world is inferior to the world to come. If God is able to make a world that is temporarily less than best, why can't he create a world that is never the absolute best? And is it not possible that God wants to display his grace by creating beings who are less than perfectly excellent?

Nevertheless, there is a valid insight in the greater-good defense. Scripture provides many examples of God's bringing good out of evil. And we know that on the last day, God's justice, mercy, and righteousness will be so plain to all that nobody will accuse him of wrongdoing. Rather,

> All nations will come
>   and worship before you,
> for your righteous acts have been revealed. (Rev. 15:4)

When all of God's actions are added up, it will be plain that the sum total of his works is righteous. From the evils of history he has brought unquestionable good, worthy of the highest praise. Remember the following points, however:

1) It is important for us to define *greater good* theistically. The greater good should be seen, first of all, not as greater pleasure or comfort for us, but as greater glory for God. Certainly there are events that are hard to justify as benefits to the people involved, the chief one being eternal punishment.

But God is glorified in the judgment of sinners, and that is a good thing. Nevertheless, God has promised that what brings glory to him will, in the long run, also bring benefits to believers. So Romans 8:28 declares that "in all things God works for the good of those who love him, who have been called according to his purpose."

2) Unless God's standards govern our concept of goodness, there can be no talk of good or evil at all. If there is no personal Absolute, values must be based on impersonal things and forces, like matter, motion, time, and chance. But values cannot be based on any of these. They arise only in a context of personal relationships, and absolute standards presuppose an absolute person. Thus, the Christian can turn the tables on the unbeliever who raises the problem of evil: the non-Christian has a "problem of good." Without God, there is neither good nor evil.[26]

3) If we are to evaluate God's actions rightly, we must evaluate them over the full extent of human history. The Christian claim is not that the world is perfect as it is now; in fact, Scripture denies that it is. But the full goodness of God's plan will be manifest only at the end of redemptive history. For his own reasons, God has determined to "write" history as a story taking place over millennia.[27] Evil would not be such a problem if it were created and overcome supratemporally (as in Barth's *Geschichte*) or in a period of, say, three seconds. The problem is with the long wait for God's salvation.[28] But for him, of course, a thousand years are as a day (Ps. 90:4). And when we look back upon our sufferings in this world, they will seem small to us as well, "not worth comparing with the glory that will be revealed in us" (Rom. 8:18). It is then that we will see how God has worked in all things for our good (Rom. 8:28). Even Paul, who underwent much more suffering than most of us, says that "our light and momentary troubles are achieving for us an eternal glory that far outweighs them all" (2 Cor. 4:17).

4) God often surprises us by the ways in which he brings good out of evil. Certainly Joseph was surprised at the means God used to lift him from being a slave and a prisoner to being Pharaoh's prime minister. Certainly the Israelites were surprised at the miracles by which God brought them out of Egypt and sustained them in the wilderness. But the chief example of God's astonishing ways is found in the cross of Jesus. The prophets promised

---

26. See *Apologetics to the Glory of God*, 89–102, for a fuller treatment of this argument.

27. I describe this author-character model in *The Doctrine of God*, 156–59.

28. God's relation to time is not only transcendent but also immanent. Recall the many biblical texts urging patience in waiting for God's time, including Hab. 2:3; Matt. 6:34; Rom. 8:25; Phil. 4:6–7; Heb. 10:36; James 1:3–4; 5:7–11.

God's judgment on Israel's disobedience but simultaneously promised that
he would forgive and bless. How could he do both? Israel's disobedience
merited nothing less than death. How could God be just in dealing with
their sin and still bring them his promised blessings? Certainly this problem was quite impenetrable, until Jesus died in our place. His death was at
the same time judgment and grace: judgment upon Jesus for our sin, and
grace to the true Israel, those of us who are elect in him. And if God acted
so wonderfully and surprisingly to bring good out of evil, when it seemed
most impossible, can we not trust him to bring good out of the remaining
evils that we experience?

5) Since the ultimate theodicy is future, we must now deal with the
problem of evil by faith. We cannot total up the present evils against the
present goods and from that calculation exonerate God of blame. But
our inability to do this does not require us to surrender to those who use
the problem of evil to deny the existence of God. For the burden of proof
is, after all, not upon us. It is the objector who must show that the evils
of this world cannot be part of an overall good plan. I have shown many
ways in which God brings good out of evil, even when it seems impossible for the good to prevail. Can the objector prove that God is unable
to integrate the present evils into an overall good plan? This burden of
proof is a heavy one, for the objector must prove a negative: that there
is *no* way for God to vindicate his justice on the last day. I do not believe
that burden has been met.

6) Does the greater-good defense presuppose that the end justifies the
means? It does say that God's good purposes justify his use of evil. When
we criticize someone for holding that the end justifies the means, we are
saying that he thinks that a noble end will justify means that would otherwise be accounted wicked. In this case, is God's act to bring about evil
normally a wicked action, which he justifies ad hoc because of his noble
purpose? But how would we judge in this context what is "normally" the
case? If God brought about moral evil in some sense, that act was quite
unique. Ultimately, evil came into the world only once, and even then
God did not *do* evil. Other "hardenings" of people's hearts in history are
actions that only God can perform. Who are we to claim that such actions
are "normally" wicked, rather than confess that they are a unique divine
prerogative? When a man kills an innocent person, his act is normally
murder. But when God takes human life, he acts within the proper authority
of his lordship. Why should we not say the same thing about his agency

in bringing evil to pass?[29] At least, we must say again that the burden of proof is on the objector.

7) Since the burden of proof is on the objector, it is not necessary for us to come up with a full theodicy, a complete justification of God's ways. In this world, we walk by faith, not by sight (2 Cor. 5:7). We shall see later that seeking a theodicy can actually be sinful when people demand of God an explanation for the ills that have befallen them.

My conclusion on the greater-good defense, then, is that God does not *do* but certainly does *will* evil for a good purpose. The good he intends will be so great, so wonderful and beautiful, that it will make present evils seem small. But we are not under any obligation to show in every case how God's past and present actions contribute to the final good, and the unbeliever has no right to demand such an explanation.

Although the greater-good defense is basically sound, it leaves us with a sense of mystery. For it is hard to imagine *how* God's good purpose justifies the evil in the world.

Evil and God's Agency

We have seen that natural evil is a curse that God placed on the world in response to man's sin. We also saw earlier that God does harden hearts, and that, through his prophets, he predicts sinful human actions long in advance, indicating that he is in control of free human decisions. Now theologians have found it difficult to formulate in general terms how God acts to bring about those sinful actions. Earlier in this chapter, we saw Gilson arguing that God is not the cause of sin and evil, because evil is nonbeing and therefore has no cause. Gilson is willing to say that God is the "deficient" cause—which sounds like a contrast to "efficient" cause—meaning that he creates mutable beings but does not determine the specific defects that constitute sin. I found his privation theory, and his view of libertarian freedom, inadequate. But the discussion brings out an issue that we all must think about. Do we want to say that God is the "cause" of evil? That language is certainly problematic, since we usually associate cause with blame. So it seems that if God causes sin and evil, he must be to blame for it.

Therefore, there has been much discussion among theologians as to what verb best describes God's agency in regard to evil. Some initial possibilities: *authors, brings about, causes, controls, creates, decrees, foreordains, incites, includes within his plan, makes happen, ordains, permits, plans,*

29. The ontological difference between God and man lies behind these moral distinctions.

predestines, predetermines, produces, stands behind, and *wills*. Many of these are extrascriptural terms; not one is easy to define in this context. So theologians need to consider carefully which of these terms, if any, should be affirmed, and in what sense. Words are the theologian's tools. In a situation like this, none of the possibilities is fully adequate. Each term has its advantages and disadvantages. Let us consider some of those that are most frequently discussed.

1) The term *authors* is almost universally condemned in the theological literature. It is rarely defined, but it seems to mean both that God is the efficient cause of evil and that by causing evil he actually does something wrong. So the Westminster Confession of Faith says that God "neither is nor can be the author or approver of sin" (5.4). Despite this denial in a major Reformed confession, Arminians regularly charge that Reformed theology makes God the author of sin. They assume that if God brings about evil in any sense, he must therefore approve it and deserve the blame. In their view nothing less than libertarian freedom can absolve God from the charge of authoring sin.

But as we noted earlier, libertarian freedom is incoherent and unbiblical, and in some sense God does bring about sinful human actions. To deny this, or to charge God with wickedness on account of it, is not open to a Bible-believing Christian. Somehow, we must confess both that God has a role in bringing evil about and that in doing so he is holy and blameless. In the last section, I tried to show how the greater-good defense, properly understood, supports this confession. God does bring sins about, but always for his own good purposes. So in bringing sin to pass, he does not himself commit sin. If that argument is sound, then a Reformed doctrine of the sovereignty of God does not imply that God is the author of sin.

2) *Causes* is another term that has led to much wrestling by theologians. As we recall, Gilson, with the Thomistic tradition, denies that God is the cause of evil[30] by defining evil as a privation. Reformed writers have also denied that God is the cause of sin. Calvin teaches, "For the proper and genuine cause of sin is not God's hidden counsel but the evident will of man,"[31] although in the context he also states that Adam's fall was "not without God's knowledge and ordination."[32] Here are some other examples:

30. Except, of course, as a *deficient* cause.
31. John Calvin, *Concerning the Eternal Predestination of God* (London: James Clarke, 1961), 122. Calvin accepts the privation theory, as is evident on p. 169.
32. Ibid., 121.

See that you make not God the author of sin, by charging his sacred decree with men's miscarriages, as if that were the cause or occasion of them; which we are sure that it is not, nor can be, any more than the sun can be the cause of darkness.[33]

It is [God] who created, preserves, actuates and directs all things. But it by no means follows, from these premises, that God is therefore the cause of sin, for sin is nothing but *anomia*, illegality, want of conformity to the divine law (1 John iii. 4), a mere privation of rectitude; consequently, being itself a thing purely negative, it can have no positive or efficient cause, but only a negative or deficient one, as several learned men have observed.[34]

According to the Canons of Dordt, "The cause or blame for this unbelief, as well as for all other sins, is not at all in God, but in man" (1.5).

In these quotations, *cause* seems to take on the connotations of the term *author*. For these writers, to say that God "causes" evil is to say, or perhaps imply, that he is to blame for it. Note the phrase "cause or blame" in the Canons of Dordt, in which the terms seem to be treated as synonyms. But note above that although Calvin rejects *cause* he affirms *ordination*. God is not the "cause" of sin, but it occurs by his "ordination." For the modern reader, the distinction is not evident. To ordain is to cause, and vice versa. If causality entails blame, then ordination would seem to entail it as well; if not, then neither entails it. But evidently in the vocabulary of Calvin and his successors there was a difference between the two terms.

For us, the question is whether God can be the efficient cause of sin without being to blame for it. The older theologians denied that God was the efficient cause of sin because they held the privation theory, and also because they identified cause with authorship. But if, as I recommend, we reject the privation theory, and if, as I believe, the connection between cause and blame in modern language is no stronger than the connection between ordination and blame, then it seems to me that it is not wrong to say that God causes evil and sin. Certainly we should employ such language *cautiously*, however, in view of the long history of its rejection by theologians.

33. Elisha Coles, *A Practical Discourse on God's Sovereignty* (Marshallton, DE: National Foundation for Christian Education, 1968), 15; originally published in 1673.
34. Jerome Zanchius, "Observations on the Divine Attributes," in *Absolute Predestination* (Marshallton, DE: National Foundation for Christian Education, n.d.), 33; originally written in 1562. Compare the formulations of the post-Reformation dogmaticians Polan and Wolleb in Heppe, *Reformed Dogmatics*, 143, and of Mastricht, 277. All of these base their arguments on the premise that evil is a mere privation.

It is interesting that Calvin does use *cause*, referring to God's agency in bringing evil about, when he distinguishes between God as the "remote cause" and human agency as the "proximate cause." Arguing that God is not the "author of sin," he says that "the proximate cause is one thing, the remote cause another."[35] Calvin points out that when wicked men steal Job's goods, Job recognizes that "the LORD gave and the LORD has taken away; may the name of the LORD be praised" (Job 1:21). The thieves, being the proximate cause of the evil, are guilty of committing it, but Job does not question the motives of the Lord, the remote cause. Calvin, however, does not believe that the proximate-remote distinction is sufficient to show us *why* God is guiltless:

> But how it was ordained by the foreknowledge and decree of God what man's future was without God being implicated as associate in the fault as the author and approver of transgression, is clearly a secret so much excelling the insight of the human mind, that I am not ashamed to confess ignorance.[36]

He uses the proximate-remote distinction merely to distinguish between the causality of God and that of creatures, and therefore to *state* that the former is always righteous. But he does not believe that the distinction solves the problem of evil.

At least, the above discussion does indicate that Calvin is willing in some contexts to refer to God as a cause of sin and evil. Calvin also describes God as the sole cause of the hardening and reprobation of the wicked:

> Therefore, if we cannot assign any reason for his bestowing mercy on his people, but just that it so pleases him, neither can we have any reason for his reprobating others but his will. When God is said to visit mercy or harden whom he will, men are reminded that they are not to seek for any cause beyond his will.[37]

3) Consider now the term *permits*. This is the preferred term in Arminian theology, in which it amounts to a denial that God causes sin. For the Arminian, God does not cause sin; he only permits it. Reformed theologians have also used the term, but they have insisted that God's permission of sin is no less efficacious than his ordination of good. Calvin denies that there is any "mere permission" in God:

35. Calvin, *Concerning the Eternal Predestination of God*, 181.
36. Ibid., 124.
37. Calvin, *Institutes*, 3.22.11; cf. 3.23.1.

From this it is easy to conclude how foolish and frail is the support of divine justice afforded by the suggestion that evils come to be not by [God's] will, but merely by His permission. Of course, so far as they are evils, which men perpetrate with their evil mind, as I shall show in greater detail shortly, I admit that they are not pleasing to God. But it is a quite frivolous refuge to say that God otiosely permits them, when Scripture shows Him not only willing but the author of them.[38]

God's permission is an *efficacious* permission. Heinrich Heppe describes it as such (*voluntas efficaciter permittens*[39]) and quotes J. H. Heidegger:

Nor whether He is willing or refusing is God's permission like man's permission, which admits of an eclipse which he neither wills nor refuses, as the LOMBARD and with him the Scholastics assert. It is effective, mighty, and not separate from God's will at all. Otiose permission of sin separated from God's will is repugnant both to the nature of the First Cause and to the divine and almighty foresight, to His nature and to Scripture.[40]

If God's permission is efficacious, how does it differ from other exercises of his will? Evidently, the Reformed use *permit* mainly as a more delicate term than *cause*, suggesting that God brings sin about with a kind of reluctance born of his holy hatred of it.

This usage does reflect a biblical pattern. When Satan acts, he acts, in an obvious sense, by God's permission.[41] God allows him to take Job's family, wealth, and health. But God will not allow Satan to take Job's life (Job 2:6). So Satan is on a leash, acting only within limits set by God. In this respect, all sinful acts are similar. The sinner can go only so far before he meets the judgment of God.

It is appropriate, therefore, to use *permission* to refer to God's ordination of sin. But we should not assume, as Arminians do, that divine permission is anything less than sovereign ordination. What God permits or allows will happen. God could easily have prevented Satan's attack on Job if he had intended to. That he did not prevent that attack implies that he intended it

---

38. John Calvin, *Concerning the Eternal Predestination of God*, 176. Calvin's use of the term *author* raises questions. He probably means that God authors evil happenings without authoring their evil character. But the use of *author* here indicates something of the flexibility of his terminology, in contrast to the relative rigidity of his successors' terminology.

39. Lat. "a will, efficaciously permitting."

40. See Heppe, *Reformed Dogmatics*, 90.

41. In this use, and in the Reformed theological use, *permission* has no connotation of moral approval as it sometimes has in contemporary use.

to happen. Permission, then, is a form of ordination, a form of causation.[42] The fact that it is sometimes taken otherwise is a good argument for not using it but perhaps not a decisive argument.

The discussion above should be sufficient to indicate the need for caution in our choice of vocabulary and also the need to think carefully before condemning the vocabulary of others. It is not easy to find adequate terms to describe God's ordination of evil. Our language must not compromise either God's full sovereignty or his holiness and goodness.

None of these formulations solves the problem of evil. It is not a solution to say that God ordains evil but does not author or cause it (if we choose to say that). As important as it is, this language is not a solution to the problem, but only a way of raising it. For the problem of evil asks *how* God can ordain evil without authoring it. And, as Calvin pointed out, the distinction between remote and proximate cause is also inadequate to answer the questions before us, however useful it may be in stating who is to blame for evil. Nor is it a solution to say that God permits, rather than ordains, evil. As we have seen, God's permission is as efficacious as his ordination. The difference between the terms brings nothing to light that will solve the problem.

I should, however, say something more about the nature of God's agency with regard to evil. God's relationship to free agents is in some respects like the relationship of an author to his characters. Let us consider to what extent God's relationship to human sinners is like that of Shakespeare to Macbeth, the murderer of Duncan.

I borrow the Shakespeare-Macbeth illustration from Wayne Grudem's excellent *Systematic Theology*.[43] But I do disagree with Grudem on one point. He says that we could say that either Macbeth or Shakespeare killed King Duncan. I agree, of course, that both Macbeth and Shakespeare are responsible, at different levels of reality, for the death of Duncan. But as I analyze the language that we typically use in such contexts, it seems clear to me that we would not normally say that Shakespeare killed Duncan. Shakespeare wrote the murder into his play. But the murder took place in the world of the play, not the real world of the author. Macbeth did it, not Shakespeare. We sense the rightness of Macbeth paying for his crime. But we would certainly consider it very unjust if Shakespeare were tried and put to death for killing Duncan. And no one suggests that there is any problem in reconciling Shakespeare's benevolence with his omnipotence over the

---

42. Traditional Arminians agree that God is omnipotent and can prevent sinful actions. So we wonder how they can object to this argument. If God could prevent sin but chooses not to, must we not say that he has ordained it to happen?
43. Grand Rapids: Zondervan, 1994, 321–22.

world of the drama. Indeed, there is reason for us to praise Shakespeare for raising up this character, Macbeth, to show us the consequences of sin.

The difference between levels, then, may have moral, as well as metaphysical, significance.[44] It may explain why the biblical writers, who do not hesitate to say that God brings about sin and evil, do not accuse him of wrongdoing. The relationship between God and us, of course, is different in some respects from that between an author and his characters. Most significantly, we are real and Macbeth is not. But between God and us there is a vast difference in the kind of reality and in relative status. God is the absolute controller of and authority over nature and history. He is the lawgiver, and we receive his laws. He is the head of the covenant; we are the servants. He has devised the creation for his own glory; we seek his glory, rather than our own. He makes us as the potter makes pots, for his own purposes. He has many rights and prerogatives we do not. Do these differences not put God in a different moral category as well?

The transcendence of God plays a significant role in biblical responses to the problem of evil. Because God is who he is, the covenant Lord, he is not required to defend himself against charges of injustice. He is the judge, and we are not. Very often in Scripture, when something happens that calls God's goodness into question, he pointedly refrains from explaining. Indeed, he often rebukes those people who question him. Job demanded an interview with God, so that he could ask God the reasons for his sufferings (Job 23:1–7; 31:35–37). But when he met God, God asked the questions: "Brace yourself like a man; I will question you, and you shall answer me" (38:3). The questions mostly revealed Job's ignorance about God's creation: if Job does not understand the ways of the animals, how can he presume to call God's motives into question? He does not even understand earthly things; how can he presume to debate heavenly things? God is not subject to the ignorant evaluations of his creatures.[45]

44. The metaphysical difference between the Creator and the world of which evil is a part may indicate the true connection between the ethical and the metaphysical, as opposed to the false connection posited by the chain-of-being thinkers mentioned earlier in this chapter. It may also indicate that there is a grain of truth in the privation theory: there is a metaphysical difference between good and evil, but it is not the difference between being and nonbeing; instead, it is the difference between uncreated being and created being.

45. To say this is not to adopt the view of Gordon H. Clark, who argued that God, being above the moral law, is not subject to it. See his *Religion, Reason, and Revelation* (Philadelphia: Presbyterian and Reformed, 1961). Certainly God has some prerogatives that he forbids to us, such as the freedom to take human life. But, for the most part, the moral laws that God imposes upon us are grounded in his own character. See Ex. 20:11; Lev. 11:44–45; Matt. 5:45; 1 Pet. 1:15–16. God will not violate his own character. What Scripture denies is that man has sufficient understanding of God's character and his eternal plan (not to mention sufficient authority) to bring accusations against him.

It is significant that the potter-clay image appears in the one place in Scripture where the problem of evil is explicitly addressed.[46] In Romans 9:19–21, Paul appeals specifically to the difference in metaphysical level and status between the Creator and the creature:

> One of you will say to me, "Then why does God still blame us? For who resists his will?" But who are you, O man, to talk back to God? "Shall what is formed say to him who formed it, 'Why did you make me like this?'" Does not the potter have the right to make out of the same lump of clay some pottery for noble purposes and some for common use?

This answer to the problem of evil turns entirely on God's sovereignty. It is as far as could be imagined from a free will defense. It brings to our attention the fact that his prerogatives are far greater than ours, as does the author-character model.

One might object that this model makes God the author of evil. But that objection confuses two senses of the word *author*. As we have seen, the phrase *author of evil* connotes not only causality of evil, but also blame for it. To author evil is to do it. But in saying that God is related to the world as an author to a story, we actually provide a way of seeing that God is *not* to be blamed for the sin of his creatures.

This is, of course, not the only biblical response to the problem of evil. Sometimes God does not respond by silencing us, as above, but by showing us in some measure how evil contributes to his plan—what I have called the greater-good defense. The greater-good defense refers particularly to God's lordship attribute of control—that he is sovereign over evil and uses it for good. The Romans 9 response refers particularly to God's lordship attribute of authority. And his attribute of covenant presence addresses the emotional problem of evil, comforting us with the promises of God and the love of Jesus, from which no evil can separate us (Rom. 8:35–39).

Many persons, Christians included, seem to be unaware that a particular form of suffering caused by evil characterizes much of the world in the first decade of the twenty-first century—oppression. In the next chapter apologist Bill Edgar addresses the difficult issues of economic and sexual oppression within the context of a biblical theology of suffering.

---

46. The problem is raised, of course, in the book of Job and in many other places in Scripture. But to my knowledge, Romans 9 is the only passage in which a biblical writer gives an explicit answer to it. Job never learns why he has suffered.

8

SUFFERING AND OPPRESSION

WILLIAM EDGAR

In the overdeveloped West we tend to reduce suffering to pain, whether physical or mental. Certainly such suffering is real enough. When it hurts, it hurts. As a child I suffered from debilitating migraine headaches, and unless you have had these, it is almost impossible to describe the agony. Yet human suffering is both wider and deeper than pain. The Bible describes suffering in a thousand ways, but surely one of the most comprehensive categories for it is oppression.

Human Bondage

Scripture gives various depictions of the broad category of oppression. Oppression is real and widespread. Wherever it occurs there are disenfranchised human beings. Lack of access to power is one of the most distressing results of oppression. Most crucially, according to Scripture, such subjugation is a sign of religious apostasy. In his litany of evils perpetrated by Israel, the prophet Amos exclaims, "You trample on the poor and force him to give you grain. . . . You oppress the righteous and take bribes and you deprive the poor of justice in the courts" (Amos 5:11–12).[1] The primary evil behind these all-too-real manifestations is Israel's disdain of the Lord God, leading to his consequent judgment against this people (Amos 5:7, 21; 6:8). So there is a cause-and-effect relation between oppression and God's displeasure. Put the opposite way, one of the most telling signs of a people's faithfulness to God is the way they treat disadvantaged people (Deut. 14:29; 26:12). Such a concern is simply the reflection of God's own concerns. He is "a father to the fatherless, a defender of widows" (Ps. 68:5; Deut. 10:18).

The oppressor's victim, in one form or another, is a slave. Again, slavery is real, but it is also part of a larger picture. The Exodus story, as it describes the misery of the enslaved Israelites and then their glorious liberation, is something of an archetype for the human condition in a fallen world, followed by the emancipation of God's people by his power. "When we were children," Paul wrote, "we were in slavery under the basic principles of the world" (Gal. 4:3). Now we are sons and daughters. The gospel gives us a new identity. Being crucified with Christ, "the body of sin . . . [is] done away with, that we should no longer be slaves to sin," he tells the Romans (Rom. 6:6). Now we are free from sin's dominion (Rom. 6:14). Slavery, though a real condition, is thus also a metaphor.

Slavery Alive Today

Despite an impression of progress, there is actually more slavery in today's world than in any previous generation. And as in the biblical accounts, slavery is both real and emblematic. In our twenty-first century, conservative estimates put the number of actual slaves at around twenty-seven million. If you add the slave-like condition of bonded labor, then the number is closer to one hundred million. The number of slaves today is greater than the entire number deported from West Africa to North America during the era of chattel slavery. Slavery is found on every continent. In Niger, about seven percent of the population, over eight-hundred-forty thousand people, are slaves. Women from Eastern Europe are bonded to work in West Africa, while men are sent into forced labor in Brazil. In India, Nepal, and Pakistan, millions of people are working in slave-like conditions. The most common form is debt bondage, or working to pay off real or alleged debts. Shamelessly exploited people are found in every sector: agriculture, mines and quarries, the gem industry, textiles, and private households.

1. Unless otherwise indicated, Scripture quotations in this chapter are taken from *The Holy Bible: New International Version* (NIV).

We learn more and more about this plight from today's crusaders against slavery. Gary Haugen of International Justice Mission (IJM) travels around the world with the purposes of uncovering cases of slavery and abuse and bringing justice and relief where possible. IJM believes that most people, including Christians, are ignorant of the extent of these evil practices and that they desperately need to be educated. At the heart of injustice, Haugen argues, are two basic components: coercion and oppression.[2] Using distressing case studies, he explains that coercion and deception work together in a devilish partnership to deprive people of freedom and keep the abused from detection.

A sad but not unusual example is that of ten-year-old Shama, one of over fifteen million children sold into bonded labor by her impoverished family. Lacking money for the medical needs of her younger sister, the family sold her into servitude to a local money lender, known as a *mudalali*. Her work is to sit on the floor and close cigarettes with a small knife for thirteen hours a day, with only a fifteen-minute break for lunch. The lender requires that she pay back the entire debt with interest before she can be free but pays her so little that this can never happen: "Through the coercion of economic desperation, the deception of hidden interest charges and the threat of abuse if she does not comply, the mudalali is able to capture Shama's income stream in perpetuity, rob her of her childhood and destroy any hope of her ever breathing a breath of freedom in her youth."[3]

More shocking, if possible, than classic slavery or debt bondage, is the worldwide practice of sex trafficking. Numbers are difficult to come by, but it is likely that tens of millions of people, mostly women and children (boys as well as girls), are currently serving as sex slaves in brothels on every continent. Human trafficking is not new, but what is new is the global dimension of this harrowing phenomenon, with its sophistication and control. Those who are working against such horrors know that coercion and deception are systemic, not simply isolated. What appears to be "just the way things are" is in fact rooted in a larger social fabric, with participants at many levels.

Most people directly involved in enslaving other human beings do so under a cloak of legitimacy. I have spent time in several countries in West Africa where one can witness the layers behind various forms of abuse. For example, taxi drivers will be stopped by police and required to hand over large portions of their earnings. If they do not, they are beaten and their

2. See Gary Haugen, *Good News About Injustice: A Witness of Courage in a Hurting World* (Downers Grove, IL: InterVarsity, 1999), 124–41.
3. Ibid., 128.

cars destroyed. The police argue that they are levying a sort of taxation. But behind them is a government that will not pay policemen enough, so they are encouraged to make up their pay with these oppressive means. For anyone hoping to bring reform it is difficult to know where to begin.

Fortunately, there is light at the end of this dark tunnel. If we begin with biblical principles, and then take an honest look at the way things are, we will find some good answers for the issues surrounding oppression, slavery, and the suffering that ensues. Typically, those answers fall into two basic categories. The first is understanding and the second is action.

Education First

One of the perverse results of the fall is that we imagine evil can be hidden from sight. In Isaiah's prophecy against Ariel, the symbolic name for Jerusalem, there is special condemnation for those who try to conduct their crimes in secret: "Woe to those who go to great depths to hide their plans from the LORD, who do their work in darkness and think, 'Who sees us? Who will know?'" (Isa. 29:15). Understanding slavery takes some biblical education, as well as some powers of observation. But it particularly requires the courage to bring dark things into the light.

We said above that the Exodus story is paradigmatic for sin and deliverance. But the Bible begins not with the Exodus but with Genesis. Getting this right is absolutely critical. Advocates of liberation theology, while they rightly concentrate on the issue of systemic oppression, often neglect the background of the order of creation and therefore get the problem and the answer wrong. So enthusiastic are they to identify oppression and emancipation as the center of theology that they neglect the bigger picture. James H. Cone, in *A Black Theology of Liberation*, uses the Exodus account to inform the basic structure of theology.[4] Viewed from the perspective of an oppressed minority, in this case African-American, Cone argues that all basic categories of theology ought to reflect the binary theme of oppression and freedom. Almost inevitably, whites are oppressors and blacks are victims. There is plenty of evidence for this view, and yet the way he puts it does not give us a balanced picture.

For one thing, although in North America whites were the slave owners, more often than not the purchasing of slaves from places like West Africa needed the complicity of other Africans. Furthermore, while oppression often looks one-sided, with moneyed people disenfranchising the less

---

4. James H. Cone, *A Black Theology of Liberation* (Philadelphia; New York: Lippincott, 1970). This and other texts had a large influence on other forms of liberation theology, particularly in Latin America.

powerful, victims can also become oppressors. This can happen through revenge or by participating in subversive plots to repay evil with evil. In other words, biblically, oppression is an equal-opportunity disease. Cone makes little mention of these subtleties. But most seriously, he does not really discuss either how we got into such a condition in the first place or what a fully just society would look like once there was liberation.

What is lacking is a consideration of the larger picture set forth in Scripture of creation-fall-redemption. Again, without beginning at creation Cone and many others who do not necessarily agree with all of his views still become, in effect, reductionists. They cannot see that the evil of oppression began not with European colonialists nor with Pharaoh, as recorded in the book of Exodus (which liberation theologians consider the most basic book of the Bible), but with our first parents in the garden. Without rooting the problem in the fall, which is creation gone wrong, they deprive themselves of the ability to find any solution more comprehensive than release from certain forms of bondage. While we certainly want to promote freedom from oppression, we do not want to stop short of responding to the full depth of the bondage that has invaded God's good world.

The Good and the Just

In the biblical account, the world of the original creation was profoundly good and thus profoundly just. Ensuring justice was the God who brought the world into being. It is he who determined the calling of each part of creation—the existence of light, the purpose of land and sea, the life of plants and animals. It is he who gave names to all things and entrusted part of that naming to the human race, whom he made after his image. The purpose of mankind is clearly stated in the record of the special creation of the man and the woman: "Then God said, 'Let us make man in our image, in our likeness, and let them rule over the fish of the sea and the birds of the air, over the livestock, over all the earth, and over all the creatures that move along the ground'" (Gen. 1:26). An astonishing statement for its breadth, it establishes the call of the human race as, fundamentally, *ruling*.

This marvelous vocation is further elaborated in the so-called cultural mandate in Genesis 1:28–30, and then in the more detailed chapter two. Though the creation is in its primeval stage, nevertheless the principles of justice are well expressed. Mankind was to rule, to have dominion, as God's image bearer, as his vice-regent here on earth. And humanity was to grow, spread, and fill the pages of unwritten history. Indeed, childbearing was to be a primary way by which this cultural mandate would be fulfilled.

The original creation was "good and very good" (see Gen. 1:31). This goodness radiated throughout all aspects of the world, including human social life. The man and the woman, who would certainly have different roles, were equally image bearers. Adam would greet his newly created spouse as "bone of my bones and flesh of my flesh" (Gen. 2:23). There was to be no struggle between the sexes or between those of Eve's progeny. In addition to the general condition of goodness and right rule, there was to be a special probation whereby this condition would be tested. A special instruction was given: do not eat of the fruit of the tree of the knowledge of good and evil. Many in the Reformed tradition understand this test to be eschatological, that is, to look forward to a time of permanent, consummate bliss should our first parents refuse the temptation and joyfully accept God's good intentions. While having a confrontation with evil, they should not have succumbed. If they had not, they would have guided their descendants into greater and greater enjoyment of goodness and rule by justice.

The point here is that if one does not begin with this understanding of the goodness of creation then one will be at a loss to find it later. The struggle against oppression is not a struggle against the order of creation. Often, those who engage in liberation theologies rightly identify oppression as structural rather than only individual, but they wrongly reduce the battle to good guys who are victims against bad guys who are rulers. What they miss is that all peoples, from every race, living out every calling, are "good guys" because they are made in the image of God. We are called to rule God's earth, *all* the earth, as Genesis puts it. And they also miss the subtleties of the way justice looks in our highly differentiated modern societies. Rule is not wrong in itself. It is a necessary and happy feature of social organization.

The Catastrophe

The story continues. Rather than exercising rule under God's terms, Adam and Eve rebelled and chose to trust the voice of the tempter rather than the voice of the Lord. It is significant that the tempter used, as a primary argument, the claim that God was unjust. You won't die, the serpent argued, but your "eyes will be opened," as though God had arbitrarily and unfairly (oppressively) kept them shut, pushing those poor creatures down. The tempter argued that they would be like God, knowing good and evil—as though bearing God's image was not enough, as though they could not grow in their knowledge of good and evil without having to commit to evil. It was all perversely plausible.

There is an important point to be noted: God fully intended for the human race to grow in its understanding of right and wrong.[5] Biblical sages are meant to grow in their understanding. There is a way to grow in understanding evil without having to succumb to evil. The author of Hebrews tells us it is by constant use and training that the mature person comes to "distinguish good from evil" (Heb. 5:14). No one escapes this training ground, not even Jesus, the incarnate Lord, who, "Although he was a son, . . . learned obedience from what he suffered" (Heb. 5:8).

Adam and Eve failed, however. And now, in solidarity with our first parents, the human race has been plunged into the deepest misery. Having been "good guys," we all became "bad guys," capable of the worst. We are still God's image bearers, but we are inclined to evil. We know this story well, but we do not often understand its full force. What was introduced into the world in this act of "cosmic treason"[6] has resulted in nothing less than a curse across every sphere of life (Gen. 3:8–19). Our primary religious engagement, our friendship with God, has been broken. Instead of free access, we are naked and ashamed. To cover ourselves we invent counterfeit religions and lifestyles. Childbearing, which was to be a major joy, is now a major hardship. Our relation to God's good earth has been broken. The extent of our rule over the world is such that, now that we are no longer right with God, the world is no longer right with us. We now want to ruin this place. But it will ruin us too. Strain and difficulty characterize our efforts at bringing forth food from the ground. Indeed, all of natural life is set against us. Though we were made from the ground, so that we could live and give life to it, in the end we will die, and the ground will reclaim us.

Significantly for our considerations, we have become a race of oppressors. According to the biblical account, the desire to rule would replace marital harmony (Gen. 3:16). Whatever else the cryptic words "desire" and "rule" may mean, they do not speak of a healthy relationship, but rather of a struggle for power. Power became distorted throughout human society. Just one generation from Adam and Eve, jealousy incited one brother to murder another. The twin evils of coercion and oppression mentioned earlier came to inhabit a world that knew nothing of them before.

Now, it must be stressed that our depravity does not eradicate the image of God. The fall does not abrogate the creation. As Albert Wolters puts it, not the structures of creation but their direction have been altered: "Sin introduces an entirely new dimension to the created order. There is no

---

5. This point is admirably made by Geerhardus Vos in his *Biblical Theology* (Grand Rapids, MI: Eerdmans, 1948), 39–43.
6. I first heard this expression from R. C. Sproul in an explanation of Original Sin.

sense in which sin 'fits' in God's good handiwork. Rather, it establishes an unprecedented axis, as it were, along which it is possible to plot varying degrees of good and evil."[7] This allows us to fight against evil without fighting against the created order or against the Creator who brought it into being. Indeed, the created order continues to function, by God's grace, so that humanity still rules and may seek to effect justice.

Even as things go from bad to worse in the biblical story, hope remains and grace exists to apply justice to the fallen world. Early on there are accounts of oppression leading to slavery. The Joseph story is a poignant account of the jealousy of brothers against a younger sibling who had their father's special favor more than they (Genesis 37ff.). One can debate whether Joseph was entirely wise to share his dream about ruling his brothers. What is not debatable is the heinous revenge they took: selling him into slavery to Midianite merchants, plunging their father, Jacob, into despair, and condemning Joseph to misery. Of course, we know the marvelous conclusion to the story: an evil plan is turned into the greater good of Israel (Gen. 50:20). God ordered history such that the very oppressors who made Joseph a slave were blessed with redemption. We also know that not long after, the seventy who entered Egypt to live under Joseph's rule became a great multitude.

Yet now, all of God's people were plunged into slavery: "Then a new king, who did not know about Joseph, came to power in Egypt" (Ex. 1:8). Using the tactics of fear, the Egyptians made the lives of the Israelites bitter, condemning them to slave labor in both the cities and the fields. As many have pointed out, the oppression of Israel had several levels:[8] (1) a political level—the people became victims of oppressive policies, and instead of having any recourse their voice within the Egyptian state was removed; (2) an economic level, though the two are related—the Israelites were more and more exploited and forced into labors whose fruits only benefited the oppressors; (3) a social level—the state not only became tyrannical but genocidal toward Israel, attempting systematically to eliminate all male newborns; (4) the religious level—in one way this is an all-pervasive category since all of life is religion, but here we shall describe it somewhat more narrowly as service, or worship. The slavery of the Israelites was a great hindrance to their worship of the Lord. The point is made poignantly

7. Albert M. Wolters, *Creation Regained: Biblical Basics for a Reformational Worldview* (Grand Rapids, MI: Eerdmans, 1985), 47.
8. Here I will use the categories suggested by Christopher J. H. Wright in *The Mission of God* (Downers Grove, IL: InterVarsity, 2006), 268–72, although I substitute "religious" for his "spiritual."

in the Hebrew text because the word for "service" (*'ābad*) is the same as the word for "slavery." Thus, Moses told Pharaoh to let God's people go so that they might *serve* (worship) him, which would have been understood as a confrontationally stated alternative to their present *service* of slavery (Ex. 4:22–23; cf. 2:23).

We should have no difficulty drawing the parallels to the entire human condition. All of us, whether conscious of it or not, are under the yoke of oppression. It has many levels. Although some are the actual oppressors, even they are under the rule of slavery to sin. Thus it misses the mark to say that there are the guilty ones (the oppressors) and the innocent ones (the oppressed). To be sure, the oppressors will be judged the more severely. But even in their oppression they show themselves to submit to the tyranny of sin, from which they too need delivery. We remember the story of Zacchaeus, a corrupt tax collector who saw the light and promised Jesus he would give half of his considerable possessions to the poor and repay four times the amount to those he extorted. To this Jesus said, "Today salvation has come to this house, because this man, too, is a son of Abraham," adding, "For the Son of Man came to seek and to save what was lost" (Luke 19:9–10). This puts a very different light on things than liberation theology does. "Bad guys," too, are children of Abraham, and can be found by Jesus.

So what can be done? At this point, one may certainly raise the larger issue of theodicy. How is it that, in a world created by God and governed by God, we could have fallen into this condition? While the Scripture does not fully elaborate on this issue, it does state two things forcefully. First, God is fully sovereign, yet his authority over humanity does not make him the author of evil. His sovereignty is, indeed, a guarantee of our freedom and responsibility, not an impediment to it. Put clearly, we alone are accountable for the introduction of evil into the world. Second, God has had mercy on us, looks down at our suffering, and provides a way out.

Full Redemption

Just as the Lord responds to all of the dimensions of need mentioned in the Exodus story, so he fully meets all of our needs as people in bondage. It is crucial to understand that God's response comes from his heart. When the people of Israel cried out and groaned in their slavery, God *heard* them. This signifies more than simply being attuned to the people's cry. It means he is there, he has compassion, he is not silent. "God heard their groaning and he remembered his covenant" (Ex. 2:24). Furthermore, the Lord "looked on the Israelites and was concerned about them" (Ex. 2:25). The word translated "concern" is far stronger than our English word, which gives the impression of just being worried or caring for the people. The root is *yada*, "to know." Knowledge of his people is a constant theme in the Old Testament. To be known by God is to be loved, to be in the best place you could possibly be. This is because now God bears the burden, not the people. Knowledge here means full acknowledgment and commitment to intervene. In the midst of his own oppressive suffering, Job cries out that he cannot see God. "But," he says, "he *knows* the way that I take; when he has tested me, I will come forth as gold" (Job 23:10). God's knowledge is of great comfort to Job, because it means that in the end, he will do something about his condition.

God remembers his covenant. Again, to remember is not simply to recall. It is to bring to the forefront the great promises that were made to the patriarchs, beginning with Abraham and reiterated to Isaac and Jacob. Everything hinges on these covenantal promises. Since God swore by himself and proved his sincerity with signs of several kinds, it is impossible for that covenant not to be fulfilled (Heb. 6:13). Thus, the Lord's knowledge of his people's plight has a basic foundation not simply in his omniscience but in his great promise, sealed forever with testimonies to the fathers. When Christ was on the cross, the thief asked him to remember him when he came into his kingdom (Luke 23:42). His response, "Today you will be with me in paradise," flowed out of the guaranty of the covenant that he remembered (Luke 23:43).

To make the point another way: oppression is not just any condition of servitude. It is denying people their dignity as God's image bearers. The oppressed are denied access to their rights before God. While the expressions of human rights in the modern world often coincide with the biblical picture of God's intentions for humanity, they may not always be the same thing. This is particularly true of the struggle for justice. For example, to become president of a company is not my right. To have the opportunity to work in healthy conditions is. To call homosexual partnerships a civil right is not an acceptable principle of justice. This is because marriage is a creation ordinance, established by God, and meant to be heterosexual. To allow legitimate partnerships for the purpose of jointly owning property or running a company is a different matter. Christians ought to be hard at work to promote true justice for all. Such justice is not simply what might seem rationally warranted. It must stem from the divine requirements.

Christ and Redemption
We stated above that there are two categories of answers to the problem of oppression. The first is understanding. The next step is to move from

understanding to action. And here, of course, the Exodus account tells us about a God who is fully engaged in action. When the Lord appeared to Moses from the burning bush—a sign that Israel was in the fire but would survive unscathed—he said these powerful words: "I have indeed *seen* the misery of my people in Egypt. I have *heard* them crying out because of their slave drivers, and I am concerned about their suffering." Notice the verbs. God understands. But then he adds, "So I have *come down* to rescue them from the hand of the Egyptians and to *bring them up* out of that land" (Ex. 3:7–8). Understanding is followed by action. God is a God of action and not of empty promises.

One important aspect of God's active intervention is worth noting: God is a *gōʾel*. That is, he is a redeemer. This means he is a hero who comes to purchase his people back (see Ex. 15:16). But it means much more. The *gōʾel* in the ancient world was typically a member of the wider family whose duty it was to protect that family when it met with adversity or came into need. It meant something like "kinsman protector," or, really, the "family champion." He might need to avenge unjustly shed blood (Num. 35:12, 19), or to provide an heir, as in the memorable case of Boaz with Ruth. It most significantly meant the redemption of land or slaves. If a family member fell into debt and sold himself as a bonded servant, the *gōʾel* was to purchase his freedom (Lev. 25:25–28). Well, the Lord God identifies himself as the *gōʾel* of his people: "I will free you from being slaves to them [the Egyptians], and I will *redeem* you with an outstretched arm and with mighty acts of judgment" (Ex. 6:6). Other verbs tell us of God's strong commitment to intervention: he *brings out*, he *delivers*, he *saves*, he *causes to go up*, and so forth. In all of these cases it is clear that God himself takes the initiative, because he is faithful to his promises.

The Exodus account describes the reality of slavery and salvation from all aspects of its bondage. But this is only a *type*, or a paradigm, in the larger picture of salvation history. The *antetype* is, of course, Jesus Christ. He quite literally understood, and then came down to earth as the incarnate Son of God, in order to bring us up with him to the promised land of eternal life in the heavenly places. And he did so not by judging the world, as God had judged the Egyptians, but by his judgment on bondage itself. He effected the death of death in his own death. Being sinless, he was able to rise up from the dead and to bring justification to all who believe in him (Rom. 4:25). So now, when we come to God through Christ, we may have both justification, as Christ's righteousness is imputed to us, and sanctification, whereby we are transformed from our own slavery to sin to full freedom to serve our God. He is a God, as the *Book of Common Prayer* puts it, "whose service is perfect freedom." To be sure, at the end of this world's history he will come again to establish full justice on the earth, in a judgment of fire. But for now, he does it incrementally, not bruising the dimly burning wick but fanning it into flame.

Christ is the true *gō'el* who comes to redeem his people, purchasing them at a terrible price. The risen Christ then leads his people in a mission of redemption for the world. Following the divine pattern, the church must bring the message of forgiveness to the world and also bring relief to its slaves. These two tasks cannot be separated. As Harvie Conn and others have pointed out, as followers of Christ we refuse to isolate the so-called physical from the so-called spiritual. To do so is to break up a divinely ordered unity. Just as a body without a spirit is a corpse, so a spirit without a body is a ghost![9]

A powerful approach to this fully-integrated mission of the church is found in the book of James. In his polemic against a religion of good intentions and of claims to being justified by a faith that is alone, the author describes authentic spirituality this way: "Religion that God our Father accepts as pure and faultless is this: to look after orphans and widows in their distress and to keep oneself from being polluted by the world" (James 1:27). The word translated "to look after" is *episkeptomai*. It has a variety of meanings, but they all center on the idea of "looking upon in order to help." A closely related term is *episkopos*, the overseer, or bishop, whose duty it is to guard the soul, to see that things are done right in the church. The Old Testament equivalent is often *phaqar*, which contains the idea of looking down with grace or mercy. The Septuagint uses the word *episkeptomai* or its equivalent in places such as Genesis 21:1, where the Lord is gracious to Sarah and gives her a child. And it is represented several times in the Exodus story, in exactly the way we have been discussing. God commands Moses to report to the elders that he has "*watched over you* and . . . seen what has been done to you in Egypt" (Ex. 3:16; see 4:31; 13:19).

Often understood as a kind of injunction to visit elderly people on a Sunday afternoon, this admonition is far stronger. It says that if we are Christians at all, we will look for disenfranchised people, those without proper access to power, and will help them gain it. According to Scripture, Jesus Christ is particularly identified with suffering people. In the parable of the sheep and the goats, those righteous people are blessed who gave him food when he was hungry and drink when he was thirsty, who clothed him, cared for him (our

9. Harvie M. Conn, *Evangelism: Doing Justice and Preaching Grace* (Phillipsburg, NJ: P&R, repr. 1992).

word *episkeptomai* again) in sickness, and saw him in prison. To do these things for the least of his people is to do it for him (Matt. 25:34–40). These injunctions are not given to us to turn the Christian faith into a religion of works. They are to remind us that the evidence of true faith is caring for, even more, seeking justice for, those who are disenfranchised.

Relief for Today's Slaves

When the church begins to understand these principles, then moving into action should be almost natural. Almost, because our actions must be informed not only by the theological foundation of God's mission to the world but by biblical wisdom as it applies to the contemporary expressions of sin and evil. What does the pursuit of justice look like in the modern era, where slavery continues to keep its shackles around the necks and souls of oppressed peoples?

Let us reflect briefly on the experience of African-Americans. While many other examples can be cited, this one is particularly powerful in that enslaved Africans in North America embraced the Christian faith and then lived out their oppression and emancipation in its light. Sylvia Frey explores this transformation in *Come Shouting to Zion*:

> The passage from traditional religions to Christianity was arguably the single most significant event in African-American history. It created a community of faith and provided a body of values and a religious commitment that became in time the principal solvent of ethnic differences and the primary source of cultural identity. It provided African-Americans with an ideology of resistance and the means to absorb the cultural norms that turned Africans into African Americans. The churches Afro-Christians founded formed the institutional bases for these developments and served as the main training ground for the men and women who were to lead the community out of slavery and into a new identity as free African-American Christians.[10]

Accordingly, it comes as no surprise that the enslaved Africans strongly identified with the people of Israel. They loved Moses, who was God's spokesman against Pharaoh. And, especially, they loved King Jesus, the great redeemer who was God's chosen one to scatter the proud, bring down rulers, and lift up the humble (Luke 1:51–52).

Not surprisingly, the enslaved Africans were deeply knowledgeable about the Bible as well. They developed a unique interpretive approach to the

10. Sylvia Frey and Betty Wood, *Come Shouting to Zion: African-American Protestantism in the American South and British Caribbean to 1830* (Chapel Hill: University of North Carolina Press, 1998), 1.

Scriptures. In the second half of the eighteenth century, a self-conscious hermeneutic emerged in which the Bible gave hope for emancipation but also helped interpret the horrific condition of chattel slavery. We are coming to appreciate the work of these early exegetes in a new way. Historically, two schools of thought have more or less prevailed. The one says that African-American Christianity was basically emotional, derived from the revival meetings. The other states that black religion was a free-will Arminianism that could not accept God's cruel providence.

As we look more closely at the actual sermons and writings, we find quite another picture emerging. Many of the early biblical interpreters were Calvinists with a strong sense of God's providence and of the finality of Christ's work. One of the most remarkable, John Marrant, a freeborn African-American minister in Boston, told his fellow blacks that if they wanted to see themselves "presented on the level . . . with the greatest kings on earth," they must "study the holy book of God." He went on to argue that the evil of the day was passing away, giving way to the era wherein the poor in spirit and those that mourn would inherit the kingdom of God.[11]

A school of thought grew, represented by outstanding black exegetes like Lemuel Haynes, Quobna Ottobah Cugoano, and especially the famous Olaudah Equiano, the friend and mentor of William Wilberforce, that saw the Bible as a great tool to attack the evils of the slave trade. It did this not by finding verses against slavery or by arguing against the slaveholders' misreading of Old Testament history but by pointing to the finished work of Christ.[12] For example, rather than questioning the perverse historiography that traces the black race to Ham, their argument was that at the atonement of Christ, any curse from times past was removed. But it went further. Equiano believed that there were strong historical parallels between the Ibo (his people) and the Israelites. Both practiced sacrifices, both believed in a Creator God, both practiced circumcision. And both practiced a milder, Mosaic form of slavery. But then in Christ all of that was fulfilled and the shadows removed. Therefore, the African slavery of his time was a return to the past and a wicked one at that. Whatever one may think of Equiano's historiography, this was a powerful argument, as John Saillant explains:

11. From "A Sermon Preached on the 24th Day of June, 1789 . . . " in *Black Atlantic Writers of the Eighteenth Century*, ed. Vincent Carretta (Lexington: University Press of Kentucky, 1996).
12. See, for example, *The Interesting and Other Narratives*, rev. ed. (New York: Penguin Classics, 2003).

Lawful slavery among the Israelites as well as among West Africans was revealed, after the Atonement, to be a misinterpretation, even if a necessary one, of God's commands. The idea that both Israelites and Africans inevitably misinterpreted God's word allowed Equiano and Cugoano to see themselves as converted Africans and to praise West African culture for its Old Testament nobility even as they criticized the African segments of the slave trade and slavery.[13]

Besides this, another type of argument was employed. Providence, which had been used to justify slavery, was turned upside down and was used by this school of thought to prove that God could use even the harshest means to bring people to the knowledge of himself. Both Equiano and Cugoano argued that the abuses they suffered at the hands of white men came from the "invisible hand of God" to allow them to come to know him. This was very different from the white case for slavery being a providential move to "civilize" the blacks. Providence would never lead to such systematic evil, this school argued. In fact, as the Calvinist Lemuel Haynes explained, slaves had been kept "under the greatest ignorance, and Blindness, and they are scersly Ever [sic] told by their white masters whether there is a Supreme Being that governs the universe."[14] No, providence could lead only to benefits, so modern slavery had to be a temporary hardship on the journey to Christian freedom.

A Long Way from Home

A great deal of water has flowed over the dam from the eighteenth century to our own times. Yet even today full freedom, with justice, is not available to people of color in Europe and North America. But almost every time that there has been progress in the struggle for social justice, the biblical narrative is in the fabric. The Southern Freedom Movement and the Southern Christian Leadership Conference would make no sense without the backdrop of the Bible. Martin Luther King Jr., Fannie Lou Hamer, and so many others constantly employed terms of the biblical imagery of slavery and emancipation. King frequently used the images of the Promised Land, the "least of these," justice rolling down like waters, and the like in his powerful rhetoric.

13. John Saillant, "Origins of African-American Biblical Hermeneutics in the Eighteenth-Century Black Opposition," in *African-Americans and the Bible: Sacred Texts and Social Textures*, ed. Vincent L. Wimbush (New York: Continuum, 2003), 240.
14. Quoted by Saillant in "Origins of African-American Biblical Hermeneutics," 243. The ancient spelling is in the original.

Despite this, there was arguably an important deficiency. Their language did not fully attain the robust scriptural requirements for justice. Here is the battle for today. While correctly making the parallel between racial discrimination and oppression in biblical terms, there has been a confusion of the biblical idea of liberation with the American dream which has actually stopped short of full emancipation. This means that many leaders never made a separation of church from state, at least in their rhetoric. Their common problem is one that Haynes, Cugoano, and Equiano would have recognized. It is to confuse human rights with American destiny. It is to confuse the biblical requirements for justice with a kind of faith in one nation that might be privileged to have special favor with God. Put another way, it is to fail to recognize that justice must be expressed in every sphere of society, not just in schools or simply from the government down but in a variety of God-given institutions.

If James Skillen is right in his assessment of the scope of biblical justice, then both blacks and whites have missed the deeper requirements of justice in our highly differentiated society.[15] The civil rights movement rightly fought for justice over against discrimination in significant pockets of society. Led mostly by black Christians, its goals were accepted, sometimes grudgingly, by whites. Yet, while looking at the problems and solutions from different vantage points, blacks and whites both shared a common understanding of America's call and of its civil religion. According to this view, which took a long time to develop, America is called as a special nation under the kind and watchful eye of the Almighty. At its center is the idea of freedom—not biblical freedom but a generalized idea of utopian American life, one that ensures the individual liberty of all its citizens. This is a fine thing in itself but very different from a fully biblical ideal of justice in every sphere of society.

While whites debated the role of government in forcing racial integration, with the more conservative ones rejecting government interference and the more liberal ones welcoming it when necessary, both defined justice merely in terms of freedom—particularly individual freedom, often assuming that the nation had a special destiny under God's providence to spread that freedom around the world. And while blacks debated the relative merits of force versus nonviolence, both understood America to be a promised land, resembling Palestine in the Old Testament. Thus, while both blacks and whites supported the end of racial discrimination in schools and

15. James W. Skillen, *In Pursuit of Justice: Christian-Democratic Explorations* (Lanham, MD: Rowman & Littlefield, 2004), 82–92.

workplace, neither significantly wrestled with the deeper question of what justice looks like throughout a differentiated society, where government has a limited role to play. To extend the famous quip by G. K. Chesterton: whites believed that America was a nation with the soul of a church,[16] while blacks believed that America was a church with the soul of a nation.[17] But neither fully recognized the differentiated society we live in, where neither should civil law be determined by vague religiosity, nor should an entire nation be considered church-like. Justice means fully understanding the difference between a modern nation and the calling of the Old Testament Israelite theocracy, which was uniquely chosen by God to be his people. Skillen clarifies this:

> Our republic can be just and do justice only as a community of citizens under public law. A just polity is one that upholds equal and fair treatment under law for people of all races as they exercise responsibilities in their families, churches, schools, businesses, and other organizations. A just polity is one that recognizes and gives equal treatment to people of all faiths, all colors, and all ethnic backgrounds, but it cannot overcome all sin or bring in the Kingdom of God to America.[18]

At the deepest level, then, people are not defined by their color, but as image bearers of God, living and having their being in many different spheres of life.

What is true of America is true of nations around the world. In the struggle against slavery worldwide, justice should be promoted in every sphere of existence. Certainly the governments of many countries will need to be called to task. But so will families, schools, churches and mosques, businesses, and artists' studios. As Christians, we believe in promoting biblical justice across the board. Because God looks down with compassion on all who are oppressed, we must in turn look for opportunities to visit his justice in every place it is ignored. Everyone has a role to play. For everyone can find opportunities in the varied world we live in to "look after orphans and widows in their distress" (James 1:27). Once we recognize the true extent of suffering, then, with God's power we may be agents of

---

16. G. K. Chesterton, *What I Saw in America*, Collected Works, vol. 21 (Ft. Collins, CO: Ignatius Press, 1990), 37.

17. This was suggested to me by James Melvin Washington, "The Making of a Church with the Soul of a Nation," in *African American Religious Thought: An Anthology*, ed. Cornel West and Eddie S. Glaude Jr. (Louisville: Westminster, 2003), 414.

18. Ibid., 90.

transformation, called to bring people out of bondage and into true and meaningful freedom.

While this chapter's treatment of worldwide and corporate suffering is important, so are individual cases of suffering. And that is what the next two chapters provide. First, David Calhoun tells his story of coping for almost twenty years with a form of cancer that was supposed to kill him in one year. Then, John Feinberg concludes our volume with his gripping story of loving his wife, Pat, as she has endured a crushing neurological disorder that has gradually robbed her of physical and mental abilities.

9

POEMS IN THE PARK

My Cancer and God's Grace

DAVID B. CALHOUN

Not long before he died of cancer in 1991, Howard Nemerov, professor emeritus at Washington University in St. Louis and former Poet Laureate of the United States, wrote this poem of two sentences:

> What rational being, after seventy years,
> When Scripture says he's running out of rope,
> Would want more of the only world he knows?
>
> No rational being, he while he endures
> Holds on to the inveterate infantile hope
> That the road ends but as the runway does.[1]

Nemerov makes two points in his little poem of forty-six words: one, this life is pretty miserable, especially as one gets older; two, people hold

---

1. Howard Nemerov, "Trying Conclusions," in *Trying Conclusions: New and Selected Poems, 1961–1991* (Chicago: University of Chicago Press, 1991), 159; used by permission.

on to the childish, irrational hope that there is life after death. Perhaps the words *death after death* could sum up the poet's view.

Many centuries ago another—and far greater—poet also reflected on this life and what lies beyond it. His immortal words are found in the Twenty-third Psalm—the most beloved of all the psalms, probably the best known of all the chapters of the Bible, and perhaps the most memorable fifty-three words (in the Hebrew text) ever written in any language.

> The LORD is my shepherd; I shall not want.
> He makes me lie down in green pastures.
> He leads me beside still waters.
> He restores my soul.
> He leads me in paths of righteousness
> for his name's sake.
>
> Even though I walk through the valley of the shadow of death,
> I will fear no evil,
> for you are with me;
> your rod and your staff,
> they comfort me.
>
> You prepare a table before me
> in the presence of my enemies;
> you anoint my head with oil;
> my cup overflows.
> Surely goodness and mercy shall follow me
> all the days of my life,
> and I shall dwell in the house of the LORD
> forever.

The psalmist also makes two points: one, this life is sometimes delightful and sometimes hard; two, though our circumstances change, the Lord does not. He is with us, his people, all the way through this life, and after this life we shall dwell in his house forever. We could sum up the psalm with the words "life after life."

These two very different poems, one modern and one ancient, illustrate the power of poetry to express our deepest yearnings, our darkest fears, our most baffling questions, our greatest hopes, and our strongest certainties.

Virginia Woolf wrote that "English, which can express the thoughts of Hamlet and the tragedy of Lear, has no words for the shiver and the headache. . . . The merest school girl, when she falls in love, has Shakespeare and Keats to speak for her; but let a sufferer try to describe a pain in his head for a doctor and language at once runs dry."[2] But there are words for the sufferer—with a pain in his head or an ache in her heart—in poems. General William Lennox, superintendent of West Point Military Academy, teaches a course on war poetry. He has said, "For those who are in combat, it's very hard for them to articulate what they experience. They go through a whole series of emotions: joy, elation, horror, fear. What genre allows you to portray that better than poetry?"[3]

The Lithuanian-Polish poet Czeslaw Milosz has described physical pain perceptively in this age of Alzheimers. "Wise thoughts fail in its presence" and "starry skies go out," he writes; "this body so fragile and woundable . . . will remain when words abandon us."[4]

The English romantic poet John Keats describes the deeper pain of the human condition in his "Ode to a Nightingale." He addresses the little bird, which, he says, has never known:

> . . . The weariness, the fever, and the fret
> Here, where men sit and hear each other groan;
> Where palsy shakes a few, sad, last grey hairs,
> Where youth grows pale, and spectre-thin, and dies;
> Where but to think is to be full of sorrow.[5]

In a few words, Irish poet W. B. Yeats explains the source of that sorrow:

> But is there any comfort to be found?
> Man is in love and loves what vanishes,
> What more is there to say?[6]

The most profound poetry—describing our suffering in its many dimensions and giving voice to our cries of lament—is the poetry of the Bible. Close to one-third of the Old Testament is poetry—a little in the narrative books, more in the Prophets, and a large part of Psalms, Proverbs, Lamenta-

---

2. Virginia Woolf, "On Being Ill," quoted in Kristin M. Swenson, *Living through Pain: Psalms and the Search for Wholeness* (Waco: Baylor University Press, 2005), 40.

3. Gen. William Lennox, quoted by Peggy Rosenthal, "Singing of War," *Books & Culture*, vol. 12, no. 6 (November/December 2006): 8.

4. Czeslaw Milosz, "Body," in *New and Collected Poems, 1931–2001* (New York: HarperCollins, 2001), 639.

5. John Keats, "Ode to a Nightingale," in *The Poetical Works of John Keats*, ed. H. Burton Forman (New York: Thomas Y. Crowell, 1895), 292–93.

6. W. B. Yeats, "Nineteen Hundred and Nineteen," in *The Collected Poems of W. B. Yeats* (New York: Collier, 1983), 208.

tions, Job, and Ecclesiastes. In *Living Through Pain: Psalms and the Search for Wholeness*, Kristin M. Swenson writes in a chapter with the title "Pain and the Psalms, Beyond the Medicine Cabinet" that the "psalms provide a vocabulary and language for expressing pain, a grammar of pain, which continues to resonate for people struggling with difficulties understanding and describing their particular experiences of suffering."[7]

John Calvin described the psalms as "an anatomy of all the parts of the soul, for there is not an emotion of which any one can be conscious that is not here represented as in a mirror. Or rather, the Holy Spirit has here drawn to the life all the griefs, sorrows, fears, doubts, hopes, cares, perplexities . . . with which the minds of men are wont to be agitated."[8] Calvin himself translated six psalms into French for congregational singing before turning over the task to other and better poets.[9]

Hebrew poetry is characterized by terseness, parallelism, repetition, chiasm, figures of speech, and sometimes assonance—most of which can be preserved in translations. "The rhetorical impact of biblical poetry is considerable and its aesthetic dimensions manifold," writes Adele Berlin. "The prophets used it to convince, the wise to instruct, the psalmists to offer praise."[10] We find in the words of the psalms not only the wisdom to teach and convince but also the power to comfort and sustain. The psalms provide us with thoughts to think and words to speak when we don't know how to think and what to say.

Paul Minear urges Bible scholars to study the "exegesis" of the great composers, such as Bach and Brahms, who have set biblical texts to music. "Composers are such superb interpreters of experiences of mortality, whether in modern life or in ancient literature, that all other interpreters of the same texts would do well to listen acutely to them," he wrote.[11] Christian poets, too, are often excellent exegetes of biblical truth, and non-Christian poets, blessed with God's common grace, may express not only the sadness, bleakness, and brokenness of human life and the tragedies of history, but also sometimes see, if only dimly, that this is not the way it is supposed to be.

7. Swenson, *Living Through Pain*, 74.
8. John Calvin, *Commentary on the Book of Psalms*, trans. James Anderson (Grand Rapids, MI: Eerdmans, 1949), 1:xxxvii.
9. Ford Lewis Battles, trans. and ed., *The Piety of John Calvin: An Anthology Illustrative of the Spirituality of the Reformer* (Grand Rapids, MI: Baker, 1978), 137–65.
10. Adele Berlin, "Poetry, Biblical Hebrew," in *The Oxford Companion to the Bible*, ed. Bruce M. Metzger and Michael D. Coogan (Oxford University Press, 1993), 599.
11. Paul Minear, *Death Set to Music: Masterworks by Bach, Brahms, Penderecki, Bernstein* (Atlanta: John Knox, 1987), 5.

During a period of intensive chemotherapy treatment some years ago, I found that it helped me to walk. Day after day I walked around and around a half-mile path in a park across the street from my house. I usually took with me a little book of poems or a small hymnbook. As I walked, I read the poems and hymns slowly, out loud. As the medicine flowed into my body each week in the hospital next to the park, so the words of the poetry flowed into my heart and mind every day as I walked, giving me a new infusion of courage, patience, hope, and trust.

There was no plan to my reading in the park. My choice of books and poets was almost accidental—which is another way of saying that it was completely providential. The book had to be small so I could hold it easily and read as I walked. And the poems had to be, for the most part, plain. The Lord commanded Habakkuk to "write the vision; make it plain on tablets, so he may run who reads it" (Hab. 2:2). I did not have the mental energy to struggle over obscure poetry. I made an exception, however, for Gerard Manley Hopkins, T. S. Eliot, and a few others. Hopkins wrote to a friend who found his poems obscure that he should not bother with the meaning but "pay attention to the best and most intelligible stanzas."[12]

The poets who helped me most were those who shared my Christian convictions. They represented many parts of the Christian tradition and reflected diverse theological and spiritual perceptions. I tried to avoid the sentimental, the falsely triumphant, the overly pious, the dishonest, and the sloppy in thought or language. Poetry did not have to be great poetry to help me, but it had to be honest and true. Through poetry I began to see and hear things in a new way. Francis Thompson wrote:

O world invisible, we view thee,
O world intangible, we touch thee,
O world unknowable, we know thee,
Inapprehensible, we clutch thee!

Thompson promised that if we would only listen we would hear the wings of the angels beating at our own "clay-shuttered doors." If we would only look we would see "the many-splendoured thing."[13] In his *Reflec-*

12. Gerard Manley Hopkins, quoted in Frederick Buechner, *Speak What We Feel (Not What We Ought to Say): Reflections on Literature and Faith* (San Francisco: HarperSanFrancisco, 2001), 10.
13. Francis Thompson, "In No Strange Land (The Kingdom of God Is Within You)," in Ben Witherington III and Christopher Mead Armitage, eds., *The Poetry of Piety: An Anthology of Christian Poetry* (Grand Rapids, MI: Baker, 2002), 119–20.

tions on the Psalms, C. S. Lewis describes the poetry of the psalms as "a little incarnation, giving body to what had been before invisible and inaudible."[14] The psalms, as well as hymns and the words of honest and thoughtful poets, can become little incarnations, enabling us to see the many-splendored things.

Barbara Kingsolver has written that "it's not such a wide gulf to cross . . . from survival to poetry."[15] Those who have suffered and endured are often compelled to write about it. This is especially true for Christians. *Fraser: Not a Private Matter* is a book about a young Scottish minister and his long battle with kidney failure. Fraser Tallach's youngest brother, John, writes in the book's introduction, "As I thought about God's care over those whose experiences are told in this book it occurred to me that the grace of God, though given in a way which is intimately personal, is not a private matter. Rather it is a public statement about himself which God makes to the world, through the lives of those to whom this grace is given."[16]

It is not such a wide gulf to cross from survival to poetry or, we could add, from poetry to survival. In *The Anatomy of Hope: How People Prevail in the Face of Illness*, Jerome Groopman, professor at Harvard Medical School and chief of experimental medicine at the Beth Israel Deaconess Medical Center in Boston, asserts that "clear-eyed hope gives us the courage to confront our circumstances and the capacity to surmount them. For my patients, hope, true hope, has proved as important as any medication I might prescribe or any procedure I might perform." "Hope," Dr. Groopman came to believe, "is as vital to our lives as the very oxygen that we breathe."[17] Groopman's thesis is dramatically illustrated by the movie *To End All Wars* and the book by Ernest Gordon on which it is based, *Through the Valley of the Kwai*.[18] Gordon and other Scottish and British prisoners, forced by the Japanese to build the infamous Burma-Siam "Railway of Death," taught each other philosophy, Shakespeare, and the Bible. The meaning they found gave them hope and helped them survive the relentless brutality of the prison camp.

---

14. C. S. Lewis, *Reflections on the Psalms* (Glasgow: Collins, 1958), 12.
15. Barbara Kingsolver, quoted in Swenson, *Living Through Pain*, 1.
16. Fraser Tallach, with John and David Tallach, *Fraser: Not a Private Matter. A Human Story of Grace and Suffering* (Edinburgh: Banner of Truth, 2003), x.
17. Jerome E. Groopman, *The Anatomy of Hope: How People Prevail in the Face of Illness* (New York: Random House, 2004), xiv, 208.
18. Ernest Gordon, *Through the Valley of the Kwai* (New York: Harper, 1962).

I began this reflection with Psalm 23 for a reason. This inspired (in both senses of the word) poem shaped and organized the lessons that I learned through my reading of poems in the park.

My Shepherd

Psalm 23 is labeled "A Psalm of David"—which could mean "to David" (in dedication), "of David" (belonging to David), or "for David" (to be used by David in worship). It seems right to believe that David himself was the author. Perhaps he wrote it when he was an old man looking back over his life, as suggested by Frank Crossley Morgan in his *Psalm of an Old Shepherd*.[19] C. S. Lewis said that the psalms need "no historical adjustment."[20] They are immediately and directly accessible to us. We do not have to know the historical context of Psalm 23 nor do we have to understand sheep and their ways to appreciate its significance, although books on the psalm by shepherds offer enriching insights.[21] The "Shepherd's Version" of Psalm 23 is in Scottish dialect:

> Wha is my Shepherd, weel I ken,
>   The Lord Himsel' is He;
> He leads me whaur the girse is green,
>   An' burnies quaet that be.
>
> Aft times I fain astray wad gang,
>   An' wann'r far awa';
> He fin's me oot, He pits me richt,
>   An' brings me hame an' a'.
>
> Tho' I pass through the gruesome cleugh,
>   Fin' I ken He is near;
> His muckle crook will me defen',
>   Sae I hae nocht to fear.
>
> Ilk comfort whilk a sheep could need,
>   His thoctfu' care provides;
> Tho' wolves an' dogs may prowl aboot,
>   In safety me He hides.

19. F. Crossley Morgan, *A Psalm of an Old Shepherd: A Devotional Study of Psalm Twenty-Three* (London: Marshall, Morgan & Scott, n.d.).
20. C. S. Lewis as quoted in Nancy Lammers Gross, "The Shepherd's Song: A Sermon," in *Lament: Reclaiming Practices in Pulpit, Pew, and Public Square*, ed. Sally A. Brown and Patrick D. Miller (Louisville: Westminster, 2005), 39.
21. See J. Douglas MacMillan, *The Lord Our Shepherd* (Bryntirion: Evangelical Press of Wales, 1983) and Phillip Keller, *A Shepherd Looks at Psalm 23* (Grand Rapids, MI: Zondervan, 1970).

His guidness an' His mercy baith,
    Nae doot will bide wi' me;
While faulded on the fields o' time,
    Or o' eternity.[22]

"The Lord is my shepherd." Those words tell me who God is—and who I am. Human beings are not "the ultimate measure of things, the controller of their world, or the determiner of their destiny."[23] God is in control. I am not. He is the shepherd. I am one of his sheep. This basic truth, on which all other truths are based, is expressed in the Bible, hymns, and poetry in many different ways. Psalm 23 draws a lovely and peaceful picture, although it is not without deep trouble. Another picture, raw and startling but no less reassuring, is presented in Dorothy Sayers's play *The Just Vengeance*. "The Airman" utters these words as he plunges to his death:

This is it. This is what we have always feared—
The moment of surrender, the helpless moment
When there is nothing to do but to let go. . . .
"Into Thy hands"—into another's hand
No matter whose; the enemy's hand, death's hand,
God's. . . . The one moment not to be evaded
Which says, "You must," the moment not of choice
When we must choose to do the thing we must
And will to let our own will go. Let go.
It is no use now clinging to the controls,
Let some one else take over. Take, then, take . . .
There, that is done . . . into Thy hand, O God.[24]

Green Pastures . . . Still Waters . . . Paths of Righteousness
The Shepherd leads his sheep into pleasant and refreshing places and along the best paths. He calms us down, strengthens our trust, and restores our souls.

I walked almost every day on the path around a small pond with ducks and geese, the sky and clouds above, the grass and trees below. In the spring the wildflowers grew in the sun and waved in the wind. In the fall the trees turned from green to a variety of colors, often on the same tree, almost

22. I found these words on the wall of a croft in the Scottish Highlands. The source is unknown to me.
23. Bernhard W. Anderson, *Out of the Depths: The Psalms Speak for Us Today*, 3rd ed. (Louisville: Westminster, 2000), 181.
24. Dorothy L. Sayers, *The Just Vengeance: The Lichfield Festival Play for 1946* (London: Victor Gollancz, 1946), 76; used by permission.

overnight. In the winter ice formed on the pond, and snow sometimes covered the ground, bringing its own freshness and interpreting God's creation in yet another delightful way.

C. S. Lewis wrote that "the same doctrine [of creation] which empties nature of her divinity also makes her an index, a symbol, a manifestation of the Divine."[25] The psalmists and the poets helped me to see God's creation with greater appreciation and understanding. Gerard Manley Hopkins showed me "the grandeur of God" everywhere. "The Holy Ghost over the bent world broods with warm breast and with ah! bright wings," he wrote.[26] Hopkins exhorts us to "look at the stars! look, look up at the skies! O look at all the fire-folk sitting in the air!"[27] He calls on us to praise God "for dappled things" and for "the wildness and wet" of a waterfall.[28] Hopkins's heart was "stirred" by the "brute beauty and valour and act" of the windhover, a small falcon, he praises for "the mastery of the thing!"[29]

For William Cowper "poetry was the spontaneous reaction to encountering God's wonders," including animals and birds.[30] In "The Winter Walk at Noon," Cowper describes a robin hopping from icy twig to twig, "pleas'd with his solitude," and a "squirrel, flippant, pert, and full of play."[31] Cowper's three pet rabbits lifted his often despondent spirits. Stating his opposition to shooting rabbits, Cowper wrote to a magazine explaining what "amiable creatures" rabbits are, "of what gratitude they are capable, how cheerful they are in spirits, what enjoyments they have of life."[32]

I sometimes saw rabbits playing in the grass when I walked in my park. I always saw birds. Sidney Lanier, Confederate soldier, musician, and poet, wrote about "dim sweet woods . . . the dear dark woods . . . the heavenly woods and glades, that run to the radiant marginal sand-beach within the

---

25. Lewis, *Reflections on the Psalms*, 70.

26. Gerard Manley Hopkins, "God's Grandeur," in *Poems and Prose of Gerard Manley Hopkins* (New York: Penguin, 1953), 27.

27. Hopkins, "The Starlight Night," in *Poems and Prose*, 27.

28. Hopkins, "Pied Beauty" and "Inversnaid," in *Poems and Prose*, 30, 50–51.

29. Hopkins, "The Windhover," in *Poems and Prose*, 30.

30. George M. Ella, *William Cowper: The Man of God's Stamp* (Dundas, Ontario: Joshua Press, 2000), 97. Ella calls Cowper "the poet of the barber's shop, the linen draper's, the village church, the afternoon walk and, above all, the cosy fireside chair" (91).

31. Quoted in Ella, *William Cowper*, 98–99.

32. Davis and DeMello, *Stories Rabbits Tell*, quoted by Agnieszka Tennant, "The Rabbit Habit," *Books & Culture*, vol. 12, no. 5 (September/October 2006): 29. Poet Norman Nicholson concluded his biography of Cowper with this sentence: "In his precarious pilgrimage he looked at the few feet of grass about him, at the creatures he saw, or the fireside he knew, with a love wide enough to include all Nature and all his fellow-men, and with the sharp tenderness of a long Good-bye." Norman Nicholson, *Collected Poems*, ed. Neil Curry (London: Faber and Faber, 1994), xxiv.

wide sea-marshes of Glynn" in his native Georgia. And he drew a lesson from the birds that lived there:

> As the marsh hen secretly builds on the watery sod,
> Behold I will build me a nest on the greatness of God:
> I will fly in the greatness of God as the marsh hen flies
> In the freedom that fills all the space 'twixt the marsh and the
>   skies.[33]

William Cullen Bryant describes how the waterfowl wanders alone "but not lost" because "there is a Power whose care teaches" the little bird its way along the "pathless coast" of New England. Weary, the waterfowl flies on but:

> Soon that toil shall end;
> Soon shalt thou find a summer home, and rest,
> And scream among thy fellows; reeds shall bend,
> Soon, o'er thy sheltered nest.[34]

Many times I saw Anne Porter's "Wild Geese Alighting on a Lake" happen in my park:

> I watched them
> As they neared the lake
>
> They wheeled
> In a wide arc
> With beating wings
> And then
>
> They put their wings to sleep
> And glided downward in a drift
> Of pure abandonment
>
> Until they touched
> The surface of the lake

33. Sidney Lanier, "The Marshes of Glynn," in *Poems and Letters* (Baltimore: Johns Hopkins, 1945), 46, 48.
34. William Cullen Bryant, "To a Waterfowl," in *Eerdmans Book of Christian Poetry: A Treasury of Poems and the Stories of Their Writers*, comp. Pat Alexander (Grand Rapids, MI: Eerdmans, 1981), 49.

Composed their wings
And settled

On the rippling water
As though it were a nest.[35]

Elizabeth Barrett Browning sought patience in the midst of "dreary life" from the birds, the ocean, the stars, and even from "a blade of grass" that "grows by, contented through the heat and cold."[36]

In "A Ballad of Trees and the Master," Sidney Lanier imagined Christ's night on the Mount of Olives:

Into the woods my Master went,
    Clean forspent, forspent.
Into the woods my Master came,
    Forspent with love and shame.
But the olives they were not blind to Him,
The little gray leaves were kind to Him:
The thorn-tree had a mind to Him
    When into the woods He came.

Out of the woods my Master went,
    And He was well content.
Out of the woods my Master came,
    Content with death and shame.
When Death and Shame would woo Him last,
From under the trees they drew Him last:
'Twas on a tree they slew Him—last

    When out of the woods He came.[37]

Was Jesus helped by the quietness and beauty of nature? Did he even notice the trees? Were "the little gray leaves" kind to him? In a passage full of music young John Calvin wrote, "For the young birds, singing, sing to

35. Anne Porter, "Wild Geese Alighting on a Lake," in *Living Things: Collected Poems* (Hanover, NH: Zoland, 2006), 154; used by permission. The foreword describes Porter as a modern American poet who has "found a language to transmit her Franciscan joy in created things," xiv.

36. Elizabeth Barrett Browning, "Patience Taught by Nature," in *Eerdmans Book of Christian Poetry*, 50.

37. Lanier was disabled by illness, harassed by financial problems, and distracted by conflicting goals. He hoped that the gospel of love and beauty would redeem a world sick with materialism. Far from orthodox in his theology, there is in him a yearning for something great, good, and transforming.

God; the beasts shout aloud to Him; the elements proclaim His might; the mountains echo Him; the rivers and fountains sparkle to Him; the herbs and flowers smell sweet to Him."[38]

"When despair for the world grows in me," writes Wendell Berry, the Kentucky farmer-poet, he finds solace in "the peace of wild things who do not tax their lives with forethought of grief."[39]

All his married life B. B. Warfield, professor at Princeton Seminary, lovingly cared for his wife, Annie, who suffered from a nervous condition brought on apparently by a fearful lightning storm. Warfield was a great theologian, not a great poet, but his little poem "Trusting in the Dark" spoke to me one stormy spring day as I walked in my park:

> Said Robert Leighton,[40] holy man,
> Intent a flickering faith to fan
> Into a steady blaze—
> "Behold yon floweret to the sun,
> As he his daily course doth run,
> Turn undeclining gaze."
>
> "E'en when the clouds obscure his face,
> And only faith discerns the place
> Where in the heavens he soars,
> This floweret still, with constant eye,
> The secret places of the sky
> Untiringly explores."
>
> "Look up, my soul! What can this be
> But Nature's parable to thee?
> Look up, with courage bright!
> The clouds press on thee, dense and black,
> Thy Sun shines ever at their back—
> Look up and see His light!"[41]

---

38. From an anonymous foreword to Olivetanus's French translation of 1535; after 1545 it was associated with Calvin. *Corpus Reformatorum* 9, 823ff. See W. de Greef, *The Writings of John Calvin: An Introductory Guide* (Grand Rapids, MI: Baker, 1993), 90–92.
39. Wendell Berry, "The Peace of Wild Things," in *Collected Poems: 1957–1982* (San Francisco: North Point Press, 1985), 69.
40. Leighton, Archbishop of Glasgow from 1670 to 1674, combined deep-seated Calvinism with devotional piety. He tried to bring about unity between the Scottish Presbyterians and Episcopalians.
41. B. B. Warfield, "Trusting in the Dark," in *Four Hymns and Some Religious Verses* (Philadelphia: Westminster, 1910), 12.

"Nature's parable" in Warfield's poem leads us further into Psalm 23, where the clouds, "dense and black," press on us.

Valley of the Shadow of Death

The first three verses of Psalm 23 describe the delightful experiences of the Christian's life—green pastures, still waters, paths of righteousness. But in verse four the picture suddenly changes, and we find ourselves in the valley of the shadow of death. John Bunyan's *The Pilgrim's Progress* follows the Christian pilgrim through a varied landscape. There are "Delectable Mountains," but there is also "the Slough of Despond." There is "House Beautiful," but there is also "Hill Difficulty." There is "the Country of Beulah"—where birds always sing, flowers always bloom, and the sun shines night and day—and there is also "the valley of the shadow of death."

The valley of the *shadow* of death is not death itself but a place of darkness, sadness, affliction, and trial. In *The Pilgrim's Progress*, Christian came to this valley, and he "must needs go through it, because the way to the celestial city lay through the midst of it." "Now this valley," Bunyan explains, "is a very solitary place. The prophet Jeremiah thus describes it: a wilderness, a land of deserts and of pits, a land of drought, and of the shadow of death."[42] We experience this dark valley in different ways—in trials of illness, depression, addiction, abuse, rejection, bitter disappointment, and other hard experiences of life. Until that day when "death shall be no more, neither shall there be mourning, nor crying, nor pain anymore" (Rev. 21:4) there will be the valley of the shadow of death. And like Bunyan's Christian, we "must needs go through it."

Gerard Manley Hopkins's most intense suffering came in 1885 and 1886 when he wrote what a friend called his "terrible sonnets"—filled with desperation, exhaustion, and a sense of God's absence:[43]

> I wake and feel the fell of dark, not day.
> What hours, O what black hours we have spent
> This night! what sights, you, heart, saw; ways you went!
> And more must, in yet longer light's delay.
>
> With witness I speak this. But where I say
> Hours I mean years, mean life. And my lament
> Is cries, countless, cries like dead letters sent
> To dearest him that lives alas! away.[44]

42. John Bunyan, *The Pilgrim's Progress* (Edinburgh: Banner of Truth, 1977), 64.
43. See Buechner, *Speak What We Feel*, 19–20.
44. Hopkins, "Carrion Comfort," in *Poems and Prose*, 62.

Psalm 88 (sometimes described as the one psalm without hope) ends with the words, "You have caused my beloved and my friend to shun me; my companions have become darkness" (v. 18). Kathryn Greene-McCreight described her own experience with mental illness in a book whose title, *Darkness Is My Only Companion*, is taken from this verse.[45] For all its darkness, however, Psalm 88 contains a message of hope. It is a cry to the Lord, as are Hopkins's "terrible sonnets" and Kathryn Greene-McCreight's testimony. In another of his poems—described by Frederick Buechner as a "breathless, ragged poem"[46]—Hopkins, still obsessed with the darkness, came in the poem's last line to speak of the "now done darkness" (it is over and done with) as he "lay wrestling with (my God!) my God."[47] T. S. Eliot wrote that when we come to the place of letting go into the hands of God, we find that "the darkness shall be the light, and the stillness the dancing."[48] If we keep on reading beyond Psalm 88, we will come to Psalm 139:12—"Even the darkness is not dark to you; the night is bright as the day, for darkness is as light with you."

Nicholas Wolterstorff entered the darkness of the valley of the shadow of death when a mountain climbing accident killed his son, Eric. Wolterstorff searched for solace in music. In his deeply moving *Lament for a Son*, he wrote: "The music that speaks *about* our brokenness is not itself broken. Is there no broken music?"[49] There is broken music, and there is broken poetry, as we find in the poem "Denial" by George Herbert. The speaker's "disorder" is illustrated and emphasized by the failure of his poem to rhyme fully.

> When my devotions could not pierce
>   Thy silent ears,
> Then was my heart broken, as was my verse:
>   My breast was full of fears
>   And disorder.

---

45. Kathryn Greene-McCreight, *Darkness Is My Only Companion: A Christian Response to Mental Illness* (Grand Rapids, MI: Brazos, 2006).
46. Buechner, *Speak What We Feel*, 27.
47. Hopkins, "Carrion Comfort," in *Poems and Prose*, 61. At Hopkins's death only five of his minor poems had been published, although he was sure that "our Lord" valued his work. He died of typhoid fever a few weeks before his forty-fifth birthday. In one of his last poems, he pled with God to renew his spirit and his poetry in the prayer: "O thou lord of life, send my roots rain" ("Thou Art Indeed Just, Lord, if I Contend," in *Poems and Prose*, 67).
48. T. S. Eliot, "Four Quartets—East Coker," in *The Complete Poems and Plays 1909–1950* (New York: Harcourt Brace, 1950), 127.
49. Nicholas Wolterstorff, *Lament for a Son* (Grand Rapids, MI: Eerdmans, 1987), 52.

My bent thoughts, like a brittle bow,
    Did fly asunder:
Each took his way; some would to pleasures go,
     Some to the wars and thunder
       Of alarms.[50]

As good go any where, they say,
    As to denumb
Both knees and heart, in crying night and day,
    "Come, come, my God, O come,"
      But no hearing.

Oh that Thou shouldst give dust a tongue
    To cry to Thee,
And then not hear it crying! All day long
My heart was in my knee,
    But no hearing.

Therefore my soul lay out of sight,
    Untuned, unstrung:
My feeble spirit, unable to look right,
    Like a nipped blossom, hung
      Discontented.

O cheer and tune my heartless breast,
    Defer no time;
That so Thy favors granting my request,
    They and my mind may chime,
      And mend my rhyme.

In my own time of suffering, I returned again and again to the poems of George Herbert. His "Bitter-Sweet" captures the spirit of the laments of the psalmists:

Ah my dear angry Lord,
Since thou dost love, yet strike;
Cast down, yet help afford;
Sure I will do the like.

I will complain, yet praise;
I will bewail, approve;

50. Often pronounced "alarums," meaning a call to battle.

> And all my sour-sweet days
> I will lament, and love.

Herbert's "Jesu" is witty and profound:

> Jesu is in my heart, his sacred name
> Is deeply carved there: but th' other week
> A great affliction broke the little frame,
> Ev'n all to pieces; which I went to seek:
> And first I found the corner, where was *J*,
> After, where *ES*, and next where *U* was graved.
> When I had got these parcels, instantly
> I sat me down to spell them, and perceived
> That to my broken heart he was *I ease you*,
>   And to my whole is *JESU*.

One day, as I walked in the park and through my own personal valley, I read "Litany to the Holy Spirit" by Robert Herrick. The poet prays for the Spirit's comfort when temptation oppresses, when doubts confuse, and when doctors fail:

> When the artless doctor sees
> No one hope, but of his fees,
> And his skill runs on the lees,[51]
>   Sweet Spirit, comfort me!
>
> When his potion and his pill
> Has or none or little skill,
> Meet for nothing but to kill,
>   Sweet Spirit, comfort me!

This is not a cry for deliverance from the troubles of life, but a plea for comfort and help in all that comes. I read these words at a time when the chemotherapy threatened to kill me before the cancer did. Herrick's poem comforted as it amused me. Most of my doctors and nurses have been skillful and sympathetic, but one experience deeply distressed me. During that time the poet helped me to pray for comfort from the "Sweet Spirit" of God.

A burden can become a cross, John Calvin asserts, when we willingly accept it as coming from God and gladly bear it with trust and patience.[52]

51. Meaning "his skill is drained to the last drop."
52. John Calvin, *Institutes of the Christian Religion* (Philadelphia: Westminster, 1960) 1:702–12.

William Henry Sheppard, Southern Presbyterian missionary to the Congo, knew about cross bearing. An African-American, Sheppard was born in Virginia to former slave parents near the end of the Civil War. In Africa he faithfully preached the gospel and courageously stood against the brutal exploitation and mass slaughter of the Congolese people by the agents of the European rubber trade. He wrote:

> God laid upon my back a grievous load,
> A heavy cross to bear along the road;
> I staggered on, till lo! One weary day,
> An angry lion leaped across my way.
> I prayed to God, and swift at His command
> The cross became a weapon in my hand.[53]

African-American spirituals are songs of sorrow and strength—from a people who knew plenty of both. One of those songs often puzzled me:

> Nobody knows the trouble I've seen,
> Nobody knows like Jesus;
> Nobody knows the trouble I've seen,
> Glory, Hallelujah.

The last two words did not seem to fit. I could understand, "Nobody knows the trouble I've seen, woe is me!" But "Glory, Hallelujah"? One day as I was reading these words in the park, I remembered Paul's encouragement to the Corinthians: "For this light momentary affliction is preparing for us an eternal weight of glory beyond all comparison" (2 Cor. 4:17). Today's cross is tomorrow's crown. Glory, Hallelujah!

A poet who understood what it is to walk through the valley of the shadow of death was Anne Bradstreet, author of the first published book of verse to be written in the New World. She struggled, along with the other Pilgrim settlers of the Massachusetts colony, to survive the New England winters and the disease and dangers of life in a remote and primitive place. When her house was destroyed by fire, this mother of eight children wrote about the shock of seeing everything lost. In one of the poem's nine verses, she described her feelings:

> And, when I could no longer look,
> I blest his Name that gave and took,

---

53. William Henry Sheppard, "The Cross," in Pagan Kennedy, *Black Livingstone: A True Tale of Adventure in the Nineteenth-Century Congo* (New York: Viking, 2002), vii.

> That laid my goods now in the dust:
> Yea so it was, and so 'twas just.
> It was his own: it was not mine;
> Far be it that I should repine.

But Anne Bradstreet knew that she had not lost everything. She reminded herself that she already had another house:

> Thou hast an house on high erect
> Fram'd by that mighty Architect,
> With glory richly furnished,
> Stands permanent tho' this be fled.
> It's purchased, and paid for too
> By him who hath enough to do.

One early spring day I took a little book of Bradstreet's poems to the park, and I read these words:

> As spring the winter doth succeed,
> And leaves the naked trees do dress,
> The earth all black is cloth'd in green;
> At sunshine each their joy express.
>
> My sun's returned with healing wings,
> My soul and body doth rejoice,
> My heart exults and praises sings
> To him that heard my wailing voice.

Trouble comes back as sure as winter comes again, and it has, in fact, for me. I write these words just after learning that my cancer, in remission for three years, has returned. Even in the winters of life, Anne Bradstreet knew that she had "a shelter from the storm" in God "who is . . . so wondrous great."

Francis Thompson experienced the dark valley as he struggled with mental distress, opium addiction, homelessness, and suicidal thoughts. In one of his poems his desperate cries are answered at last:

> But (when so sad thou canst not sadder)
> Cry;—and upon thy so sore loss
> Shall shine the traffic of Jacob's ladder
> Pitched betwixt Heaven and Charing Cross.

> Yea, in the night, my Soul, my daughter,
> Cry,—clinging Heaven by the hems;
> And lo, Christ walking on the water,
> Not of Gennesareth, but Thames!

There are many ways of saying David's words to the Lord, "I will fear no evil, for you are with me." "Autumn," by Rainer Maria Rilke, an Austrian writer born in Prague, put it this way:

> We are all falling. This hand's falling too—
> all have this falling-sickness none withstands.
>
> And yet there's One whose gently-holding hands
> this universal falling can't fall through.[54]

The last two lines bring to mind a favorite Scripture text: "The eternal God is your dwelling place, and underneath are the everlasting arms" (Deut. 33:27).

In one of her books Dorothy Sayers speaks through Balthazar—a wise man who has experienced famine, plague, wars, and the "burden of fear." Yet all this is nothing, he asserts, "if I may look upon the hidden face of God" and read in his eyes "that He is acquainted with grief."[55]

God is not indifferent, William Blake assures us. God, who himself became "a man of woe," cares:

> Think not thou canst sigh a sigh
> And thy maker is not by;
> Think not thou canst weep a tear
> And thy maker is not near,
>
> O! he gives to us his joy
> That our grief he may destroy;
> Till our grief is fled and gone
> He doth sit by us and moan.[56]

How often I thought of these words during dark nights of sickness and suffering. Where is God? What is he doing? I know where he is. I know

---

54. Rainer Maria Rilke, "Autumn," in *Poems* (New York: Alfred A. Knopf, 1996), 20.
55. Dorothy Sayers, Prologue to *He That Should Come*, in *Two Plays About God and Man* (Norton, CT: Vineyard Books, 1977).
56. William Blake, "On Another's Sorrow."

what he is doing. He is sitting by me and he is moaning. "Suffering is there," wrote Eugene Peterson, "and where the sufferer is, God is."[57]

William Cowper helps me to "fresh courage take" as I experience the mystery of God's providence in taking me through the valley:

> God moves in a mysterious way his wonders to perform;
>   he plants his footsteps in the sea, and rides upon the storm
>
> Deep in unfathomable mines of never failing skill
>   he treasures up his bright designs, and works his sovereign will.
>
> Ye fearful saints, fresh courage take; the clouds ye so much dread
>   are big with mercy, and shall break in blessings on your head.
>
> Judge not the Lord by feeble sense, but trust him for his grace;
>   behind a frowning providence he hides a smiling face.
>
> His purposes will ripen fast, unfolding every hour;
>   the bud may have a bitter taste, but sweet will be the flow'r.
>
> Blind unbelief is sure to err, and scan his work in vain;
>   God is his own interpreter, and he will make it plain.[58]

Every line, almost every word, is, like the clouds, "big" with meaning and mercy. Large books have been written about God's providence with less success than Cowper's hymn.

I experienced extreme hoarseness and difficulty in speaking after a course of radiation burned my vocal cords. As a teacher who could talk only fifteen minutes at a time, I felt that I had become useless. Others have struggled with similar feelings, including the great Puritan poet John Milton at the onset of his blindness:

> When I consider how my light is spent,
> Ere half my days, in this dark world and wide,
> And that one talent which is death to hide,
> Lodged with me useless, though my soul more bent
> To serve therewith my Maker, and present
> My true account, lest he returning chide,
> "Doth God exact day labour, light denied?"

57. Eugene H. Peterson, *Five Smooth Stones for Pastoral Work* (Grand Rapids, MI: Eerdmans, 1992), 114.
58. William Cowper, "God Moves in a Mysterious Way."

> I fondly ask! But Patience, to prevent
> That murmur, soon replies, "God doth not need
> Either man's work or his own gifts; who best
> Bear his mild yoke, they serve him best; his state
> Is kingly: thousands at his bidding speed,
> And post o'er land and ocean without rest;
> They also serve who only stand and wait."

T. S. Eliot's "Four Quartets," dense and complex like most of his poetry,[59] are filled with brilliant insights that flare forth from time to time. He writes that

> The dance along the artery
> The circulation of the lymph
> Are figured in the drift of stars.[60]

These words suggest that there is pattern and purpose in everything—including the circulation of the lymph, an image sure to catch the attention of someone like me who has lymphoma.[61] Not only is there a purpose in everything, but there is a person who cares:

> The wounded surgeon plies the steel
> That questions the distempered part;
> Beneath the bleeding hands we feel
> The sharp compassion of the healer's art
> Resolving the enigma of the fever chart.[62]

The good shepherd who leads us in the valley of the shadow of death is also the great physician, who, wounded himself, knows firsthand our pain, and who is so compassionate that he hurts to heal. Toward the end of *Four Quartets*, Eliot asks the inescapable question, "Who then devised the torment?" He gives a one-word answer: "Love."[63]

We are pilgrims, not wanderers. Or, to follow the image of Psalm 23, we are sheep. Our shepherd knows what is the best path for us to take. Sometimes

---

59. An exception is *Old Possum's Book of Practical Cats.* I read and reread these poems for fun.

60. Eliot, "Four Quartets," in *Complete Poems and Plays*, 118.

61. I read these words in a book by John Carmody in which he speaks to God: "You work my death. All the little cells, cancerous or benign, strut their stuff at your behest. I can't begin to comprehend the nearly infinite delicacy and beauty of how you've arranged our cells and nerves. . . . You are playing through us, circulating in our lymph. The harmonies of the spheres are echoing in our blood. Perhaps even the chorus of the 144,000 is sounding." John Carmody, *Cancer and Faith* (Mystic, CT: Twenty-Third Publications, 1994), 32–33. The allusion in the last sentence is to Revelation 14:3—"And they were singing a new song before the throne."

62. Eliot, "Four Quartets," in *Complete Poems and Plays*, 127.

63. Ibid., 144.

our lives may seem disconnected and erratic. We may find it difficult or impossible to see any pattern. But there is a plan. There is a pattern, and someday (perhaps to some extent in this life, certainly and completely in heaven) we will look back over it all and be amazed at how perfect it was. Time spent in the valley is not wasted; it is part of God's plan for us. There we are blessed with his presence, comforted by his rod and staff, and learn more fully what it means to be "his people, and the sheep of his pasture" (Ps. 100:3).

Table . . . Oil . . . Cup

Verse four of Psalm 23 introduces another quite different image. The Lord is both the good shepherd who cares for his sheep and the gracious host who offers hospitality and protection. The two pictures come together, according to Bernhard Anderson, in the pastoral way of life that still prevails in some parts of the world today. The shepherd leads and cares for his sheep and welcomes travelers to the hospitality and safety of his tent.[64]

In the tent we find that God blesses us abundantly even when we are experiencing life's most difficult times. Like the famous opening sentences of *A Tale of Two Cities*, illness can be both the worst of times and the best of times. There is anxiety and suffering. There are blessings to be counted and good things to enjoy. The psalmist wrote, "It is good to give thanks to the LORD, to sing praises to your name, O Most High" (Ps. 92:1). George Herbert began one of his poems with the words, "Thou that hast giv'n so much to me, / Give one more thing, a grateful heart."[65]

First-century Jewish prayer not only offered a blessing over every meal but also at the spontaneous events of everyday life; benedictions are prescribed at the sight of meteors, earthquakes, lightning, thunder, wind, mountains, sea, rivers, even desert, as well as when building a new home or buying new clothes.[66]

On several of my walks, I took with me to the park a book of poems by Robert Louis Stevenson. His *Child's Garden of Verses* has a little two-line poem called "Happy Thought":

> The world is so full of a number of things,
> I'm sure we should all be as happy as kings.[67]

---

64. Anderson, *Out of the Depths*, 181.
65. Herbert, "Gratefulness," in *The Works of George Herbert*, 123.
66. See David Crump, *Knocking on Heaven's Door: A New Testament Theology of Petitionary Prayer* (Grand Rapids, MI: Baker, 2006), 112.
67. Robert Louis Stevenson, *Selected Poems* (London: Penguin, 1998), 75.

After recovery from a time of deep despair, young G. K. Chesterton wrote in his notebook:

> You say grace before meals.
> All right.
> But I say grace before the play and the opera,
> And grace before the concert and the pantomime,
> And grace before I open a book,
> And grace before sketching, painting,
> Swimming, fencing, boxing, walking, playing, dancing;
> And grace before I dip the pen in the ink.[68]

In God's tent the table is graciously and abundantly spread, not only in the presence of the hostile powers of this age but also in the presence of "the last enemy" (1 Cor. 15:26).

All the Days of My Life

During one of my walks around the park, I read and reread John Newton's "Amazing Grace." That day, a few days after I had received a discouraging report from my oncologist, I focused on this verse:

> The Lord has promised good to me,
>   His word my hope secures;
> He will my shield and portion be,
>   As long as life endures.[69]

As I spent much of the fifth and sixth decades of my life struggling with cancer and cancer treatment, I realized not only that was serious illness was threatening me, but also that old age was coming on fast. Was my physical decline caused by cancer or old age or both? In a poem called "As One Oldster to Another," C. S. Lewis captures something of the pathos of aging. Some things are lost, but not everything:

> Well, yes the old bones ache. There were easier
> Beds thirty years back. Sleep, then importunate,
>   Now with reserve doles out her favours;
>   Food disagrees; there are draughts in houses.
>
> . . . .

68. G. K. Chesterton, quoted in Buechner, *Speak What We Feel*, 119.
69. John Newton, "Amazing Grace."

Still beauty calls as once in the mazes of
Boyhood. The bird-like soul quivers. Into her
　　Flash darts of unfulfill'd desire and
　　　　Pierce with a bright, unabated anguish.[70]

House of the Lord

Psalm 23 assures us that death is not the end. There is something more and
something better. Following the words "surely goodness and mercy shall
follow me all the days of my life," there is not a period but a comma (in our
Bible translations) and the word "and." My last day on earth is not my last
day. The road will end but it "ends . . . as the runway does." I will die, but I
will dwell "in the house of the LORD forever."

No greater contrast can exist than that between the Christian view of
departing this life and the darkness of death as represented in the ancient
world. For the latter, death was a flower crushed, a ship wrecked, a race lost,
a harp with strings snapped and all the music gone. For Christians death is
the dawn of an eternal day, the gate to life, the end of the journey, a home-
coming, and, in the words of C. S. Lewis, the beginning of "Chapter One
of the Great Story, which no one on earth has read: which goes on forever:
in which every chapter is better than the one before."[71]

I love the poem by John Donne "Hymn to God, My God, in My Sickness."
The first verse of six reads:

Since I am coming to that holy room
　　Where, with Thy choir of saints for evermore
I shall be made Thy music, as I come
　　I tune the instrument here at the door,
　　And what I must do then, think here before.

Anticipating death, Donne prepares for heaven. He writes in the last
verse:

So, in His purple wrapped receive me Lord,
　　By these His thorns give me His other crown;
And as to others' souls I preached Thy word,
　　Be this my text, my sermon to mine own:
　　Therefore, that He may raise, the Lord throws down.

70. C. S. Lewis, "As One Oldster to Another," in *Poems*, ed. Walter Hooper (San Diego: Harcourt
Brace Jovanovich, 1964), 41–42.
71. C. S. Lewis, *The Last Battle* (New York: Collier, 1956), 184.

As a minister who has preached to others for over fifty years, I am moved by Donne's words as I come closer to the end of my journey and anticipate the nearer presence of God.[72]

The witty, bold, and compact poetry of Emily Dickinson intrigues me, even when her meaning eludes me. But I do understand, I think, something of this little poem:

> I heard a Fly buzz—when I died—
> The Stillness in the Room
> Was like the Stillness in the Air—
> Between the Heaves of Storm—
>
> The Eyes around—had wrung them dry—
> And Breaths were gathering firm
> For that last Onset—when the King
> Be witnessed—in the Room.[73]

God, the King, is in charge of life and death. All is in his hands. All the rest is circumstance—and all that is in his hands, too. We wait and we learn to accept his timing of things, as did Puritan Richard Baxter:

> Lord, it belongs not to my care,
>   Whether I die or live;
> To love and serve Thee is my share,
>   And this thy grace must give.
>
> If life be long I will be glad
>   That I may long obey;
> If short—yet why should I be sad
>   To soar to endless day?
>
> Christ leads me through no darker rooms
>   Than he went through before;
> He that unto God's kingdom comes,
>   Must enter by this door.
>
> Come, Lord, when grace has made me meet
>   Thy blessed face to see;
> For if thy work on earth be sweet,
>   What will thy glory be![74]

---

72. According to Isaac Walton, Donne's contemporary biographer, this poem was written only eight days before Donne's death in 1631, although other accounts put it earlier.
73. Emily Dickinson, "I Heard a Fly Buzz When I Died."
74. Richard Baxter, "Lord, It Belongs Not to My Care."

Christina Rossetti spent her life caring for her widowed mother, serving the needy, and writing poems, including this one:

> If I might only love my God and die!
> But now he bids me love him and live on,
> Now when the bloom of all my life is gone,
> The pleasant half of life has quite gone by.
> My tree of hope is lopped that spread so high;
> And I forgot how summer glowed and shone,
> While autumn grips me with its fingers wan,
> And frets me with its fitful windy sigh.
> When autumn passes then must winter numb,
> And winter may not pass a weary while,
> But when it passes spring shall flower again:
> And in that spring who weepeth now shall smile,
> Yea, they shall wax who now are on the wane,
> Yea, they shall sing for love when Christ shall come.[75]

John Berryman reflected on Polycarp's courageous witness when "facing the fire" and the poet prayed that whatever comes at the end of his time—"cancer, senility, mania"—he, too, would be ready with his witness.[76] As a church history professor and cancer patient, I embraced these words with eagerness.

Jane Kenyon, poet laureate of New Hampshire, was diagnosed with leukemia and died the next year at the age of forty-seven. Her quiet, simple poems, inspired by thoughtful observation of ordinary life and by the Bible and hymns, contain psalm-like utterances of great beauty. She concludes one of her poems with the words, "Let it come, as it will, and don't be afraid. God will not leave us comfortless, so let evening come."[77]

Wandering far from his homeland and from the Calvinistic faith of his loving parents, Robert Louis Stevenson could not forget the "dull, cold northern sky" and the "brawling Sabbath bells" of Scotland.[78] In "Evensong," written in faraway Samoa, he returned to the simple trust and joys of a child:

---

75. Christina Rossetti, "If Only."

76. John Berryman, "Eleven Addresses to the Lord," in *Love and Fame*, 2nd ed. (New York: Farrar, Straus and Giroux, 1970), 90. Polycarp was martyred at Smyrna in A.D. 155 or 156.

77. Jane Kenyon, "Let Evening Come," in *Collected Poems* (Saint Paul, MN: Graywolf, 2005), 213. Kenyon believed that the words of this poem were given to her by the Holy Spirit. See *Books & Culture* (January/February 1997): 22.

78. Stevenson, "O Dull, Cold Northern Sky," in *Selected Poems*, 16.

The breeze from the embalmèd land
Blows sudden from the shore,
And claps my cottage door.
I hear the signal, Lord—I understand.
The night at Thy command
Comes. I will eat and sleep and will not question more.[79]

C. S. Lewis's "Evensong" looks beyond the evening to the coming dawn:

Slumber's less uncertain
Brother soon will bind us
—Darker falls the curtain,
Stifling-close 'tis drawn:
But amidst that prison
Still Thy voice can find us,
And, as Thou hast risen,
Raise us in Thy dawn.[80]

Welsh poet Henry Vaughan wrote this beautiful "Easter Hymn":

Death and darkness get you packing,
Nothing now to man is lacking,
All your triumphs now are ended,
And what Adam marred is mended;
Graves are beds now for the weary,
Death a nap, to wake more merry;
Youth now, full of pious duty,
Seeks in thee for perfect beauty,
The weak, and aged tired, with length
Of days, from thee look for new strength,
And infants with thy pangs contest
As pleasant, as if with the breast;
Then, unto him, who thus hath thrown
Even to contempt thy kingdom down,
And by his blood did us advance
Unto his own inheritance,
To him be glory, power, praise,
From this, unto the last of days.

79. Stevenson, "Evensong," in *Selected Poems*, 239.
80. Lewis, "Evensong," in *Poems*, 128.

Vaughan celebrates Christ's and therefore our victory over death, as John Donne does in his better known "On Death":

> Death, be not proud, though some have called thee
> Mighty and dreadful, for thou art not so;
> For those whom thou thinkst thou dost overthrow
> Die not, poor Death, nor yet canst thou kill me.
> From rest and sleep, which but thy pictures be,
> Much pleasure—then, from thee much more must flow;
> And soonest our best men with thee do go,
> Rest of their bones and soul's delivery.
> Thou'rt slave to fate, chance, kings, and desperate men,
> And dost with poison, war, and sickness dwell;
> And poppy or charms can make us sleep as well,
> And better than thy stroke. Why swellest thou then?
> One short sleep past, we wake eternally,
> And death shall be no more. Death, thou shalt die.[81]

George Herbert's "Dialogue Anthem" makes the same point:

> Christian.   Alas, poor Death, where is thy glory?
>   Where is thy famous force, thy ancient sting?
>
> Death.   Alas poor mortal, void of story,
>   Go spell and read how I have kill'd thy King.
>
> Christian.   Poor death! and who was hurt thereby?
>   Thy curse being laid on him, makes thee accurst.
>
> Death.   Let losers talk: yet thou shalt die;
>   These arms shall crush thee.
>
> Christian.   Spare not, do thy worst.
>   I shall be one day better than before:
>   Thou so much worse, that thou shall be no more.[82]

Here are the words of the priest in John Henry Newman's "The Dream of Gerontius":

---

81. John Donne, "On Death." The correct punctuation of the last line is a major point of the movie "Wit." I remember shouting out the last line during a cold winter walk in my empty park.
82. Herbert, "Dialogue Anthem."

> Go forth upon thy journey, Christian soul!
> Go from this world! Go, in the name of God,
> The Omnipotent Father, who created thee!
> Go, in the Name of Jesus Christ, our Lord,
> Son of the Living God, who bled for thee!
> Go, in the Name of the Holy Spirit, who
> Hath been pour'd out on thee! Go, in the name
> Of Angels and Archangels, in the name
> Of Thrones and Dominations, in the name
> Of Princedoms and of Powers, and in the name
> Of Cherubim and Seraphim, go forth!
> Go, in the name of Patriarchs and Prophets,
> And of Apostles and Evangelists,
> Of Martyrs and Confessors, in the name
> Of holy Monks and Hermits, in the name
> Of holy Virgins, and all Saints of God,
> Both men and women, go! Go on thy course,
> And may thy place today be found in peace,
> And may thy dwelling be the Holy Mount
> Of Zion—through the Same, through Christ, our Lord.[83]

Now, that is a send-off!

Jane Kenyon looks back to this life in her "Notes from the Other Side" and asserts that "God, as promised, proves to be mercy clothed in light."[84]

The famous poem written by Dylan Thomas for his dying father begins:

> Do not go gentle into that good night,
> Old age should burn and rave at close of day;
> Rage, rage against the dying of the light.[85]

Thomas's words of despair at the dying of the light contrast with the moving farewell of Norman Nicholson as he thinks of the times he has looked from his beloved Cumbrian coast at the sunset over the "sea to the west" and prays, "Let my eyes at last be blinded not by the dark but by dazzle."[86]

83. John Henry Newman, "The Dream of Gerontius." Newman's work has been set to music by Edward Elgar and two of the poems in it are well known as hymns—"Firmly I Believe and Truly" and "Praise to the Holiest in the Height."

84. Kenyon, "Notes From the Other Side," in *Collected Poems*, 267.

85. Dylan Thomas, "Do Not Go Gentle into That Good Night," in *The Oxford Book of Twentieth-Century English Verse* (Oxford: Oxford University Press, 1973), 474.

86. Norman Nicholson, "Sea to the West," in *Collected Poems*, 339. The closing lines of the poem are now on Nicholson's west-facing tombstone in the churchyard at Millom, the English Lake District town, where he had lived in the same small house for the whole of his seventy-three years.

By God's grace, I sometimes have caught a glimpse of "the many-splen-doured thing" in the words and images of the poets, and my eyes were daz-zled for a moment. Someday I shall see that greater light, a light that shall never fade, a light of which all our glimpses of glory are faint reflections, the light of the New Jerusalem, a city that has "no need of sun or moon to shine on it, for the glory of God gives it light, and its lamp is the Lamb" (Rev. 21:23). In that light the problem of pain will disappear and sickness and suffering will be no more "for the former things have passed away" (Rev. 21:4). The words of the poets will take physical shape, and faith will become sight and what we love will never vanish. "The grace of the Lord Jesus be with all. Amen" (Rev. 22:21).

10

A JOURNEY IN SUFFERING

Personal Reflections on
the Religious Problem of Evil

JOHN S. FEINBERG

W hy do bad things happen to good people? If God really loves us, why
doesn't he stop the bad things that befall us? How can I serve or even
worship a God who rewards my faithfulness with affliction? Most of us
have probably asked these questions at some time or other. In fact, these
are issues that for most of us instigate our thinking about God and evil.
They raise the personal dimension of the problem of evil.

Some years ago Alvin Plantinga wrote about the religious problem of
evil in his work *God, Freedom, and Evil*. After writing of the more abstract
theological/philosophical problem of evil, he noted that there is also a
religious problem that confronts the theist:

> In the presence of his own suffering or that of someone near to him he may
> find it difficult to maintain what he takes to be the proper attitude towards
> God. Faced with great personal suffering or misfortune, he may be tempted
> to rebel against God, to shake his fist in God's face, or even to give up belief in

God altogether. But this is a problem of a different dimension. Such a problem calls, not for philosophical enlightenment, but for pastoral care.[1]

I read that statement many years ago. Intellectually I agreed with it, but experientially I didn't fully understand it. I had always viewed the problem of evil as a major hindrance that keeps unbelievers from turning to Christ and sometimes causes believers to turn away. I thought that as long as one had intellectual answers that explained why God allowed evil in the world and as long as one could point to specific benefits that might accrue in the life of the sufferer, the sufferer would be satisfied. When I saw others struggle over their relationship with God because of some tragedy, I naïvely thought that if I could just offer them some answers that would resolve everything. I was somewhat impatient with those who seemed unable to move past their struggles. In principle, I agreed that sufferers need pastoral care, but I thought that a lot of that care involved explaining intellectually God's purposes in allowing evil. Maybe the religious problem isn't about philosophical enlightenment, but a healthy dose of philosophy couldn't hurt. Or so I thought.

More than fifteen years ago my perceptions on this matter changed dramatically as a result of experiences of evil that befell my family. Before these things happened, I couldn't have written this chapter, for I operated under the misguided ideas already mentioned. Even for a long time afterward I found it too painful to speak about this, let alone write about it. I offer it now as an illustration of my point that the religious problem of evil is a different kind of problem from the others we have discussed. However, my primary reason for writing about these experiences isn't to evoke sympathy or pity, but hopefully to help those who suffer and those who minister to the afflicted.

Like many people, I grew up, went to school, got married, and began a career in relatively trouble-free circumstances. I had problems and afflictions as most people do, but nothing you would consider catastrophic or truly tragic. I knew that those who take a stand for Christ can expect to suffer, so I figured there were more troubles coming. But I figured that they would be like the rest I had endured—annoying, frustrating, and painful to a certain degree, but nothing totally devastating. After all, I reasoned, once one goes a certain distance with Christ and reaches a certain level of spiritual maturity, even really big problems aren't likely to derail spiritual growth. There might be temporary disruption in one's relation to the Lord, but that would soon be put to rest.

All of that changed for me on November 4, 1987, when I learned something far beyond my worst nightmare. For some years my wife, Pat, had expe-

1. Alvin Plantinga, *God, Freedom, and Evil* (New York: Harper & Row, 1974), 63–64.

rienced certain physical difficulties, though they weren't painful, and we didn't think they were serious. They were symptoms of something, but we had no idea of what. As the years passed, they became more pronounced. We decided that we had to find out what the problem was and get it corrected. My wife eventually wound up at a neurologist who made the diagnosis—Huntington's chorea.

I had no idea what that was. Huntington's disease is a genetically transmitted disease involving the premature deterioration of the caudate nucleus of the brain. Symptoms are both physical and psychological. On the physical side, it involves the gradual loss of control of all voluntary bodily movement. Psychologically, it involves memory loss and depression, and as the disease progresses, it can lead to hallucinations and paranoid schizophrenia. Symptoms do not begin until around thirty years of age at the earliest, though some who have it show no signs until their later thirties or early forties. It is a slowly developing disease, but over ten to twenty years it takes its toll, and it is fatal. Currently, there are some medications to help with symptoms, but there is no known cure. Only a few years prior to my wife's diagnosis had doctors even discovered the chromosome involved. At the time of her diagnosis, the exact genetic marker was unknown, but through ongoing research, doctors and scientists have isolated the gene for this disease. Still, we are a good distance from a cure.

As bad as that news was, the story gets even worse. Huntington's disease is controlled by a dominant gene. This means that only one parent needs to have it in order to transfer it to their children. Each child has a fifty-fifty chance of getting it, but as mentioned, symptoms don't show up until about thirty at the earliest. We have three children, all born prior to Pat's diagnosis.

Since Huntington's is controlled by a dominant gene, those who have the gene get the disease. If they don't get the disease, they can't be a carrier. There are now tests that accurately tell whether someone at risk for the disease has the gene and will get the disease. However, there is a real dilemma over whether one should take this test. If a person takes the test and learns that he or she will get the disease, it may be impossible to get health insurance or employment. And some who have tested positive have committed suicide rather than endure this lengthy and difficult disease. On the other hand, if one doesn't know, he or she must make decisions in the dark about career, marriage, and children.

After this news came, my immediate response was shock and confusion. How could this be happening? Before we were married, we knew that my wife's mother had mental problems. At the time of our wedding, she had been in a mental institution for five years. We asked several people, including doctors, how likely it was that this might happen to my wife, believing all along that it was a purely psychological problem. Psychologists assured us that if my wife were to have such problems, they would have already surfaced. Since she was in her twenties and nothing had happened, there was no need to worry. We never imagined that there was a physiological base to my mother-in-law's problems or that the difficulty could be passed genetically to my wife. Nor did anyone else. Immediate family members knew nothing about this, and others who might have known said nothing. My father-in-law had at one time heard the name of the disease but didn't ask for details about what it was. Before we started our family, we checked again to see if anything hereditary that might harm the children could be passed on. Again, we were told there was nothing to fear.

So then, none of this could possibly be happening—yet it was. I struggled to accept the doctor's diagnosis, especially since he had done nothing more than observe Pat's symptoms and ask about her family history. No other tests were done that day, but the diagnosis was given. I complained that this was all too inferential. Such minimal data didn't warrant that conclusion. No philosopher would accept that kind of argument. For several months I was torn between hope that it wasn't true and fear that Pat's problems could be nothing else. A second opinion by a specialist doing research on the disease confirmed the diagnosis. All hope that it wasn't true was lost.

Initial Reactions

After the initial diagnosis and later confirmation, I was besieged by a host of emotions. Even to this day, I still wrestle with those feelings. The predominant reaction I experienced was a feeling of hopelessness. There had been problems before, but usually there was some way out. In fact, usually, I could figure out something to do and do it. But not this time. I would have to watch my dear wife slowly deteriorate and die. Maybe as the disease progressed, she wouldn't even know me. Or possibly worse, she would know me but would turn against me as she imagined that I had turned against her. After all, my mother-in-law had misjudged my father-in-law's reasons for putting her in a mental institution for the last years of her life. Ultimately, Pat would die, and yet it still wouldn't be over. The same thing could happen to each of our children. I remember thinking that this threat of doom would hang over my family for the rest of our lives. There was no morally acceptable way out. There was only one person who could do anything about this, and it appeared at that time that he wasn't. The situation seemed hopeless.

Beyond the hopelessness, I felt helpless to do anything. I was experiencing physical problems myself that were only exacerbated by the stress from this news. Before long I was barely able to do my work. And I wasn't much help to my family either. I wanted at least to comfort my wife and help her deal with this distressing news. But all along she has handled this situation far better than I. Somehow God gave her strength and victory over the situation, and she didn't seem to need my help. I felt locked out of her life at this most critical time and unable to help. Whatever therapeutic value there might be for me in comforting her was lost.

Along with those feelings came a sense of abandonment. There seemed to be no answer and no one to help. Yes, there were friends and family, but what could they do? Even the doctors did not have a cure for this disease, so what could others do? Something else heightened the feeling of abandonment. Invariably when news like this comes, people are concerned but tend to stay away for fear of saying the wrong thing. Nobody wants to be like Job's comforters who over time became his accusers! But staying at a distance only serves to confirm the worst fears of the person suffering. He feels abandoned, and by keeping your distance you communicate that he is. And the problem isn't just that one feels abandoned by friends at this point but that God is no longer there. It doesn't matter how much you have sensed God's presence in your life before. At a time like this, he seems absent. And when you know that he is the only one who can do anything about your problem, it is especially painful to sense this absence.

These emotions were also accompanied by anger. The anger may not have been particularly rational, but it was real. I never expected exemption from problems just because I am a Christian, but I never thought something like this would happen. In one fell stroke, we learned that my whole family was under this cloud of doom. That kind of catastrophe wasn't supposed to happen. Since I had known before I married that God wanted me in the ministry, and having been raised in the home of a well-known Christian educator and minister, I knew that the life I would lead would require lots of time and effort. Given that mind-set, had I known the truth about my wife's family medical history, I wouldn't have married her. Pat has said that had she known, she probably wouldn't have married at all. If we had known, we wouldn't have had children. Nobody wants to put people they most love in this kind of jeopardy! I was angry at family members who knew and didn't tell us, at the doctors who knew and never explained it to the family, and at family members who didn't know but could have asked the doctors for an explanation but didn't. If anyone had given us the information before we married, I could have avoided this situation.

Though I didn't want to admit it, I was also angry at God. I knew that was foolish. After all, God hadn't done this. Nor could I think of anything in or out of Scripture that obligates God to keep this from happening. Beyond that, it was foolish to be angry at the one person who could do anything about it. Anyway, who was I, the creature, to contest the Creator? As Paul says (Rom. 9:19–21), the creature has no right to haul the Creator into the courtroom of human moral judgments and put him on trial as though he has done something wrong. God has total power and authority over me.

I felt that God had somehow misled me, even tricked me. When Pat and I first met, we were sure there was no way we would marry. I was headed into teaching, and she was headed to the mission field. One night I went to break off the relationship, because I was sure God couldn't want us to fight his will to send us in different directions. As Pat and I talked, we began to realize that she had a definite call to full-time ministry, but there was no clear call to missions. We continued to see each other and prayed about this whole thing, asking the Lord to break it off (as painful as that would be) if he didn't want us together. Rather than destroying the relationship, the Lord made it abundantly clear in various ways that he wanted us to marry.

The Lord knew I was going into a very demanding ministry and that if I was really to give myself to it, I would need a relatively healthy wife. My mom had suffered with various physical problems, and I had seen the strain that had put on Dad and his ministry. But Mom was never incapacitated so that she couldn't function in the home on a consistent basis. Beyond that, those who had been asked about whether Pat could have the same problems as her mother had assured us there was nothing to worry about. Now I had learned the horrible truth, and I felt that I had been tricked.

With the anger came a sense of confusion. None of this made any sense. God is the supremely rational being, and yet it appeared that he was actualizing a contradiction in my life! The news of my wife's illness seemed to contradict the Lord's leading in my life over the previous fifteen years. At one point, I thought about Abraham. God had given him Isaac, the child of promise, only to tell him to sacrifice Isaac on Mount Moriah. That must have made no more sense to Abraham than my situation made to me. And yet Abraham believed anyway. He believed that if he sacrificed Isaac, God would resurrect Isaac from the dead (Heb. 11:19). What incredible faith! Surely, his situation should comfort and encourage me. But it didn't. I remembered only too quickly that it was reasonable for Abraham to believe, because God had made very specific promises about this son (Gen. 12:1–3; 15:4–6; 17:15–19). God had made no such promises to me about my wife and children.

He had made it clear that Pat and I should marry, and he had seen to it that the information that would have kept us from having children was hidden. But he had never promised that there would be no catastrophic illness, or that we would have long, healthy lives. Yes, God could perform a miracle (as Abraham expected in Isaac's case) and heal all of them, but there were no promises that he would.

I was also confused for another reason. I was raised around people who suffered greatly; my mother had one physical problem after another and this in part sparked my interest at an early age in the problem of pain and suffering. In seminary, I wrote my master of divinity thesis on Job. Later, my master of theology thesis was on God's sovereign control of all things and how that relates to human freedom. My doctoral dissertation even focused on the problems of evil and led to my book *The Many Faces of Evil*.[2] If anyone had thought about this and was prepared to face affliction, surely it was I. And yet when the events I have recounted happened, I found little comfort in any of it. I had all these intellectual answers, but none of them made any difference in how I felt. The emotional and psychological pain was unrelenting, and the physical results from the stress and mental pain were devastating.

Why didn't all the years of study, reflection, and writing on the problem of evil help at this moment of personal crisis? As I reflected on this, I came to what for me was an especially significant realization. All my study and all the intellectual answers were of little help because the religious problem of evil isn't primarily an intellectual problem but is fundamentally an emotional problem! People wrestling with evil, as I was, do not need an intellectual discourse on how to justify God's ways to man in light of what's happening. That's what is needed to solve the abstract theological/philosophical problem of evil. This, on the other hand, is a problem about how someone experiencing affliction can live with this God who doesn't stop it.

This doesn't mean that no spiritual truths or intellectual answers can help the sufferer. It does mean that many of those answers won't help with a particular problem and that others that do won't help at all stages in the sufferer's experience. They must be used at times when the emotional pain has healed enough so that the sufferer is in a particular frame of mind.

It was at this point that I understood experientially Plantinga's point about the religious problem requiring pastoral care, not philosophical discussion. And I would urge you to take this very seriously, if you want to

---

2. John S. Feinberg, *The Many Faces of Evil: Theological Systems and the Problems of Evil*, rev. ed. (Wheaton, IL: Crossway Books, 2005).

help those struggling with the religious problem. As an illustration, think of a young child at a playground who falls and skins her knee. She runs to her mother for comfort. Now, her mother can do any number of things. She may tell her daughter that this has happened because she was running too fast and not watching where she was going. She must be more careful the next time. The mother, if she knew the laws of physics and causation, might even explain to her child how these laws were operating to make her child's scrape just the size and shape it is. The mother might even expound for a few moments on the lessons God is trying to teach her child from this experience. If she then pauses and asks her daughter, "Do you understand, Sweetheart?" don't be surprised if the little girl replies, "Yes, Mommy, but it still hurts!" Even the most thorough explanation at that moment doesn't stop her pain. The child doesn't need a discourse; she needs her mother's hugs and kisses. There will be time for the discourse later; now she needs comfort.

The same is true for each of us as we struggle with the religious problem of evil. We don't immediately need a lengthy lecture to appeal to our mind, because this isn't primarily an intellectual matter. What we need is something to take away the pain.

Things That Don't Help

If the religious problem of evil isn't primarily about justifying God's ways to man but about how one can live with this God, how can we help people through this difficult time in their life? I can only answer in terms of things that did and didn't help me. Hopefully, this will help you, whether you are struggling with suffering or hoping to minister to those who are.

Invariably, people will try to say something they hope will help. Let me mention some things that are inappropriate to say. Someone may say, "There must be some great sin you've committed; otherwise this wouldn't be happening to you." I am truly thankful that no one said this to my family. This was the reaction of many of Job's miserable comforters. While God does punish sin, and the wicked will have a day of judgment, Scripture is clear that sometimes the ungodly prosper (Psalm 73) and the righteous suffer (Job 1:8; 2:3; 1 Pet. 4:12–19). The truth is that in most instances we don't really know whether someone suffers as a righteous person or as a sinner. If someone is suffering as punishment for sin, that person will likely know it without our saying a thing. If that person doesn't realize it, it is still probably better to ask him what he thinks God is saying through the affliction, rather than to offer our opinion. And, if someone is suffering for righteousness' sake, as was Job, it won't help if those who aren't suffering assume an attitude of moral superiority and accuse the sufferer of sin.

Another mistake is to focus on the loss of things rather than the loss of people. Some years ago a relative who was on vacation learned that her home had burned to the ground, trapping and killing her son who was unable to escape. Her pastor made little attempt to see her or allow her to talk out her feelings. And the few times he did say something, he expressed concern over the loss of her house and possessions and missed the point of her grief. By his insensitivity, he missed the opportunity to minister to her in her time of crisis and hindered rather than helped the healing process in her life.

Sometimes people try to comfort us by convincing us that what has happened spares us from other problems. One of my students and his wife had their first baby, who then suddenly died. After the funeral and toward the end of the term, he shared with the class some things not to say to someone experiencing such grief. He told us how some people had said, "You know, it's probably a good thing that your son died. He probably would have grown up to be a problem. Maybe he'd have been a drug addict or would have refused to follow Christ. God knows these things in advance, and he was probably just saving you from those problems." I trust that no one thinks this is an appropriate thing to say. Such a loss is extremely painful, and the pain isn't eased, let alone removed, by insensitive speculations about the future. Moreover, the comment is wrong because it in effect says that it is good that evil has happened. I don't see how that can ever be an appropriate attitude for a Christian. Yes, James says we are to count it all joy when we fall into various afflictions (James 1:1–2), but the affliction is not joy but evil. The cause for joy is that in spite of the evil and in the midst of affliction, God is with us and can accomplish positive things in our life. But the affliction isn't a good thing.

There are other comments that don't help either, and here I speak from personal experience. Not long after we learned about my wife's condition someone said to me, "Well, everyone's going to die from something. You just know in advance what it is in your wife's case." Even if this were true, which it might not be, in what respect can it be a comfort? Another typical comment I heard is one I have made myself at times when visiting the sick or the bereaved. As we fumble for something to say that will comfort our friend or loved one, somehow it seems appropriate to say, "I know how you must feel at a time like this." Through my experiences, I have learned how unhelpful this comment can be. One problem is that it isn't true, and the sufferer knows it. Hence, it sounds phony when you say it. Even if you think you know how I feel, and even if the same thing happened to you, you don't and you can't know how I feel because you are not me with my particular personality and emotions, with my background and experiences, with my particular family and the relations to one another we share.

Now, it may be, especially if something similar has happened to you, that you tell me this because you think I might be encouraged by seeing that others have suffered greatly and yet have survived it. If that is your point, then simply say that. What helps is not knowing you feel like I do but knowing that you care! Remember, the sufferer feels helpless, hopeless, and abandoned. He doesn't need us to identify with his situation but to care and show it by helping however we can. He doesn't need us to share his feelings; he needs us to share his burdens!

Let me mention another set of comments I found thoroughly unhelpful. As the months wore on after my wife's diagnosis, I longed to have someone to talk to about how I felt. A dear, godly colleague who has been a friend for many years offered to listen. I explained how perplexed I was and how it seemed that God had hidden information about my wife prior to our marriage and prior to having children. I noted that, for a Calvinistic conception of God that sees God in control of all things, this was especially troublesome. But even if I were more inclined toward an Arminian notion of God, it still seemed God should have intervened in our behalf. After all, hadn't we prayed that God would lead us and keep us from making a wrong decision about whether to marry? My friend replied that I was too focused on various models of God and that I needed to recognize that God is bigger than all those conceptions.

There is something right about what my friend said, but I still found it unhelpful. My friend in essence was saying that things would be better for me if I just changed my notion of God. Now, it is true that a sufferer who is an atheist needs to change her perception of God. A Christian who has little training in theology might also need a better understanding of God, and even a theology professor could hardly be hurt by adjusting his views to a more accurate picture of God.

But there is still a major problem in thinking that this will resolve the religious problem of evil; it treats what is fundamentally an emotional problem as if it were an intellectual problem. The sufferer may have a wrong notion of God, and at some point, we may need to help her get a better picture of God. But if the religious problem is, as I suggest, at root an emotional hurt, then that must be handled first.

Other forms of this error are also common among Christians. One is, "You know, if you were a Calvinist, you'd see that God is in control of all of this, and then you could rest in him." Another is, "If you weren't so Calvin-istic, you wouldn't think God has his hand so directly in everything, and then you'd stop blaming him for what's happened to you." Or, "When things like this happen, aren't you glad you're a Calvinist? Isn't it great to know that God is ultimately in control of it all, and he's already planned the way out of your problem?" The first two of these comments are really saying that this whole thing will be all right if you just change your view of God. The third doesn't tell the sufferer to get a new concept of God but tells him to take comfort in his beliefs about God. But don't assume this will in fact comfort everyone. I am a Calvinist, and I found that comment distressing, not helpful. In fact, I remember thinking quite frequently that everything that had happened to me and my family would be easier to take if I were an Arminian. At least then I wouldn't see God so actively and directly in control of what had happened.

Was it that I really needed to discard my Calvinism as inadequate? Not at all. Had I been an Arminian, what had happened would still hurt ter-ribly. Indeed, there is a time for explanation and reflection upon what one knows to be true of God. If one's ideas about God are wrong, there is also a time for changing them. But not when the hurt is so deep and so new! Remember the little girl with the skinned knee. In answer to her mother's explanations she says, "Yes, Mommy, but it still hurts."

Remember as well Plantinga's point. This isn't a problem that requires philosophical or theological discourse but pastoral care. In any given case, no one can predict how long it will take for the pain to subside to the point where the sufferer is ready to think seriously about concepts of God. But until it does, it won't help the afflicted to tell them to change their view of God or simply meditate on what they believe about him.

One other thing was unhelpful in the midst of this emotional and spiri-tual turmoil and upheaval. I was concerned about my response to our situation. After all, Christians are supposed to rejoice in all things and persevere no matter what. Beyond that, as one in a position of Christian leadership, people would be looking all the more closely at me to see how I handled this. Still, I was finding it hard to cope, and for six months I was even physically and emotionally unable to preach. One day I listened to a Christian radio program, on which parents who had lost a daughter in her twenties in an automobile accident gave their testimony and recounted how, as a result of these events, various people had come to know the Lord. They concluded that even though the loss of their daughter was hard, it was all for the best. I heard that and felt more guilt. It seemed the height of Christian maturity to take life's harshest blows and say that it was good that this had happened. If that was what it meant to be victorious in the midst of affliction, I knew I was far from that. I couldn't rejoice over the evil that had befallen and would befall my family. But I thought I was supposed to, so my sense of inadequacy increased.

When I talked with my friend and colleague, as I mentioned above, some things he said weren't helpful. But what he said on this matter was most helpful. I told him I knew I was supposed to respond Christianly in this situation. But did that mean I had to like what was happening? Without batting an eyelash he responded, "You do have to learn to live with this, but that doesn't mean you have to like it!" This may sound like heresy to some. Popular Christian belief reminds us to rejoice in everything and count it all joy when trials come our way. One isn't really "with it" spiritually unless he can say the affliction was a good thing—or so we are told. But I beg to differ. Thinking that way won't help you cope with your grief; it will only add to it, as you feel guilty about your inability to do what you think you are called to do.

My friend was right, and I came to see why as I reflected on this over the following weeks and months. Those verses don't say the affliction is good or that it is a cause for rejoicing. They say that we are to rejoice when these things happen, because God is sufficient in the midst of trials and because of what God accomplishes in spite of them. Affliction may prove to be the occasion for God to do good things in our life, but the suffering itself isn't good but evil.

Because the affliction is evil I am neither required to like it nor should I. We live in a fallen world, which is why it is even possible for these things to happen. Scripture is clear that people die because of sin (Rom. 5:12). If people are going to die, they must die from something, and that means there will be diseases that take life. But if what is happening to my wife is ultimately the consequence of living in a sinful, fallen world, how can I applaud it? As a Christian, I am called to resist sin and its consequences in all forms. How, then, can I like it when the consequences of sin befall anyone, let alone a loved one? No, you don't have to like it, and if you properly understand why this is happening, you had better not like it!

Suggesting that the sufferer likes what is happening is also wrong because it ignores our humanness. Grief and sorrow in the face of tragedy are real human emotions. Unless they are admitted and expressed, they will remain inside us and destroy us. Healing can't come if we deny what we are feeling and act as though it is good that evil has occurred. Those negative feelings must be admitted, expressed, and dealt with, not hidden so that the sufferer acts as though everything is all right. Realizing that I didn't have to like what was happening relieved a great burden from me. In the rest of this chapter I want to turn from things that didn't help to things that did. These things didn't all happen at once, and in some cases it took a while for their import to sink in. If you are wrestling with the religious problem of evil, none of these comments may help you now, but at some point they may, so don't hesitate to come back to this later.

Things That Help

One thing that did help over time came in a conversation with my father several weeks after we first received my wife's diagnosis. I was bemoaning the fact that the situation looked hopeless. I couldn't see how I would be able to handle it as Pat got worse. On top of that there was the prospect of having to go through the same thing with one or more of our children. At that point Dad said, "John, God never promised to give you tomorrow's grace for today. He only promised today's grace for today, and that's all you need!" In that one comment I was reminded both of God's grace and of my need to take each day one at a time.

Eventually I saw that I don't have to live my tomorrows today. I don't know how I'll cope when my tomorrows come, but I know that they will come only one day at a time, and with each day, even as now, there will be grace to meet each new challenge. That doesn't mean it will be fun, but it does mean that for each day God will provide the strength needed. As a result of those truths, I began to readjust my focus from the future to the present. I would begin each day asking God for just the grace needed to sustain me that day. As that prayer was answered day after day, I gained more assurance that God would be there when things got worse. As a result, I found that I worried less about the future and focused more on the present day and its responsibilities.

Another major factor in helping me to cope, though I didn't realize it at the time, was seeing that God and others really do care. In the midst of my sense of abandonment and helplessness, God used various people to show me that he and others knew what I was going through and cared. Several incidents in particular were especially meaningful. Shortly after the news came about my wife, my brother came to encourage me. He said that though I might feel abandoned at that moment, God hadn't abandoned me, and neither had he nor the rest of my family. At that point I was still in such shock that I didn't realize that I was feeling a sense of abandonment. But God knew it and sent my brother to reassure me.

I remember as well an important visit from my pastor. We hadn't asked that he come but he knew we were hurting and cared enough to come. I remember well his first words. He told me that he couldn't begin to know how I felt, but he wanted me to know that he really cared about what was happening, and he and the church wanted to help in any way possible. It was exactly what I needed to hear. He didn't say much more, but he was willing to be there and listen. His presence said enough: he cared. At a time when it seemed impossible to survive the trial and when everything appeared hopeless, I needed to know that someone cared and would help.

After that first visit, there were other visits, and words were matched with actions. My pastor had noticed that our home needed some decorating and put together a group of people from the church to help. It was a way of saying they loved us, were sorry about what had happened, and wanted to do something tangible to express that care. I remember thinking that this was God's way of showing me that in a future day when I needed more involved help to care for my wife, his people would be there.

Colleagues, students, and those in administration at my school also displayed their concern. Students on their own initiative set aside special times each week to pray for us. Colleagues also prayed for us, and both expressed their concern by asking periodically how we were doing and if they could help. And when it was difficult for me to teach many of my classes, those in administration did not scold me or threaten to take my job but responded with patience and understanding. I was scheduled for a sabbatical that first academic year when the news came, and I didn't know how I would fulfill my responsibilities. I was in sufficient physical pain, let alone emotional stress, and I didn't know how I would be able to write during my sabbatical. I mentioned this to the president and dean, suggesting that perhaps I should postpone the sabbatical. They compassionately told me to take the quarter off, to consider it a combination of a sabbatical and medical leave, and not to worry about how much writing I would accomplish. Their care, concern, and compassion toward me at this difficult time helped me realize in an even fuller way that God did care for me.

There is part of the story I have left until now. After my wife was first diagnosed, and before we went for a second opinion, we requested a copy of my mother-in-law's chart from the hospital in New York. Because she had died some ten years earlier, and because of my wife's situation, they sent us the chart. When the chart came, I began to look through it. My mother-in-law had been admitted to that hospital in 1967, five years before my wife and I met and married.

As I read the chart, I didn't understand much of it, but one thing I saw horrified me: the family medical history and the diagnosis of Huntington's disease were recorded in her chart. The information that could have saved me from this situation was there for five years before I even met my wife. The information that could have kept us from having children and saddling them with this burden was right there from 1967 onward. It had been there for twenty years, and no one had told us about it. I was furious. But in the months and years that have passed, I have come to see this in a different way. For twenty years that information had been there, and at any time we could have found it out. Why, then, did God not give it to us until 1987?

As I wrestled with that question, I began to see his love and concern for us. God kept it hidden because he wanted me to marry Pat, who is a great woman and a wonderful wife. My life would be impoverished without her, and I would have missed the blessing of being married to her had I known earlier. God wanted our three sons to be born. Each is a blessing and a treasure, but we would have missed that had we known earlier. And God knew that we needed to be in a community of brothers and sisters in Christ at church and at the seminary who would love us and care for us at this darkest hour. And so he withheld that information, not because he accidentally overlooked giving it to us, and not because he is an uncaring God who delights in seeing his children suffer. He withheld it as a sign of his great care for us. There is never a good time to receive such news, but God knew that this was exactly the right time.

So far I have written about the need to care and show it, in the midst of a person's suffering, because I am so convinced of how crucial it is. By our words and deeds, we must show those who are hurting that we really care. And, by all means, we must show it by not avoiding those who suffer but by being there, even if only to listen. It is human nature to stay away for fear that we may say the wrong thing. Be there anyway, even if you say nothing. Your presence and willingness to listen say enough. When we keep our distance from those who suffer, we confirm their worst fears that no one cares and no one will help. Show them that someone cares, not only when the initial shock comes but also in the weeks, months, and years that follow. There is a sense in which one never completely recovers from tragedy and always needs the love and concern of others.

In the midst of these problems, I was vividly reminded about how difficult it is to go on without hope. I didn't really begin to feel much relief from my pain until I began to see some rays of hope. The fact that God and others cared was reason for hope, as was the realization that God would give grace for each new day. But beyond that, friends who knew about our situation could point to specific reasons for hope. For one thing, research on this disease continues. With advances in genetic engineering in the area of gene therapy, there is legitimate reason for hope. Of course it is possible that neither a cure nor even much help will come in time to help my wife, but there is reason to be hopeful in regard to our children.

Though we must be careful not to offer false hope, when there are real grounds for hope, we should be quick to point those out. Some of my colleagues are especially sensitive to this need. When a newspaper or journal article appears that chronicles some advance in research on Huntington's, no matter how small or insignificant the development, they make a point to show me the article. They realize that it is difficult to go on without hope, so when there are legitimate grounds for it, they bring them to my attention.

Something else that helped in my situation was focusing on the fact that in spite of what happened, God is good. One particular incident made me focus on that. A little over a year after we first received news of my wife's condition, I was being considered for tenure where I teach. In the tenure review interview, I was asked a question that stopped me in my tracks. One of the committee members asked, "In light of what you've been through, can you still say that God is good?" Though I answered affirmatively, I did so somewhat hesitantly. I realized that I had been focusing so much on the problems and on what God had not done that I really hadn't paid enough attention to all the evidence of his goodness in my life.

In the months that followed, I thought a lot about how many things were going well for us. I believe that no matter how much pain and turmoil there is, it helps the sufferer to focus on ways God has shown his goodness in spite of the problems. Counting one's blessings may seem trite, but it does in fact give a different perspective on what is happening to you. In our case, there were many evidences of God's goodness. For one thing, the disease progressed very slowly in my wife's case. Given the nature of this disease, God is the only one who can do anything about it, and at least for many years, he retarded the course of the disease. There are no guarantees for its future progression, but I can always be thankful for those extra years of relative normalcy in my wife's condition.

The love and concern shown to us by other Christians continues, and periodically I am again reminded of God's goodness as I hear of people literally all over the world who somehow have heard about this and are praying for us. In addition, I have often thought that since this has happened, what a blessing it is to live at this time in history! During much of the nineteenth and early part of the twentieth century (let alone earlier), little was known about this disease. Now it is known that there is a physiological base to this disease, not a psychological one. Moreover, within the last decade or so the chromosome involved has been identified, and even the exact genetic marker has been isolated. My wife could have lived at any other time in history—that she and our children live now is a sign of God's goodness.

When I look at these and many other things, I can truly say that God has been and is good to us. It is easy to focus on what is going wrong, but much goes right and that is ample evidence of God's grace and goodness to us. Surely we don't deserve it, and he isn't obligated to give it, but he does. In recent years, I have continually been reminded of 1 Peter 5:7, which tells us to cast all our cares on him because he cares for us. Peter could have written, "Cast all your cares on him, for he is powerful enough to do something about it." That would be equally true. But it is as if Peter is saying, "Of course he's powerful enough to do something about our problems. He wouldn't be God if he weren't." What we want to know, though, is whether he cares enough to help us. And, indeed, he does care. Everywhere in our life, in spite of what may be happening, we can find evidence of God's care if we only look for it.

In spite of all these encouragements in the midst of affliction, there has still been the nagging question of how this could happen to us. After all, it isn't just that my wife is a Christian and has given her life in service to the Lord. The question of why this should happen to her is especially nagging because it couldn't be God's retribution upon her for any sin she committed in her life. That she would get this disease was decided at the moment she was conceived!

As I thought about that, I was reminded of an unpopular but very important biblical truth: things like this happen because we live in a fallen world. God told Adam and Eve that if they disobeyed him, they would die (Gen. 2:17). They disobeyed, so the curse fell on them, and Paul tells us that it fell on all of us as well (Rom. 5:12). Adam's sin and its consequences have been imputed to the whole race. And if people are to die, they must die of some cause, such as disease. When one realizes this, one understands that though my wife committed no specific sin after birth that brought this upon her, this has happened because of sin. It is her sin in Adam, though she is no more responsible than the rest of us. It is not the most comforting thought, but it is a healthy reminder that this isn't God's fault, but ultimately ours. And the human race was warned.

The main lesson to learn from this, however, is the enormity of sin and the need to hate it. Shortly after the news of my wife's disease came, I received what I thought a rather strange note of condolence from a friend who was teaching at another seminary. He expressed his sorrow over the news and then wrote, "I can imagine how angry you must be right now at sin." Frankly,

I thought at the time this was a rather odd way to console someone. Sin was the last focus of my anger, if it was a focus at all. But I realized that he was absolutely right. Our situation and other tragic events occur because we live in a fallen world. We may think our sins are a trifling matter, and to us they may be. But when you hear the diagnosis of a terminal disease, or when you stand at the grave of a loved one, as we did at my mother's grave and then at my father's, you get a vivid illustration of how terrible sin is. God has told us it will lead to this, but we don't take him as seriously as we should until tragedy strikes.

We may think sin is really a trivial thing, but that is what Adam and Eve thought, too, and look at the mess that resulted! We may also think the punishment (disease, troubles, and death) far outweighs the crime—a little sin—but that only underscores how far we are from God's perspective on these things. In light of our relative comfort with sin, a little sin doesn't seem so bad. From the perspective of an absolutely perfect God who has nothing to do with sin, it must be atrocious.

My friend was right. We need to see sin as God does and hate it. When we see it from the perspective of where it ultimately leads, we begin to understand how truly serious it is and how much we must resist it. I can't promise this will be of great comfort to you, but it may help you to focus your anger in the right direction. It may also help you to feel more comfortable with God as you realize that ultimately all of us, not God, have brought these things on ourselves. God warned us, but we didn't listen. Thank God that now in our troubles he does listen and even forgives and restores!

Other things happened that helped me to cope with our situation. I mentioned earlier that I had physical problems and that the stress from my wife's situation only made matters worse. Within a few months I came to a point where I was in great pain and was of little use to anyone. I didn't have the physical stamina to preach or the energy to make it through my classes. I not only felt that our situation was helpless and hopeless, but that I was useless and adding to the problem by requiring attention that should have been placed elsewhere. As with many people, my sense of self-worth is tied in large part to my work and productivity. When I could do little to function, my sense of hopelessness increased.

In the midst of this dilemma, the Lord gave me some opportunities to do things that helped other people. This was just what I needed at the time. It gave me a chance to get my focus off of our problems and on someone else's needs. Even more, it showed me that I still could be useful. Gradually, as I regained strength, I became increasingly thankful that I could do anything, let alone help others who had shown us so much love. For those wrestling with affliction, I would encourage the same: as you are able and when you are able, seek out ways to help others. There is therapeutic value in getting your eyes off your problems and in seeing again that you can help others. I found that this helped to lift the burden somewhat, and it showed me that when others, including my family, needed me, through God's enablement I would be able to help them.

Moving Forward

I began to ask myself what my options were for handling this problem long range. Somewhere in the grieving process I think each of us must ask ourselves what the options are for addressing our problem. In my case, there were few, but they were radically diverse. On the one hand, I could continue to grieve and fall apart. But I had already done that, and it had solved nothing. I saw little improvement in my own outlook, and I was of little help to anyone else. My wife still needed a husband, my children a father, and my students a teacher. Falling apart wouldn't help any of them. As Scripture says, there is a time to mourn, but then there is a time that one must get on with life.

Or, perhaps, instead, I could get on with my life, but just exclude God from it. Many people choose this option in the face of affliction. They either conclude that there is no God or decide that there is but they will fight him. But neither of these was acceptable for me. I had seen too many evidences of God's work in my life to decide there was no God. Rejecting his existence was unsatisfactory, but choosing to fight him was no better. God's goodness throughout my life and even now in our circumstances didn't warrant my turning from him. Besides, it is lunacy to pick a fight you can't win. Even more, it is beyond lunacy to fight someone who, rather than being the cause of your problems, is the only possible answer to them.

Maybe I could take a Kierkegaardian leap of faith that somehow this all made sense, though I could explain none of it. In other words, I could simply ignore and bypass intellect and throw myself on God in hopes that he was there. But this didn't seem a plausible option for me. Some might find it attractive, but it isn't my nature to sacrifice intellect so totally. I knew there would still be the questions and that there would be no peace until they were settled. I didn't expect to find all the answers, but I knew I had to find many of them.

The only real option for me was clear. I had to continue trusting, and yes, worshiping God, and I had to get on with my life. I needed to stop the seemingly interminable deep grieving and allow emotional healing to continue by focusing on the things I have already shared. I had to focus on answers that would satisfy the emotional dimensions of my struggle and would at the same time give enough intellectual answers to warrant peace of mind. And I realized that I couldn't wait until all those answers arrived to continue with life. Too many people needed me, and I needed to be there for them.

As I began to take this approach to my problems (and at some point all of us must decide how we will handle our problems), I began to focus more on positive things. The healing and coping process continues to this day, as it will through the rest of my life. But God has allowed me to function again, and there is progress in dealing with these problems. I am so thankful God led me to choose the option I did for handling my situation.

God is not only there when the shock of tragic news first comes. At various points along the way when we are ready to hear it, he adds a further word. One of those words of help comes from Ecclesiastes 7:13–14; the thrust of the passage is that God hides the future from us so that we will trust him. Though this might seem a rather strange source of comfort, let me share it with you. The passage reads:

> Consider the work of God,
> For who is able to straighten what He has bent?
> In the day of prosperity be happy,
> But in the day of adversity consider—
> God has made the one as well as the other
> So that man will not discover anything that will be after him.[3]

The context of these verses is significant. Commentators agree that chapter 7 contains a series of aphorisms, though they don't always agree on how they fit together. Generally, much of chapter 7 focuses on things that at first appear undesirable in order to show that in fact they have a certain benefit. Chapter 6 shows that things that look good also have a down side. The ultimate message, then, is that we can't always take things at face value, nor should we presume to understand them. And if this is true of things we do and experience, how much more is it true of God and his ways! This is the context of verses 13–14.

In the passage itself, the writer begins by emphasizing the sovereign power of God (v. 13). Verse 13b is a rhetorical question, and the answer is obvious. Some think this verse means that if God brings something we consider evil, we can't make it good (straighten it). We can't overturn God's

3. Unless otherwise indicated, Scripture quotations in this chapter are taken from the *New American Standard Bible* (NASB).

powerful hand. While this interpretation surely fits verse 14 and its teaching about God's bringing of adversity, I think the writer's point is even more general. That is, just as no one can straighten what God bends, no one can bend what he straightens. No one can overturn what God does; man must simply submit to God's providence.

All of this suggests that both adversity and prosperity are under God's hand. Verse 14 confirms that, for it says God sends both good and bad. The writer tells us to be happy in the good days. Out of fear of the future, we might be troubled even when things are going well. That worry will help us learn nothing about the future, but it may destroy the happiness in the present that we should be and could be having. The writer then says that in evil days, we should consider. He doesn't say that in evil days we should be sad, for he doesn't need to. That comes naturally. Instead, we should consider. We should think about what has happened, about the alternation of good and bad, and realize that no one knows when which will come. In fact, what appears to be good may turn out evil and vice versa. Things aren't always as they seem.

Why does God give this alternation of good and bad? Why doesn't he always reveal how things will turn out? The writer says God does this to conceal the future ("so that man will not discover anything that will be after him"). But why would God do that? Though the answer isn't explicit in the text, I think it is implicit. If we don't know what to expect, we must just simply wait on the Lord for what will come next and entrust it all to him. We may want to change what he will do, but verse 13 reminds us that we can't. We must submit to his providence and trust him. If we knew the details of our future, we might think we could figure out solutions to fixing it. In short, we might think there was no need to trust God. Yet God conceals the future so that we must trust him. You can see how this truth fit so specifically to our situation. It wasn't relevant to us only before we learned the news that was for so long available but untouched. It is relevant now as we contemplate the course of this disease and our children's futures as well.

What are the implications of this truth? If God conceals the future so that we must trust him, doesn't that mean God manipulates events to get us to love him? Maybe he can't get our love and trust any other way, so he uses circumstances to force us to trust him. If that is so, this is no God worthy of praise and worship—this isn't a good God! This is a conniving, manipulative God who has created us solely for his benefit and really doesn't care about us after all. As I thought about the implications of this truth, I realized that God isn't an evil God. By concealing the future, God does make us trust him, but I suggest that this isn't manipulative but compassionate in a number of ways.

It is compassionate because knowing the details of our future would be harmful to us. Suppose our future would be good. No doubt we would be relieved, but the joy of discovery would be gone. What could be exciting when it happens would lose its thrill as a surprise. We might even be bored. The joy of anticipation would be gone. Revealing a promising future might also make us complacent in our relation to God, or we might conclude that we don't need him. Or suppose our future would be evil. Barring the return of the Lord for the church, Scripture and common sense teach that the ultimate end of this life is death. But if we knew how or when it would end or even what evils would befall us along the way, we might be totally horrified and unable to act as fear paralyzed us. Hiding the future is compassionate because knowing it could easily harm us.

Hiding the future is also compassionate because we must not ignore the present. If the future is good and we know what it will be, we might become impatient with the present. For example, when we anticipate an exciting summer vacation, we often become impatient with the present. In essence, we overlook the good things that are happening now, and lose the present. On the other hand, if our future is evil, we might spend much of our time worrying about it or grieving over our anticipated misfortune. The net result in either case could well be a wasting of the present and never really "living" at all.

One of the things that our experiences have done for me is to focus my attention on the present. I have always been a goal-oriented person with a focus on the future. I still plan for the future but now for the near future, not the distant future. I don't want to know any more about the distant future than I already do. I find myself focusing more on the present and enjoying it more. In fact, I am better able to cope when I focus on where my wife is today, rather than on where she may be in her condition somewhere down the road. I don't have tomorrow's grace yet, and I don't need it until tomorrow! We must not be so overly occupied with the future that we lose sight of today. God has hidden the future so that we might trust him, and he is compassionate in doing so.

God is compassionate in hiding the future as well because we would probably try to change it if we knew what was to come. But as verse 13 suggests, it is impossible to change what God has decided to do. Why waste the present trying to change something you can't change? In the process, you may drive yourself crazy.

God's hiding of the future is also compassionate because we couldn't handle the information in some cases if we had it. If the future is evil and we see it all at once, it could be too horrifying for us to take. On November 4, 1987, I caught a glimpse of the future that just about destroyed me. I am more than willing now to take the future one day at a time. In most cases God compassionately reveals the details of our future moment by moment, and that is enough. As Scripture says, "Sufficient unto the day is the evil thereof" (Matt. 6:34 KJV). We don't need to know tomorrow's evil today!

Though all the things I have shared were sources of comfort and encouragement, something still seemed wrong. There seemed to be a basic unfairness about what was happening. And, frankly, I believe this is a sticking point for many people which makes it so difficult for them to live with God. Put simply, why was this happening to us and not also to other people? Wasn't it unjust of God to ask us to bear this burden, and not others? Please do not misunderstand. I wouldn't wish this on anyone, but it seemed only fair that if others escape, we should, too. If God could keep others from this fate, why couldn't he keep us from it? It's not that he owes any of us anything per se, but justice seems to show that he owes us at least as good a shake as the next person.

I suspect that most who experience significant tragedy in their life have thought this way at some point. I had those thoughts, but I came to see that they contain an error. In philosophical discussions of justice, there is a distinction between what is called distributive justice and egalitarian justice. Distributive justice refers to rendering each person what is their due. If you do good, in strict justice you are owed good. If you do evil, in strict justice you deserve punishment. Egalitarian justice, however, is giving everyone the same thing, regardless of merits or deserts.

This helped me to see where the source of the problem was. It isn't just that we think distributive justice mandates a better fate for us since we think we have done good. Our complaint is that we expect God to deal with the world with egalitarian justice. We expect him to treat everyone the same, and that means I should escape an affliction if others do. Once I realized this, I immediately asked why God is obligated to operate in these matters on the basis of egalitarian justice. Given the demands of distributive justice, all of us as sinners deserve nothing but punishment. Why, then, is God obligated to respond to us in egalitarian terms? I could not answer that. I realized that if God really did handle us according to egalitarian justice, we would all either experience the same torture or be equally blessed. Neither of those ideas squares with the God of the Scriptures. Once I realized this,

I understood that much of my anger rested on a misunderstanding of what God is expected to do.

But even this principle doesn't solve the problem. Even if God isn't obligated to give any of us more than we deserve, and even if what we deserve is punishment for sin, still God has chosen to be gracious to some. If you are suffering from some affliction, you may feel that God should have extended equal grace to you as he has to those who never confront your affliction. God must be unjust for not extending as much grace to you as to the next person. Though this objection is understandable, it is still wrong. The objection now has moved from a demand that God treat us with egalitarian justice to a demand that God dole out egalitarian grace. This is wrong in two respects. In the first place, God is no more obligated to give the same grace to everyone than he is to give the same justice to all. He is obligated only to distribute what we deserve.

The other point is that since we are talking about grace, the charge of injustice on God's part (and that is really what the sufferer means by this complaint) can't even arise. Grace is unmerited favor. That means you get something good that you don't deserve. But if I don't merit it at all, it can't be unjust that my neighbor gets more grace than I do. In fact, God isn't obligated to treat us with any kind of grace. That's why it is grace and not justice. And that is also why it can't be unjust if someone gets more grace than another. God owes none of us any grace. If he graciously chooses to give some of us a better (by our evaluation) lot than others, that is his right.

Though these principles about grace and justice won't relieve the pain of what you are experiencing, if they are properly understood, they can help dissipate anger toward God. I have found it to be liberating, and I frequently remind myself of these principles when I am inclined to lament that God has given others an easier lot than I.

I close this chapter hoping that what you have read will minister to your needs and will help you minister to others who are hurting. It hasn't been an easy chapter to write, and I would give anything not to have learned what I have learned in the way I did. But if the chapter is helpful to you, then it has been worth my effort to write it.

Here is one final thought. It is especially relevant to those who are believers and suffer as righteous individuals. It was something I needed to see, and it helped me as well when I realized it. John says the world didn't understand Christ, so we who are the children of God and follow Christ can expect to be misunderstood and persecuted as well (1 John 3:1). Jesus told his disciples that following him means bearing a cross (Matt. 16:24).

Scripture is also clear that those who follow God are engaged in a war with those who don't (Eph. 6:12; 1 Pet. 5:8–9).

Yes, we are engaged in a spiritual war. But did you think you could go to war, even be in the front lines of the battle, and never get wounded? I did. At least, I never expected a wound like the one we got. But I have come to see that this was unrealistic. The enemy is very real and has many ways of attacking those who would follow God. Knowing that there will be attacks and battle wounds doesn't mean the wounds don't hurt. But it does help us assess more accurately what has happened. One may wish exemption from the battle, but that isn't possible. One may even contemplate changing sides as many do when confronted with tragedy, but that option isn't the answer to our problems for either time or eternity.

There were other afflictions that came during the trials I have mentioned, just as I know there will be others in the future. The story isn't finished yet. Just as there have been some surprises already—some welcome, some unwelcome—God has others in store. When the wounds of battle come, and they will come, we need the comfort and care of God. I am so thankful God is there to give it!

SELECTED BIBLIOGRAPHY

Baxter, Richard. *The Saints' Everlasting Rest.* Repr. Grand Rapids, MI: Baker, 1978.

Blocher, Henri. "Christian Thought on the Problem of Evil: Part II." *Churchman* 99, no. 2 (1985): 101–30.

Bloomquist, L. Gregory. *The Function of Suffering in Philippians.* Sheffield, UK: JSOT Press, 1993.

Bridges, Jerry. *Is God Really in Control? Trusting God in a World of Terrorism, Tsunamis, and Personal Tragedy.* Colorado Springs: NavPress, 2006.

Bunyan, John. *The Pilgrim's Progress.* Edinburgh: Banner of Truth, 1977.

Calvin, John. *Suffering: Understanding the Love of God.* Edited by Joseph A. Hill. Darlington, UK: Evangelical Press, 2005.

Carmody, John. *Cancer and Faith.* Mystic, CT: Twenty-Third Publications, 1994.

Carson, D. A. *How Long, O Lord? Reflections on Suffering and Evil.* 2nd ed. Grand Rapids, MI: Baker, 2006.

Co, Adamson. "Evil and the Sovereignty of God: The Legitimacy and the Limits of Doing *Chaoskampf* Theology." PhD diss., Trinity Evangelical Divinity School, 2005.

Crenshaw, J. L. *Defending God: Biblical Responses to the Problem of Evil.* New York: Oxford University Press, 2005.

_____. *A Whirlpool of Torment: Overtures to Biblical Theology.* Philadelphia: Fortress, 1984.

Currid, John. *Why Do I Suffer? Suffering and the Sovereignty of God.* Fearn, Ross-shire, UK: Christian Focus, 2004.

Dau, Isaiah Majok. *Suffering and God: A Theological Reflection on the War in Sudan.* Nairobi: Paulines Publications Africa, 2002.

Edgar, William. "The Great Outrage." In *Reasons of the Heart: Recovering Christian Persuasion*. Phillipsburg, NJ: P&R, 1996, 2003, 95–105.

Feinberg, John S. *The Many Faces of Evil: Theological Systems and the Problems of Evil*, rev. ed. Wheaton, IL: Crossway Books, 2005.

_____. *Where Is God? A Personal Story of Finding God in Grief and Suffering*. Nashville: Broadman, 2004.

Fernando, Ajith. *The Call to Joy and Pain: Embracing Suffering in Your Ministry* Wheaton, IL: Crossway Books, 2007.

Frame, John M. *The Doctrine of God*. Phillipsburg, NJ: P&R, 2002.

Fretheim, T. E. *The Suffering of God: An Old Testament Perspective*. Minneapolis:-Fortress, 1984.

Gaertner, B. "Suffer." In *The New International Dictionary of New Testament Theology*, vol. 3. Edited by Colin Brown. Translated from the German. Grand Rapids, MI: Zondervan, 1978.

Gerstenberger, E. S., and W. Schrage. *Suffering*. Translated by John E. Steely. Nashville: Abingdon, 1980.

Greene-McCreight, Kathryn. *Darkness Is My Only Companion: A Christian Response to Mental Illness*. Grand Rapids, MI: Brazos, 2006.

Guinness, Os. *Unspeakable: Facing Up to Evil in an Age of Genocide and Terror*. San Francisco: HarperSanFrancisco, 2005.

Hafemann, Scott J. *The God of Promise and the Life of Faith: Understanding the Heart of the Bible*. Wheaton, IL: Crossway Books, 2001.

_____. "Suffering and the Spirit: An Exegetical Study of II Cor. 2:14–3:3 within the Context of the Corinthian Correspondence." WUNT 19. Tübingen: J. C. B. Mohr (Paul Siebeck), 1986.

Haugen, Gary. *Good News about Injustice: A Witness of Courage in a Hurting World*. Downers Grove, IL: InterVarsity, 1999.

Hick, John. *Evil and the God of Love*. London: Collins, 1966.

Hicks, Peter. *The Message of Evil and Suffering: Light into Darkness*. The Bible Speaks Today. Downers Grove, IL: InterVarsity, 2007.

Jervis, L. Ann. *At the Heart of the Gospel: Suffering in the Earliest Christian Message*. Grand Rapids, MI: Eerdmans, 2007.

Kaiser, W. C. *A Biblical Approach to Personal Suffering: Lamentations*. Chicago: Moody Press, 1982.

Kreeft, Peter. *Making Sense out of Suffering*. Cincinnati, OH: St. Anthony Messenger Press, 1986.

Larrimore, Mark, ed. *The Problem of Evil: A Reader*. Malden, MA: Blackwell, 2001.

Leibniz, G. W. *Theodicy*. New Haven, CT: Yale University Press, 1952.

Lewis, C. S. *A Grief Observed*. New York: Seabury, 1961.

_____. *The Problem of Pain.* New York: Macmillan, 1962.

Lloyd-Jones, David Martyn. *Why Does God Allow Suffering?* Wheaton, IL: Crossway Books, 1994.

Luhman, Reginald S. "Belief in God and the Problem of Suffering." *EvQ* 57, no. 4 (October 1985): 327–48.

MacArthur, John. *The Power of Suffering: Strengthening Your Faith in the Refiner's Fire.* Colorado Springs: David C. Cook, 1995.

McCartney, Dan G. "Suffering in James." In *The Practical Calvinist: An Introduction to the Presbyterian and Reformed Heritage in Honor of Dr. D. Clair Davis,* edited by P. Lillback. Fearn, Ross-shire, Scotland: Mentor, 2002.

_____. *Why Does It Have to Hurt? The Meaning of Christian Suffering.* Phillipsburg, NJ: P&R, 1998.

McQuilkin, J. Robertson. "The Gradual Grief of Alzheimer's: Robertson McQuilkin reflects on his wife's death after caring for her for 25 years." *Christianity Today* 48 (February 2004): 64–65.

_____. "Living by Vows." *Christianity Today* 34 (October 8, 1990): 38–40.

_____. "Muriel's Blessing: Despite the toll of his wife's Alzheimer's, a husband marvels at the mystery of love." *Christianity Today* 40 (February 5, 1996): 32–34.

McWilliams, Warren. *Where Is the God of Justice? Biblical Perspectives on Suffering.* Peabody, MA: Hendrickson, 2005.

Morgan, Christopher W., and Robert A. Peterson, eds. *Hell under Fire: Modern Scholarship Reinvents Eternal Punishment.* Grand Rapids, MI: Zondervan, 2004.

Morley, Brian. *God in the Shadows: Evil in God's World.* Fearn, Ross-shire, Scotland: Christian Focus, 2006.

Nash, Ronald H. *When a Baby Dies: Answers to Comfort Grieving Parents.* Grand Rapids, MI: Zondervan, 1999.

Oswalt, John N. *Where Are You, God? Malachi's Perspectives on Injustice and Suffering.* Nappanee, IN: Evangel, 1999.

Packer, J. I. *A Grief Sanctified: Through Sorrow to Eternal Hope (Including Richard Baxter's Timeless Memoir of His Wife's Life and Death).* Wheaton, IL: Crossway Books, 2002.

Peake, A. S. *The Problem of Suffering in the Old Testament.* London: Epworth Press, 1904.

Piper, John. *The Hidden Smile of God: The Fruit of Affliction in the Lives of John Bunyan, William Cowper, and David Brainerd.* Wheaton, IL: Crossway Books, 2001.

Piper, John, and Justin Taylor, eds. *Suffering and the Sovereignty of God.* Wheaton, IL: Crossway Books, 2006.

Plantinga, Alvin. *God, Freedom, and Evil.* Grand Rapids, MI: Eerdmans, 1974.

Plantinga, Cornelius, Jr. *Not the Way It's Supposed to Be: A Breviary of Sin.* Grand Rapids, MI: Eerdmans, 1995.

Pyne, Robert A. *Humanity and Sin.* Swindoll Leadership Library. Dallas: Word, 1999.

Robinson, H. Wheeler. *Suffering: Human and Divine.* New York: MacMillan, 1939.

Sanders, Jim Alvin. *Suffering as Divine Discipline in the Old Testament and Post Biblical Judaism.* Rochester, NY: Colgate Rochester Divinity School, 1955.

Simundson, D. J. *Faith under Fire: Biblical Interpretations of Suffering.* Minneapolis: Augsburg, 1980.

Sittser, Jerry. *A Grace Disguised: How the Soul Grows through Loss.* Grand Rapids, MI: Zondervan, 2005.

Sproul, R. C. *When Worlds Collide: Where Is God in Terrorism, War, and Suffering?* Wheaton, IL: Crossway Books, 2002.

Sutcliffe, E. *Providence and Suffering in the Old and New Testaments.* London: Thomas Nelson, 1953.

Swenson, Kristin M. *Living Through Pain: Psalms and the Search for Wholeness.* Waco, TX: Baylor University Press, 2005.

Thielicke, Helmut. *Living with Death.* Translated by Geoffrey W. Bromiley. Grand Rapids, MI: Eerdmans, 1983.

_____. *Out of the Depths.* Grand Rapids, MI: Eerdmans, 1962.

Thomas, Derek. *Calvin's Teaching on Job: Proclaiming the Incomprehensible God.* Fearn, Ross-shire, UK: Mentor/Christian Focus, 2004.

Tinker, Melvin. *Why Do Bad Things Happen to Good People? A Biblical Look at the Problem of Suffering.* Fearn, Ross-shire, UK: Christian Focus, 2006.

Wolterstorff, Nicholas. *Lament for a Son.* Grand Rapids, MI: Eerdmans, 1987.

Wright, N. T. *Evil and the Justice of God.* Downers Grove, IL: InterVarsity, 2006.

Wright, Nigel G. *A Theology of the Dark Side: Putting the Power of Evil in Its Place,* rev. ed. Downers Grove, IL: InterVarsity, 2004.

Yancey, Philip. *Disappointment with God: Three Questions No One Asks Aloud.* Grand Rapids, MI: Zondervan, 2006.

_____. *Where Is God When It Hurts?* Grand Rapids, MI: Zondervan, 2002.

GENERAL INDEX

SCRIPTURE INDEX

THEOLOGY IN COMMUNITY

FIRST-RATE EVANGELICAL SCHOLARS

take a multidisciplinary approach

to key Christian doctrines

OTHER BOOKS IN THE SERIES

The Love of God
The Glory of God
The Deity of Christ
The Kingdom of God
Fallen: A Theology of Sin
Heaven

For more information, visit www.crossway.org.

Made in the USA
Middletown, DE
14 June 2021